The Altar's Fire

The Altar's Fire

Charles Wesley's *Hymns on the Lord's Supper, 1745*
Introduction and Comment

Daniel B. Stevick

✚ EPWORTH

British Library Cataloguing in Publication data

A catalogue record for this book is available
from the British Library

0 7162 0586 6

First published in 2004
by Epworth Press
4 John Wesley Road
Werrington
Peterborough PE4 6ZP

Printed and bound in Great Britain by
Biddles Ltd, King's Lynn, Norfolk

To my dear
Laurel,
who died, March 17, 2002.

With gratitude
for fifty-three happy and loving years together.

Contents

Foreword

GEOFFREY WAINWRIGHT

Charles Wesley's hymns are a treasure historically entrusted to Methodism. Happily, some of the best from his vast output have found their way also into hymnals across a very broad swathe of English-speaking Christianity. Among hymns for times and seasons, one thinks of 'Hark! The Herald Angels Sing', 'Christ the Lord is Risen Today', 'Lo! He Comes with Clouds Descending', 'Christ Whose Glory Fills the Skies'. Of more general hymns, 'Love Divine, All Loves Excelling', 'O for a Thousand Tongues to Sing', 'Ye Servants of God, Your Master Proclaim'.

But what of the *Hymns on the Lord's Supper*, a collection of 166 eucharistic hymns published in 1745 under the joint names of John and Charles Wesley but usually thought to be largely the work of Charles? What of their reception, both domestically and ecumenically? Among Anglicans on the home territory, 'Author of Life Divine' (*HLS*, 40) figured in both *Hymns Ancient and Modern* and *The English Hymnal*, joined in the latter by 'Victim Divine' (*HLS*, 116). British Methodists have retained between a dozen and a score in their hymnals over the past two centuries. At the start of the international dialogue between the World Methodist Council and the Roman Catholic Church, the *Denver Report* of 1971 viewed the Wesleyan eucharistic hymns as offering a 'basis and hope' for doctrinal discussion on the sacrament, but in the face of Catholic enthusiasm for the hymns it was thought necessary to state that 'the eucharistic devotion of the Wesleys and the hymns of Charles Wesley are no index at all to the place of Holy Communion in the life, thought and devotion of modern Methodists'. In their remarkably positive response to Faith and Order's *Baptism, Eucharist and Ministry* (1982), however, the council of bishops of the United Methodist Church pointed to a 'vigorous renewal of liturgical theology and practice', endorsed the Lima text's use of *anamnesis* and *epiklesis* to expound the eucharist in ways that matched original Methodist teaching, and declared that 'as Wesleyans we are accustomed to the language of sacrifice, and we find BEM's statements to be in accord with the Church's Tradition and with ours'.

The likely truth of the matter is that the Wesleyan *Hymns on the Lord's Supper* enjoy a periodic revival among discerning worshippers and theologians concerned for the richness of the classic tradition of Christianity. In that line comes this attractive book, *The Altar's Fire*, the work of Daniel Stevick, an Episcopal priest from the United States. The time is ripe for this fresh examination of the hymns not only among Methodists on both sides of the Atlantic but also among Christians of other persuasions on the global scene. Discussion still surrounds the reports on the Lord's Supper presented to the Conference of the British Methodist Church in 2003, *His Presence Makes the Feast* (a title borrowed from *HLS*, 81), and to the General Conference of the United Methodist Church in 2004, *This Holy Mystery*. The magnificent hymn 'O Thou Who This Mysterious Bread' (*HLS*, 29) has been found by other Christians to fit well the pattern of Word and Table which is now widely recognised to constitute the fullness of worship for the Lord's People on the Lord's Day. In his encyclical letter of 2003, *Ecclesia de Eucharistia vivit*, Pope John Paul II called for a genuinely ecumenical eucharist in both doctrine and practice. A characteristic contribution could be made by the theme strongly present in the Wesleyan hymns, that the Church's action on earth shows and pleads the one all-sufficient sacrifice which the crucified, risen and ascended Christ shows and pleads in the heavenly sanctuary – is there anywhere a greater hymn on the subject than 'Victim Divine'? The doctrine of salvation is due for the recovery of an objective atonement to balance the subjectivism of the Abelardian account.

My prayer is that Daniel Stevick's splendid commentary on the Wesleyan *Hymns on the Lord's Supper* will help to introduce this specific treasure both to a new generation of Methodists and to a new range of Christians in other ecclesial communities who are also bound to the cause of allowing Christ's Church to be one.

Preface

Readers who come upon Charles Wesley's *Hymns on the Lord's Supper* for the first time are usually surprised and attracted by the doctrinal and spiritual depth, the variety and the intensity of what they find. Yet this quite exceptional work remains little known. In this book I invite readers to become acquainted with these strong and vivid hymns for the Holy Communion which date from the early years of the Wesleyan revival.

My own acquaintance began more than 40 years ago when a reference led me to Rattenbury's edition. I was fascinated and began to take notes. Then I found a crumbling copy of the nineteenth-century edition of Wesley's principal source, Daniel Brevint's *The Christian Sacrament and Sacrifice*, which I had rebound. My note-taking continued in such time as I could spare, but now on the two texts. I was able over the years to share a little of this material with students in a general course on the history of Christian worship. (In liturgy, not much else was going on in the eighteenth century.) But the course had to slight Wesley and hurry on to the nineteenth century and the twentieth.

Retirement has given me opportunity to return to these hymns by Charles Wesley and to the essay by Daniel Brevint that Wesley had at hand as he composed.

I seek to read these hymns in the context of their own time. But their more extended context now includes interested and perhaps at times puzzled readers of the twenty-first century. Not all present-day readers find the ideas on the sacrament which Wesley presents so passionately to be clear or congenial. Yet I have not sought to criticise or to defend so much as to present a sympathetic account of Wesley's thought.

My introductory section sets the sacramental hymns in the context of early Methodism and of the traditions of sacramental spirituality which formed Charles Wesley's mind and on which he drew.

The expository chapters follow the sequence of *Hymns on the Lord's Supper*, looking at selected hymns and stanzas, gathering up interpretive themes, and often taking note when Wesley draws important language and ideas from Brevint's small book. These chapters are followed by thematic essays which fill out the account of Wesley's sacramental thought.

The Appendices summarise some topical or technical matters.

Since I began working on Wesley and Brevint largely as a private project, I turned to libraries and to some of the leaders in Wesley studies from a previous generation. J. Ernest Rattenbury, Bernard Manning, Henry Bett, Frank Baker, Ole Borgen and others became old and trusted friends through their writings.

Rattenbury should be given special notice. His work *The Eucharistic Hymns of John and Charles Wesley*, Epworth Press, London, 1948, called the attention of the Church to *Hymns on the Lord's Supper* after many years of neglect. Rattenbury drew on ideas of Gregory Dix and of C. H. Dodd to urge the modern-day relevance of Wesley's sacramental hymns. He included in his work a slightly edited text of the hymns, which had become hard to find. For more than half a century most of the people who have known these hymns learned of them through Rattenbury. His work has worn well. Anyone who turns to the Wesley eucharistic hymns cannot but stand in debt, at first or second hand, to Rattenbury's skill as an expositor and an advocate. Anyone who writes on these hymns today is still writing footnotes to his innovative and enduring work.

As I continued my interest in Wesley, I became acquainted with some of my contemporaries who have been researching and writing in Wesley studies, often for many years. I have received encouragement and informed counsel from Charles Greene, S. T. Kimbrough, Jr, Kenneth E. Rowe, Laurence Stookey and Geoffrey Wainwright (for whose Foreword to this book I am most grateful).

I have drawn on the resources of the Methodist Archives at Madison, New Jersey, the St Mark's Library of the General Theological Seminary in New York, and the libraries of Princeton Theological Seminary and the Eastern Baptist Seminary and of the Episcopal Diocese of Pennsylvania.

Note on sources

For the text of *Hymns on the Lord's Supper* I have used the facsimile reprint of Wesley's first edition of 1745 which was reproduced in 1995 by the Charles Wesley Society, edited by Charles Green and S. T. Kimbrough, Jr. This edition includes an informative Introduction by Geoffrey Wainwright. With the period text of this edition, a reader can know what Charles Wesley actually wrote, with all of his idiosyncrasies of spelling, capitalisation and punctuation. Wesley printed GOD, LORD, CHRIST, and JESUS in small capitals. Many nouns are begun with a capital letter, but not all. Some words seem to be capitalised because they were thought important, but other important words are printed in lower case. Readers seeking consistency will not find it. When I quote full hymns or substantial passages, I follow this text. But when I cite Wesley's lines in my own commentary, I somewhat modernise the style. I have not sought to trace the changes that were made in later eighteenth-century editions of the collection, hardly any of which seem to have been substantive.

In my references to the hymns, I separate the hymn number from the stanza number by a colon and the line(s) from the stanza number by a period. Thus the line 'My Blood that speaks your Sins forgiven' is 1:4.5; that is, Hymn 1, stanza 4, line 5.

The many references to Daniel Brevint's *The Christian Sacrament and Sacrifice*, 1673, cite the full text, in the 1847 edition, rather than the abridgement that was made by John Wesley and printed with *Hymns on the Lord's Supper*. Charles seems to have followed Brevint's full text rather than his brother's précis. Comparison with a copy of the first edition, 1673, in the St Mark's Library of the General Theological Seminary in New York, indicated that the 1847 edition (for which no editor is listed) was expertly done. Apart from tempering Brevint's exuberant use of capital letters, it reproduced his seventeenth-century text very nearly as written. Passages from Brevint are identified by section and paragraph, retaining most of the punctuation and italics kept by the nineteenth-century editor.

When I cite a hymn from the 1780 *Collection of Hymns for the Use of The People Called Methodists*, I use the Bicentennial Edition, edited by Franz Hildebrandt and Oliver A. Beckerlegge, 1983, giving the number of the hymn and of the line(s).

Wesley's Bible was the Authorised Version, although for the Psalms he sometimes seems to have had in mind the version of the English Prayer Book (which is substantially Coverdale). I have used for period biblical citations a reprint of the first edition of the Authorised Version that was published by Thomas Nelson, Nashville, Tennessee (n.d.), but I have modernised the spelling.

Citations from the Book of Common Prayer are from the 1662 edition, the one that the Wesleys knew, loved and used.

For clarification of Wesley's vocabulary and usage I have frequently turned to Samuel Johnson's *Dictionary of the English Language*, which was originally published in 1755. I have used a copy of the third edition, from 1785, that was given to me years ago by my late friend and colleague, Donald F. Winslow.

Quotations from John Wesley's *Journal* are from the Everyman's Library edition, which is serviceable; and Charles Wesley's *Journal* is quoted from the Thomas Jackson edition of 1849. Both journals are cited by the date of the entry, rather than by the page in the edition used, and they are not footnoted.

Citations from John Wesley's sermons are from *John Wesley's Sermons: An Anthology*, edited by Albert C. Outler and Richard P. Heitzenrater, 1991. The texts in this anthology are those of Outler's critical edition.

In my (not very frequent) quotations from Richard Hooker I have used an edition of 1635, modernising the spelling and adding the paragraph numbers that have become standard. This may not be in every detail what Hooker wrote. For that one consults the Folger edition. But this seventeenth-century volume represents a text of the sort Wesley might have had at hand.

Quotations from Isaac Watts' hymns are from the 1753 edition of his works by David Jennings and Philip Doddridge in a handsome printing in six volumes by John Barfield, London, 1810. Watts' poetry is all in volume IV. I have cited hymn, stanza and line in the same style that I have used for the Wesley hymns.

The quotations in the Introduction, from Hooker, Anthony Sparrow, Joseph Hall, Jeremy Taylor, John Johnson, Isaac Watts, William Law and others are, for the most part, drawn from period copies in my own library.

In my discussion of the engraving which appears on page 170, several paragraphs follow generally my essay 'The Altar and the Cross: The Atonement in *Hymns on the Lord's Supper*' that was published in the *Proceedings of the Charles Wesley Society* 5 (1998), pp. 61–80. This material is used by permission.

Chronicles or eloquent discourses, may best please when they are cursorily run over; but mysteries must be studied, or they cannot well be understood; and God knows how much more is here required at our hands besides bare understanding.

Daniel Brevint

O the Grace on Man bestow'd!
Here my dearest LORD I see
Offering up his Death to GOD,
Giving all his Life to me:
God for JESU's Sake forgives
Man by JESU's Spirit lives.

Charles Wesley

Introduction

The Wesleys' Sacramental Hymns

In 1745 John and Charles Wesley published a small volume, *Hymns on the Lord's Supper*, consisting of a Preface "extracted from Dr Brevint' (about whom nothing is said), followed by 166 hymns, in five sections. The hymns, which are the Wesleys' most extensive and important expression of their sacramental doctrine and spirituality, remained in print and in widespread use among British Methodists through the rest of the eighteenth century.

The hymns, which seem to have been struck off in a period of intense creativity, are a landmark of the place that was held by the Lord's Supper at the beginning of the Methodist movement. But more significantly, in the broad literature of Christian devotion, *Hymns on the Lord's Supper* might be placed in nomination as the most spiritually profound and stylistically vigorous manual of eucharistic devotion ever written in English. The Wesley scholar Ole Borgen has described their work as 'the greatest treasure of sacramental hymnody that any church ever possessed'.[1] Yet the volume fell into neglect, and for more than two centuries its hymns have remained hardly known and little sung. The story of these hymns, their creation and their passing into obscurity, can be sketched here.

The Evangelical Revival expressed its spirit and doctrines through hymns. The Wesleys discovered the power of hymn singing from the Moravians with whom they became acquainted on their voyage to Georgia and whose pietistic hymns expressed a warm, inward love of Christ. On shipboard John learned German so that he could know the Moravian tradition better. In 1737, in Charlestown, John Wesley issued *A Collection of Psalms and Hymns*, a small work which drew heavily on the hymns of Isaac Watts and contained several of his own translations from German texts, but no hymns by his brother Charles. Although most of John's poetry is somewhat stiff, in his hymns from the German his lines flow easily, showing no marks of being translations. They may be his best work in verse.

The mission to Georgia was disappointing, and first Charles and then John returned to London in a state of spiritual discontent. Charles' restlessness was resolved in an evangelical awakening on Whitsunday, 1738, which he summarised: 'Still I felt a violent opposition and reluctance to believe; yet still the Spirit of God strove with my own and the evil spirit, till by degrees He chased away the darkness of my unbelief. I found myself convinced, I knew not how nor when' (*Journal*, 21 May 1738). Two days later John had a similar experience, when, as he tells in the best-known passage in his *Journal*, he came into a meeting at Aldersgate Street in London where he overheard Luther's *Preface to Romans* being read, and his heart was 'strangely warmed'.

On 23 May Charles remarked in his *Journal* that he had begun a hymn on his conversion. It was probably 'Where shall my wond'ring soul begin'.[2] His fresh experience released a flow of creativity, and from then until shortly before his death he wrote verse constantly. The number of his poetical works is uncertain – he never gathered a complete collection; some of his hymns were never published; some appear in more than one version or were left incomplete; and some of his poems were ephemeral celebrations of personal or family events, or even comments on public happenings. Frank Baker sets the total number of his compositions in verse at just short of 9,000. But to say how many hymns he wrote, as Eric Routley remarked, 'depends on what you call a hymn'. Most informed estimates set a figure of something in excess of 6,000, which were written over a career spanning fifty years.[3]

At the time of the publication of *Hymns on the Lord's Supper*, the Wesleyan movement was growing rapidly and the brothers were constantly on the move. Yet all through the travel, the preaching, the writing, and the organisational work of the early 1740s, Charles wrote and published hymns, issuing them in small topical collections. A volume on *God's Everlasting Love*, a stinging critique of Calvinism in verse, was published in 1741; a book of hymns for Christmas was issued in 1745; and collections for Easter, Ascension and Pentecost were published in 1746; and there were others.

The first edition of *Hymns on the Lord's Supper* was printed in 1745 by Felix Farley in Bristol under the names of both brothers, John being identified as Fellow of Lincoln-College, Oxford, and Charles as Student of Christ Church, Oxford. (In the third edition, London, 1757, both brothers were identified as 'Presbyters of the Church of England'.) All of the hymn books until the large collection of 1749 were issued as the work of John and Charles, while the books which followed carried only Charles' name.[4]

In the months preceding the publication of *Hymns on the Lord's Supper*, John and Charles were moving in different parts of England, and editorial collaboration would have been difficult. It seems certain that John contributed the essay which opens the book (an abridgement of a work by Daniel Brevint), and Hymn 85, which is a translation from Zinzendorf, and the two hymns, numbers 9 and 160, which are adaptations of poems by George Herbert. The authorship of a few other hymns has drawn question (see Appendix 3). In general, however, the hymns of this collection show consistent stylistic traits and they express passionately held ideas which do not appear in John's relatively few remarks on the Lord's Supper, and they are taken to be Charles' work.[5] They do not contradict anything that John said about the sacrament; they simply develop along independent lines. Six of the hymns that were included in *Hymns on the Lord's Supper* (numbers 9, 85, 160, 161, 163 and 164) had appeared in a 1739 volume, but the rest seem to have been written for this collection, and they must have been written in a fairly short time. *Hymns on the Lord's Supper* was republished in the eighteenth century more often than any other volume of Wesley's hymns. It remained in use and in demand.

Although the Methodist revival was growing and gathering an eager following, it was also encountering opposition. While other religious societies were taking their own way in eighteenth-century Britain, Methodism attracted more than ordinary notice. It was aggressively evangelistic, calling for conversion and an experience of 'new birth' in a population that was nominally Christian and Church of England and which was, to a great extent, baptised. It disregarded jurisdictions, asserting spiritual authority, whether episcopally authorised or not. Its field preaching attracted crowds, sometimes numbering in the thousands, including many from among the socially disinherited. To those who remembered the disruptions of the seventeenth century, this religious stir could seem not only irregular, but dangerous, even vaguely seditious.

Moreover, the eighteenth century valued decorum, and cultivated persons were scandalised by the ecstatic demonstrations that sometimes accompanied the preaching of the early Methodists. While to its followers the spiritual reality of the revival was undeniable, aspects of it almost invited misunderstanding, and it provoked enemies. Eminent churchmen denounced the Methodists; and unruly listeners, angry mobs and even riots followed them. The Wesleys themselves and their adherents were repelled from some parish churches and opposed by many incumbents. In one well-known incident, when John Wesley was denied the pulpit of his father's former church in Epworth, he preached from a tombstone in the churchyard.

These sacramental hymns give little hint of the tumult that surrounded the movement in the years in which they were written. Occasionally they express a determination to remain loyal, implying that members of the Societies might not find it easy to hold to their new-found convictions. A few of the hymns in the collection refer to conflicts with Calvinist predestinarianism and with Moravians of the 'stillness' persuasion. Generally, however, these hymns, which are expressed largely in biblical imagery, celebrate penetratingly, joyfully, and for the most part without polemic, the Sacrament of the Table.

The hymns exhibit the strong sacramental emphasis of the Wesleys and of early Methodism. John Wesley himself, throughout his long life, received the Holy Communion every four or five days, and daily during some seasons; and Charles' practice was similar. In a sermon on 'The Duty of Constant Communion' which John wrote while still at Oxford, but which he ratified as his mature opinion by publishing it late in his career, he urged that 'It is the duty of every Christian to receive the Lord's Supper as often as he can.'[6] The Wesleys never relaxed the sacramental regularity they had adopted as Oxford Methodists.

The Wesleys thought of Methodism as an evangelistic movement within the Church of England. It was their express wish that the activities of the Methodists not conflict with the services of the parish churches, at which the Wesleys' followers were expected to receive the Holy Communion. There is indication that the early Methodists, where they were welcome, eagerly filled the parish churches at the time of the sacrament. John Wesley, writing shortly after his withdrawal, with some followers, from the Fetter Lane Society, reported, 'At St. Luke's, our parish church, was such a sight, as, I believe, was never seen there before: Several hundred communicants, from whose very faces one might judge, that they indeed sought Him that was crucified' (*Journal*, Sunday, 3 August 1740). In the year of the publication of the sacramental hymns, Charles Wesley described the emotion at a sacramental occasion: 'At five I preached in the room; at eight in Kingswood, on the new Jerusalem. I administered the sacrament to all the Society; and God, the consolation of Israel, visited us. The whole congregation were moved to cry after him, either through sorrow or through joy' (*Journal*, Sunday, 31 March 1745). Some years later, Charles' *Journal* entry for Sunday, 17 October 1756, reads: 'I preached a second time at Haworth, (Mr. Grimshaw [the vicar] reading prayers) . . . The church, which had lately been enlarged, could scarce contain the congregation . . . We had a blessed number of communicants, and the Master of the feast in the midst.'

There is some uncertainty as to how Wesley's sacramental hymns were used. The Church of England was slow to adopt hymn singing, feeling that approved singing was confined to the Psalms in English meter. The long-used version by Sternhold and Hopkins, 1562, was in Wesley's day gradually being replaced by the 'New Version' by Nahum Tate and Nicholas Brady, 1696, which was often bound in editions of the Prayer Book. These metrical psalms were stylistically rather awkward, and in most churches they were 'lined out' in dreary, slow-moving fashion by a precentor. Since there was no designated place for congregational hymns in the liturgy, Wesley's sacramental hymns may have been used by Methodists as preparation for the sacrament. Evidently printed hymn books were used in homes for private and family devotion. However, in some places the hymns seem to have been sung during the administration of communion when the members of the Methodist societies, crowding the churches on sacrament Sunday, protracted the time for serving the elements. A correspondent wrote to John Wesley in 1756, '[Since] the number of communicants is generally very great, the time spent in receiving is long enough for many to feel their devotion languish for want of outward fuel.'[7] Where, in time, Methodists could observe the Lord's Supper on their own terms, these hymns could be sung freely.

Once this small book of hymns was issued, it became and remained the Wesleys' principal statement of their sacramental doctrine and spirituality. Charles Wesley returned to the subject infrequently, while *Hymns on the Lord's Supper* went through nine editions during his lifetime, with only unimportant changes. The Wesleys had declared their mind on the subject in a work which remained in print and in use.

The hymns and their reception are evidence that for the early Methodists the Holy Communion was a focus of the intense personal relation between Christ and the believer. The Supper was a celebration for converts as well as an invitation to conversion. These *Hymns on the Lord's Supper* articulated and informed the faith of the Methodists,[8] providing sacramental doctrine that could be sung.

However, in both British and American Methodism, sacramental interest and practice declined from the intention of the Wesleys.

After the tenth edition of *Hymns on the Lord's Supper* was issued in 1784, the work was reprinted once more, in 1825, and then not again until the study editions of the mid-to-late twentieth century. Seven of its hymns were included in the large and influential *Collection of Hymns for the Use of The People Called Methodists*, 1780, but, as Geoffrey Wainwright observes, 'even then their relocation in a different framework renders their eucharistic reference less obvious.'[9]

In Britain, in the early decades of the revival, the members of the

Methodist Societies were expected to receive the Holy Communion at their parish churches. But in many parishes Methodists were not welcome, and in time the necessarily non-eucharistic meetings of the Societies – meetings consisting of song, scripture, preaching, and mutual encouragement, and at times love-feasts and Wesley's Covenant Service – came to seem a complete and satisfactory form of corporate devotion.[10] Indeed, the directness, warmth and sense of community of these services may have contrasted with the staidness and impersonality that often marked the services of the churches of the Establishment. When in time it became possible for Methodists to celebrate the Holy Communion in their own meeting places, led by their own clergy, the practice of frequent communion, insofar as it had established itself, had largely lapsed. But the Wesleys had intended otherwise, and British Methodism has a way of remembering the Wesleys and recalling itself to what they had in mind. In the twentieth century, the successive British Methodist hymn books of 1904, 1933 and 1938 each included a variable selection of about 15 items from *Hymns on the Lord's Supper*.

In America, Methodism was a presence in the colonies in Wesley's lifetime, and it grew astonishingly in the nineteenth century. Eucharistic doctrine and practice of the sort that the Wesleys intended did not, however, become firmly established. *Hymns on the Lord's Supper* was never published for American Methodists, although a few of its hymns were included in the widely used *Pocket Hymn Book* (first published in England in 1784 and then revised and printed often in America after 1787). The *Sunday Service*, a communion order which John Wesley had prepared expressly for the American congregations, was little used, although parts of it were incorporated in the Discipline.[11] The Methodists, using lay preachers, were able to move with the American frontier. Few Methodist converts brought a Church of England background, and knowledge and customs which the Revival could to some extent take for granted in Britain were not present in American society. Detached from the personal authority of John Wesley and from its British, Church of England roots, American Methodism came to be marked by the activism and individualism of the then-forming style of American revivalism. (It should be said that all of the religious groups that came from Europe were affected by this powerful indigenous style.) This American religious pragmatism reduced the theological seriousness, the sense of the Church and of sacramental order that the Wesleys had cherished.

By the time that the modern, well-edited denominational hymnals began to be prepared, the hymns that Charles Wesley had written for the Supper had largely slipped from the Church's memory. Geoffrey Wainwright, speaking of American Methodism, says that 'In the twentieth-century hymnals, the *Hymns on the Lord's Supper* have been almost completely ignored.'[12] (Note should be taken of *The Wesley Hymn Book*, a small collection issued in 1958 by Franz Hildebrandt who sought to restore some of Wesley's hymns to use. It included sixteen hymns from *Hymns on the Lord's Supper*.)[13]

The Wesleyan Movement was, in the intentions of John and Charles, at the same time both evangelistic and eucharistic. However, it came to be understood among Evangelical churches in America that Christian groups which were interested in evangelism would not be interested in sacraments and that persons or churches which cared about sacraments would show little interest in evangelism. This bifurcation would have been incomprehensible to the Wesleys and to many of their earliest followers for whom conversion and sacrament formed a unity of faith and obedience. Perhaps this split is being addressed. For some decades, ecclesial and sacramental interests have grown stronger among American Methodists, although Wesley's eucharistic hymns remain little known. However, custody of these hymns does not fall solely to Methodists. The doctrine and practice of the Lord's Supper are the business of churches ecumenically. While Charles Wesley wrote his sacramental hymns with the Methodist societies in mind, he wrote as a presbyter of the Church of England. Along with an ecumenical renewal of interest in the Sacrament of the Table, there might be renewed attention to this classic body of sacramental devotion. Unaware, Wesley wrote for all churches and for the Church that is to come.

Traditions and Influences

The experience of the Wesleys placed them where traditions met. Yet the hymns make little express reference to earlier or contemporary sacramental ideas, either to agree or to disagree. Charles simply sets forth the relation of the communicant with the living Christ as he understands it, evidently thinking that when he speaks of the Lord's Supper as a meeting-place of God and a believer – a meeting-place suffused with mercy and glory, presence and sacrifice – he could draw on a shared body of understanding.

While the Wesleys were at Oxford, they read much in Pre-Reformation sources – the literature of the early Church and of the spiritual writers of the Middle Ages. They were especially attracted by Thomas à Kempis' *Imitation of Christ*. The sacramental hymns indicate that they were familiar with some of the liturgies of the early Church – possibly through the work *Principal Liturgies*, 1720, by the learned Non-juror Thomas Brett, which contained texts of early rites as well as an important 'dissertation' on them.[14] Under the influence of the Non-jurors, the 'Holy Club' had sought to follow the model – in doctrine, personal discipline, charity and sacramental practice – of the early Church as these earnest young men would have understood it.

However, there were two large, more close-at-hand contexts on which Charles Wesley's sacramental thought seems to have drawn.

Continental Protestant and English Nonconformist Thought

Luther, Calvinism and the English Puritans

The Wesleys drew from the Reformation traditions, but in a qualified way.

Both Lutherans and Calvinists affirmed Christ's presence in the eucharist. They did so against the radical Protestant parties in the sixteenth and seventeenth centuries which, reacting from the excessive Roman claims that localised Christ's very body and blood in the consecrated bread and wine, took a position of pure memorialism, recognising Christ's presence only in the hearts of faithful receivers. But, as both Luther and Calvin saw the matter, to reduce the Holy Communion to an act in which Christ is present only inwardly to the believer subverts the power which they knew the instituted sacrament to have. At the eucharist, Christians do not encounter their own faith; rather, they meet Christ himself, made known to them in the breaking of the bread. The Supper is not so much an occasion at which Christians think devoutly about Christ's past act as it is itself a present act of the living Christ. While the major churches of the Reformation affirmed the sacramental presence, they did so in somewhat different idioms.

At the time of Charles Wesley's spiritual awakening, at Pentecost, 1738, he had been reading Luther on Galatians, by which he was greatly blessed. John Wesley's evangelical awakening (or perhaps one should say one of his several moments of spiritual crisis, and the best known) occurred when at Aldersgate Street in London he overheard Luther's *Preface to Romans* being read. For a time, both brothers expressed their appreciation for Luther. They took from him the recovered Pauline doctrine of justification by faith – which, for them as for Luther, was not just one doctrine among many, but was the criterion of Christian truth. However, the Wesleys usually cited the Articles of Religion and the Homily 'On Salvation' as authority for their doctrine. Moreover, in time their understanding of the relation of justification to sanctification came to differ from that of the Lutheran tradition, and they did not take their doctrine of the eucharistic presence from Luther.

With respect to the Holy Communion, as Luther saw it, the medieval Mass had become a sacrificial work performed by a priest to obtain divine mercy for the living and the dead. By contrast, Luther regarded the Communion as the Church's grateful recognition of mercy given. It, like the redemption it signified, is God's gift to sinful humanity. The words 'this is my body' are not a miracle-working formula spoken by the priest, but words of grace and promise spoken in the Church by Christ himself. The Reformers insisted that the only sacrifice that can be made for sin has been made by God acting in Christ. All that Christians can do is to receive it trustingly.

However, although Luther strongly emphasised God's gift in the sacrament, he was able to speak of the Supper as an act of Christian sacrifice – never supplementing or repeating the sacrifice of Christ, but held within and subsumed under that one redemptive act. In the Sacrament of the Table, Luther said, we enter into Christ's sacrifice. We 'offer ourselves as a sacrifice along with Christ. That is, we lay ourselves on Christ by a firm faith in his testament and do not otherwise appear before God with our prayer, praise, and sacrifice except through Christ and his mediation. Not so we doubt that Christ is our priest or minister in heaven before God.'[15] Although Charles Wesley developed this side of eucharistic thought beyond anything Luther said, he would not have needed to think that in doing so he set himself in opposition to the German Reformer.

The Wesleys' more obvious ties were with Calvinism. Through the seventeenth century, the theological conversation of the Church of England had been with the Reformed tradition. The Wesleys' parents, Samuel and Susanna, had both come to the Church of England from Puritan Nonconformity. To this heritage we may trace John and Charles' intellectual and spiritual rigour and their characteristic plainness of style – their impatience with luxury, fineness and show. Moreover, Puritanism insisted on 'experimental religion'. Serious believers, in this tradition, monitored their own interior life for signs, more or less evident, of their election or of their immediate relation with God. The Wesleyan movement similarly required Christians to keep inward watch.

The Wesleys' debt to Calvinism was, however, somewhat mixed. When Wesley says in *Hymns on the Lord's Supper* that the gospel invitation is for *all* – 'Thy flesh for all the world is given,/ And all may live by thee' (30:7.3–4) – he is expressing his vigorous opposition to the Calvinist doctrine that in the purpose of God the effect of the atonement is limited to the elect. As evangelists, the Wesleys had to ask why they should invite persons to Christ if, by divine decree, many of them had forever been made reprobate. Similarly, the Wesleys thought that the Calvinist certainty of the perseverance of the saints opened the way to antinomianism – hence the repeated emphasis in these hymns that one who is forgiven is committed to holiness of life.

Nevertheless, the Wesleys' strong objections to some of the points of Calvinism (objections that do not seem to have been based on a deep reading of Calvin) should not obscure their indebtedness to the Calvinist tradition as it had been mediated to England through the Puritans. (While the Wesleys were consciously Arminian, most eighteenth- and nineteenth-century Anglican Evangelicals, who were in one sense of the Wesleys' school, were at least moderate Calvinists. The Wesleys, in rejecting Calvinism, created tension with some of their close associates, such as George Whitefield and Lady Huntington, and with later followers, such as Charles Simeon.) When in these hymns Wesley speaks of the 'virtue' of Christ acting in the sacrament, he means divine power. (The idea is often present even when the word 'virtue' is not.) In the sacrament, Christ acts in grace, and in his acting he is present. Calvin's eucharistic teaching expresses a similar 'virtualism', closely related to the Calvinist-Puritan emphasis on the Holy Spirit as the effecting divine agent in the human relation with God, and hence in the sacrament. Rejecting scholastic terms of 'substance', and using biblical categories, Calvin taught that in the sacrament, Christ, by the Holy Spirit, is immediately present to the believer: 'The virtue of the Holy Spirit is joined to the sacraments when they are duly received.'[16] Wesley would have found such a teaching congenial.

As to sacrifice, John Calvin, in his principal discussion of the means of grace in his *Institutes of the Christian Religion*, Bk. IV, ch. xviii, speaks of Christian sacrifices of thanksgiving, among which he included 'all our prayers, praises, thanksgivings, and whatever we do in the worship of God'. He explains that such sacrifices are not independent offerings, but that they 'finally depend upon the greater sacrifice, by which we are consecrated in soul and body to be a holy temple to the Lord'.[17] He continued, saying that the Lord's Supper, as an act in which Christians proclaim Christ's death and offer praise, is the sacrificial act of a royal and priestly people. Moreover, Christians offer what they are and have through Christ, the Great High Priest who has entered the heavenly sanctuary. This theme is clearly present in Calvin's thought, though it remained largely undeveloped in Calvin's own work and in later Calvinism.

The Puritan emphasis on the Spirit's agency in the sacrament came to expression in the 'Savoy Liturgy' which Richard Baxter, a moderate Puritan, prepared after the Restoration. Baxter's remarkable text was meant to indicate the sort of liturgy the Puritans might approve if they could have their way. Baxter's eucharistic prayer was composed entirely of phrases from the New Testament and was organised on a trinitarian scheme, its third part being a prayer for the Spirit.[18] Baxter's 'epiclesis' speaks of the Spirit in the believer, never of a relation of the Spirit to the bread and wine or to the liturgical action. Yet this Puritan Communion rite emphasised the Holy Spirit as the Prayer Books of the Church of England did not, but as Charles Wesley's eucharistic hymns would 75 years later.

Very likely Charles Wesley knew *The Communicant's Companion*, 1704, a volume of sacramental devotion by the Presbyterian divine Matthew Henry (1662–1714). Henry was a late representative of the Puritan tradition, which, as he spoke for it, had grown pastoral in tone. Henry's large Bible commentary is an enduring devotional work which the Wesleys knew and on which Charles based several hymns (none, however, in *Hymns on the Lord's Supper*).

In Henry's *Companion* (which continued in print in the English-speaking world for a century and a half) he says that the Holy Communion 'hath the whole New Testament in it'. However, in his many pages he says almost nothing of the eucharistic elements or action, and the ordinance (his preferred term) is only sacrificial insofar as it is a believer's sacrifice of thanksgiving. (Henry does not base the reality of the Christian sacrament in Christ's eternal priesthood and sacrifice.) He is principally concerned with helping the communicant to identify the inward dispositions ('frames') with which to come to and receive the sacrament. At the Holy Communion one renews one's covenant with God and finds communion with the living Christ: 'We see nothing here, if we see not the beauty of Christ; we taste nothing here, if we taste not the love of Christ' (ch. I, ii.2).[19] He says that God by the Spirit conveys to us the good things of his promise; therefore, 'receive Christ Jesus the Lord, Christ and pardon, Christ and peace, Christ and grace, Christ and heaven; 'tis all your own, if you come up to the terms on which it is offered in the gospel' (ch. II, iii.1). A generation before the Wesleys' Communion hymns, Matthew Henry's work had provided a well-expressed, deeply felt appreciation of a believer's relation to Christ in the Sacrament of the Table.

Some of Charles Wesley's sacramental emphases fall outside Reformed and Nonconformist teaching. Indeed, Baxter and Henry would have differed strongly from some of his ideas on sacrifice. Yet Wesley's understanding of the sacrament could draw on parts of the theology and spirituality of this affirmative and accessible tradition.

The Moravians

The movement known as Pietism grew up in reaction to the arid scholasticism that had come to mark much of the German Lutheran tradition in the seventeenth century. The religion of pietism was deeply inward, seeking to bring the head into the heart. The Moravians were part of this pietist stir, although the group had older, Hussite roots. The missionary impulse was powerful among the Moravians, and England became a staging-point for German missionaries who were bound for the American colonies, particularly Georgia and Pennsylvania. The Wesleys met a group of Moravians on their voyage to Georgia, and were impressed by their simplicity, their faith and sense of community. Later, after John had returned to London, he shared the leadership of the society that met at Fetter Lane with the Moravian minister, Peter Boehler.

Soon after his evangelical awakening, John went to Germany, where he lived briefly at Herrnhut and met the charismatic Moravian leader Count von Zinzendorf. He admired the devotion, the communal life and the charitable work of the Moravians, which put him in mind of the primitive Church.

The love for Christ that was openly expressed in the Moravian hymns gave a model for later Methodist hymnody. When such motifs as the believer being present at the very crucifixion, or drinking and washing in Jesus' blood, or recognising one's own sins as having brought Jesus to the cross, or references to Christ as victorious Lamb, or a fixation on Jesus' wounds, appear in Charles Wesley's hymns, they can be taken as evidence of Moravian influence (even though many such motifs also had an older medieval background).

When he returned to London, John Wesley found the society at Fetter Lane falling under the influence of a radical Moravian, Philip Molther, recently come from Germany, who contended that the inward working of God is not mediated by any 'means of grace', but is the mysterious action of God's Spirit bearing immediate witness with one's own spirit. As Molther and his followers saw it, any effort to associate grace with 'means' introduced an element of works-righteousness into the relation with God. One cannot use 'means' without in some measure trusting in them. All that one can rightly do is to wait in patience for God.

The upholders of this point of view became known as the 'stillness' group, from their frequent appeal to the text, 'Be still then, and know that I am God' (Psalm 46:10). At its most extreme, the group judged that one could receive faith without any outward means, such as sacraments, ministers, or even Scripture. John Wesley in his *Journal* for 1 November 1739 reports that Molther had persuaded one woman that she had never had any faith at all and should 'be still, ceasing from outward works' until she received faith. 'Running about to church and sacraments', he said, was folly.

After a brief hesitation, it became clear to the Wesleys that the 'stillness' teaching was an effort, in the name of spirituality, to disobey the unmistakable word of Christ; and in July 1740 they led a group out of the Fetter Lane Society; and from that time on, the Wesleys and the Moravians took separate ways.

This painful conflict occasioned several of the *Hymns on the Lord's Supper* in which Wesley argues in verse against the 'stillness' persuasion. But despite the quarrel, the relationship with the Moravians had a lasting and positive influence on the Methodist movement and its sacramental piety. John Bowmer says (referring to John, but using words that would apply to both brothers), that it was the contact with the Moravians that changed the Lord's Supper from the 'bounden duty' it might otherwise have remained for the Wesleys into a 'Gospel Feast'.[20]

The Sacramental Hymns of Isaac Watts

When Charles Wesley turned his hand to a series of hymns on the sacrament, his principal model – it may well have been his only model – would have been the group of 25 hymns 'Prepared for the Lord's Supper' by the Independent hymn-writer Isaac Watts, constituting Book III of his collection *Hymns and Spiritual Songs*, first published in 1707. While these hymns are not even in quality, they form a notable group in which Watts pioneered for English-speaking Christians what hymns on the Holy Communion should talk about, what tone they should adopt, what vocabulary they should employ. They are the first eucharistic hymns in English that show real distinction of thought and expression. Clearly the prize of the collection is Hymn 7, 'When I survey the wondrous cross', universally acknowledged as one of the great hymns in the English language, but not always recognised as a hymn written for the Holy Communion.

Watts' sacramental hymns, like Wesley's, focus on the cross: 'In lively figures here [in the sacrament] we see/ The bleeding Prince of love' (16:2.1–2). Watts celebrates a triumphal feast, 'Victorious God! what can we pay/ For favours so divine?' (21:11.1–2). Like Wesley, Watts dramatises the divine reversal in the gospel, 'He sunk beneath our heavy woes/ To raise us to his throne' (4:3.1–2); 'Jesus, the God that fought and bled,/ And conquer'd when he fell' (21:1.1–2); and:

Thy cruel thorns, thy shameful cross
Procure us heavenly crowns;

Our highest gain springs from thy loss,
Our healing from thy wounds. (23:4)

In these lines and in others, Watts speaks of Jesus' 'wounds', much as
Wesley will, 'From all his wounds new blessings flow,/ A sea of joy
without a shore' (22:4.3–4). Watts also speaks of Jesus' blood in terms as
exuberant as those Wesley will use:

Here we have wash'd our deepest stains,
And heal'd our wounds with heavenly blood:
Blest fountain! springing from the veins
Of Jesus our incarnate God. (22:5)

Watts, like Wesley, sees the Supper as a pledge of heaven: 'Come the dear
day, the glorious hour/ That brings our souls to rest!/ Then we shall need
these types no more,/ But dwell at th' heavenly feast' (15:7). As Wesley
later will, Watts speaks of the Lord's Supper as a 'recording rite'; he mentions Jesus' 'dying groan' (3:4.3); and he describes human beings in their
lowliness as 'worms' (17:1.4; 22:2.4). Both writers express sorrow for
sin, joy in undeserved grace, and confidence in final glory.

As to style, almost all of Watts' hymns are in four-line stanzas in the
most usual meters: common (8.6.8.6), long (8.8.8.8), and short (6.6.8.6).
Most of Watts' stanzas rhyme abab, but some abcb. (Wesley does not
use the rhyme scheme abcb.) Watts, like Wesley, wrote lines that are
comprised of lists: 'My life and soul, my heart and flesh,/ And all my
powers are thine' (3:3.3–4). Both writers make conscious use of alliteration.

O. A. Beckerlegge remarks that 'Watts' *Psalms and Hymns* presumably were part of the singing diet of the Holy Club.'[21] There are, of
course, many themes in Wesley's much larger collection which do not
occur in Watts' 25 hymns. Notably, Watts – following the general Dissenting tradition, and unlike the Wesleys – makes no connection between
the sacrament and Christ's heavenly high priesthood. However, a few
of Watts' emphases, such as his reading of 'the book of nature', do not
appear in Wesley. Yet there are strong similarities between the two collections in tone, themes and vocabulary. It seems certain that these eloquent
and thoughtful hymns by the revered Dr Watts were a direct influence on
the later work of Charles Wesley.[22]

Anglican Sacramental Thought

The context that most locates Charles Wesley is the spirituality and doctrine of a succession of writers of the Church of England. As Ole Borgen put it, 'Generally speaking, Wesley received his theology of the sacraments directly from the Anglican tradition.'[23]

In this tradition, first place must be given to the Book of Common Prayer. Wesley would have had in mind the form of the Lord's Supper which he had known as a worshipper and a presbyter – the form contained in the Prayer Book of 1662, understood to some extent through the teaching of the Non-jurors. The Prayer Book, as a liturgical text, communicates an understanding of the sacrament not so much by theological propositions as by its structures, its tone and the largely metaphoric language of its rhetoric – language which carries doctrinal meaning and sets some limits, but which admits more than one theological construction.

Charles Wesley, in his sacramental hymns, drew on the Prayer Book somewhat sparingly. He would have internalised its restraint, its economy and its concentration on essentials. He twice adopts the vocabulary and speech forms of the Litany; he alludes to the 'humble access' prayer; he turns a passage of the Catechism into verse; and he paraphrases the *Gloria in Excelsis*. A few of his hymns which are prayers take a form resembling a collect.[24]

The Wesleys' understanding of the Lord's Supper stands in a succession of churchly-minded Anglican writers that runs through Richard Hooker, Lancelot Andrewes, John Cosin, Herbert Thorndike, Jeremy Taylor, Simon Patrick, Robert Nelson, John Johnson, William Law, the Non-jurors and Daniel Waterland, to name only some of the most eminent.[25] This was the tradition of their father, Samuel Wesley. Unless this sixteenth- and seventeenth-century background is taken into account, Charles Wesley's ideas can seem original when they are not, and his actual originality may go unrecognised.

The shapers of the Anglican tradition differed among themselves in emphasis and idiom, yet over the generations, several affirmations concerning the eucharist gained general consent. Discussion of the sacrament was dominated by controversy – a thing which the controversialists themselves often lamented – and controversy in England (as generally in the West) centred around the two issues of eucharistic presence and eucharistic sacrifice.

Eucharistic Presence

Anglican theologians of this 'high' tradition were agreed that Christ is present in the sacrament of the table, although many of them remarked that it is not necessary to know how he is present in order to be certain of his presence and receive his benefits. Hooker, for instance, had said: 'Let it be sufficient for me presenting myself at the Lord's table to know what there I receive from him, without searching or inquiring of the manner how Christ performeth his promise' (*Ecclesiastical Polity*, V. lxvii.12). This reluctance to define was not a case of refusing to think, nor of intellectual muddle, but was based in the conviction that no theoretical account can capture the richness and mystery of Christ in the eucharist as it is known in the faith of the Church. Theories are bounded, while the sacrament, like the God who is known in the sacrament, exceeds the reach of the mind.

The Anglican writers thought that the medieval doctrine of transubstantiation, based in categories of Aristotle, was a mistaken account of sacramental presence. In the eyes of the English churchmen, when transubstantiation held that at consecration the substance of the body and blood of Christ replaces the substance of the bread and wine, it qualified the nature of the eucharistic elements – the breadness of the bread and the wineness of the wine. Hence, as the Articles of Religion charged, it 'overthroweth the nature of a sacrament' (Art. XXVIII). Most Anglicans, certainly the Wesleys, were un-speculative by temperament and impatient with metaphysical subtleties.

Anglican divines, with differences of emphasis among them and with varying degrees of clarity, found their way between transubstantiation, which, in their judgement, claimed too much for the sacrament, and receptionism, which claimed too little.

Richard Hooker (c. 1554–1600) devoted almost one third of his lengthy Book V of *The Laws of Ecclesiastical Polity* (*EP*) to the doctrine of the Holy Communion. His greatest achievement in the matter may have been to set the reality of the sacrament within the prior realities of the Church and of Christ. 'There is no union of God with man,' he said, 'without that mean between both which is both, it seemeth requisite that we first consider how God is in Christ, then how Christ is in us, and how the Sacraments do serve to make us partakers of Christ' (*EP*, V.l.3). Approaching the matter so, he develops a profound Christology and ecclesiology before he turns to the sacraments. When he does, the heart of what he had to say may be suggested by his irenic comment that on all sides there should be 'a general agreement concerning that which alone is material, namely, the *real participation* of Christ and of life in his body and blood *by means of the sacrament*' (*EP*, V.lxvii.2). Christ, by the sacrament, brings about a union between himself and the devout communicant. Hooker asks whether more than that needs to be said.

Later Church of England writers sustained this tradition. Joseph Hall (1574–1656), bishop, polemicist and author of popular meditations, wrote in 1631:

Every simple act of our faith feeds on Christ, but here [in the Sacrament] by virtue of that necessary union which our Saviour's institution hath made betwixt the sign and the thing signified, the faithful communicant doth partake of Christ in a more peculiar manner; now his very senses help and nourish his soul, and by his eyes, his hands, his taste, Christ is spiritually conveyed into his heart, to his unspeakable and everlasting consolation.[26]

The eloquent preacher, bishop, and guide of souls, Jeremy Taylor (1613–67), in his *The Worthy Communicant*, 1660, described Christ as found in the Supper, saying, 'Here the word of God is made our food in a manner so near to our understanding, that our tongues and palates feel the metaphor and the sacramental signification; here faith is in triumph and exaltation.'[27] Taylor emphasised that the sacrament is efficacious through the Holy Spirit. 'As the sacrament operates only by the virtue of the Spirit of God, so the Spirit ordinarily works by the instrumentality of the sacraments.'[28] During the Protectorate when the Prayer Book was proscribed, Taylor prepared a eucharistic rite which is virtually 'pentecostal' in citing the pervasive activity of the Holy Spirit.[29]

A writer who was a few years older than the Wesleys and whose works of moral counsel they admired was William Law (1686–1761). One of Law's early works was his reply to Bishop Hoadly's *A Plain Account of the Nature and End of the Sacrament of the Lord's Supper*, 1735. Hoadly, whose thought was of a rationalist cast, had argued that the meaning of the Lord's Supper was confined to what Jesus could have intended in his words at the Last Supper. Law responded with *A Demonstration of the Gross and Fundamental Errors of a late Book . . .*, 2nd edn, 1738. Almost pitying the thinness of Hoadly's understanding, Law argues that the institution and its promise must be read in the context of the whole gospel. 'To eat the *Body* and *Blood* of Christ, is neither more nor less than to *put on Christ*, to receive Birth and Life and Nourishment and Growth from him.' Christ in the sacrament, he says, is not past, but present, 'Neither Christ, nor his Benefits and Blessings have the Nature of things *done*, or *gone* and *past*, but are always present, always in being, always doing and never done.' Hoadly's limited grasp of what it means to remember leads Law to say, 'To remember God as absent, is but a very little way from *Atheism*.'[30] When Law in his later writings fell under the spell of the German mystic Jacob Boehme, the Wesleys turned away from him. Yet Law was a major Christian thinker of their own time who witnessed forcefully to the reality of Christ in the Supper.

The Wesleys' older contemporary, the scholarly Daniel Waterland (1683–1740), published his important work on the sacrament, *A Review of the Doctrine of the Eucharist*, in 1737.[31] Waterland wrote clearly and economically, and he argued fairly. He described the eucharist as a commemorative and representative act which communicates the virtue and grace of Christ's body and blood. Waterland summed up much of the argument that had gone before; his *Review* at once took its place as an authoritative work of Anglican eucharistic theology; and it was referred to with respect well into the nineteenth century.

Eucharistic Sacrifice

On the other matter of doctrinal contention, the eucharistic sacrifice, a succession of theologians of the Church of England expressed themselves along broadly similar lines. To cite a few of them:

Herbert Thorndike (1598–1672), one of the profoundest Anglican thinkers of the seventeenth century (though not always one of the clearest), says that in the eucharistic elements the sacrifice of Christ upon the cross 'is represented, renewed, revived, and restored . . ., and as every representation is said to be the same thing with that which it representeth; taking 'representation' here, not for a bare signifying, but for tendering and exhibiting thereby that which it signifieth.'[32]

Jeremy Taylor wrote on the sacrificial aspect of the eucharist in his early account of the life of Jesus, *The Great Exemplar*, 1649. When Taylor tells the story of the Last Supper, he digresses for an essay, 'The Institution and Reception of the Holy Sacrament of the Lord's Supper'. In this excursus he connects, as Wesley later will, the sacrifice of the cross, the eternal sacrifice in heaven, and the sacrifice of the Table:

As Christ is a Priest in heaven for ever, and yet does not sacrifice himself afresh, nor yet without a sacrifice could he be a Priest, but by a daily ministration and intercession represents his sacrifice to God, and offers himself as sacrificed; so he does upon earth by the ministry of his servants; he is offered to God, that is, he is by prayers and the Sacrament represented or offered up to God as sacrificed, which in effect, is a celebration of his death, and the applying it to the present and future necessities of the Church, as we are capable, by a ministry like to his in heaven.[33]

Writing somewhat later, Simon Patrick (1625–1707), Bishop of Chichester and later of Ely, wrote on the sacrament in two works, *The Christian Sacrifice*, 1672, and *Mensa Mystica*, 1684. In *The Christian Sacrifice* he said:

When we shew forth the inestimable value of Christ's Sacrifice, we do, as it were, offer it unto God: or rather make before him a commemoration of his Offering. And in this sense the Ancient Christians did call this Sacrament a Sacrifice: and every Christian they looked upon as a Priest and a Sacrificer, when he came to the Table of the Lord.[34]

John Wesley published an abridgement of this work by Patrick in his *Christian Library*.

In the late seventeenth century the Non-jurors argued for the essential place in the eucharistic action of 'the oblatory prayer', an element which had been in the consecration prayer of the 1549 Prayer Book, but had been relocated as a post-communion action in the Prayer Books of 1552 and 1662. In their judgement, the eucharist is the Church's sacrifice, and unless the consecration prayer itself expresses offering, a component essential to the sacramental act is missing. The Wesleys knew the works of the Non-jurors and, especially in their early years, sympathised with their liturgical programme.

The Non-juror lay-theologian Robert Nelson (1665–1715) was admired by the Wesleys; indeed, he had been a friend of their father's. In his widely used *Festivals and Fasts of the Church of England*, 1704 (a book John Wesley is known to have read while at Oxford), Nelson said that by consecration, the bread and wine of the eucharist are made symbols of the body and blood of Christ, by which 'we represent to God the Father the Passion of his Son, to the End he may for his Sake, according to the Tenour of his Covenant in him be favourable and propitious to us miserable sinners'.

Nelson's argument immediately passes to the book of Hebrews, saying, 'That as *Christ intercedes* continually for us in Heaven, by *presenting* his Death and Satisfaction to the Father; so the Church on Earth, in like Manner, may approach the Throne of Grace, *by representing* Christ unto his Father in these *holy Mysteries* of his Death and Passion.'[35]

As early as their ministry in Georgia the Wesleys were reading *The Unbloody Sacrifice and Altar* (2 vols, 1714 and 1718) by John Johnson (1662–1725), Vicar of Cranbrook in Kent. Although Johnson was not himself a Non-juror, his work – vastly learned, passionately argued and endlessly prolix – was influential among the Non-jurors. He demonstrates at length from general principles, patristic writers and early liturgies that the Holy Communion is a true sacrifice. However, as such, it does not diminish the sole saving efficacy of Christ's sacrifice:

> Since we offer nothing in the *Eucharist*, but what He by his own Insti- tution and Deputation hath made his Body and Blood, and since by offering this, we don't pretend to add to the Merits of his Death, but only to draw down to ourselves, and apply to our own Souls the Bless- ings which He purchas'd by dying for us; this is a full Demonstration that the Sacrifice of the *Eucharist* is so far from abating the Value of his Blood, that Nothing can more heighten and exalt it: For by this we fully declare our Belief, That there is no other Name under Heaven, whereby we can be saved, but that of *JESUS*, and his Passion is the Centre of all our Hopes.[36]

One of the most outspoken of the Non-jurors was Thomas Deacon (1697–1753), with whom John Wesley was acquainted. Deacon's *Devo- tions*, 1734, which John read while at Oxford, is a quite complete Prayer Book which offered a Non-juring alternative to the official liturgy of the Church of England. (In its central portions, it held closely to the fourth-century *Apostolic Constitutions*.) His doctrines, which support his *Devotions*, are expressed in *A View of Christianity* (2nd edn, 1748), which consists of two catechisms, one short and one very long. He opens his longer explanation of the sacrificial aspect of the eucharist, comment- ing:

> The greatest benefit that was ever conferred on mankind, was the redemption wrought by Christ Jesus: the most excellent worship that God ever taught his Church, is the Sacrifice of the Eucharist. Jesus Christ accomplished our redemption principally by the Sacrifice which he offered for us: and the Eucharist is a Sacrifice of praise for the Redemption wrought by him.[37]

Daniel Waterland held (contra John Johnson) that the eucharist is not a material sacrifice, but spiritual; he argued, however, that spiritual sacrifice is the highest sacrifice. The eucharist, he said, is sacrificial by reason of its relation to Christ's death. 'It is self-evident, that while we have Christ, we want neither sacrifice, altar, nor priest; for in him we have all.'[38]

This brief survey will have indicated that when Charles Wesley wrote about eucharistic presence and eucharistic sacrifice he had behind him a tradition of Anglican doctrinal affirmation that, with varieties and changes, ran back for a century and a half.

Daniel Brevint

Although the Wesleys do not otherwise identify the sources of their sacramental thought, their theological and literary debt to the seventeenth-century Anglican divine Daniel Brevint is extensive, specific and acknowledged.

The Wesleys introduce their *Hymns on the Lord's Supper* with no remarks of their own, but with an abridgement of Brevint's work *The Christian Sacrifice and Sacrament*. The abridgement, which reduces the work to about one-third of its original length, was prepared by John, who when he reproduced other people's writings usually shortened them.[39] The Wesleys say nothing about either Brevint or his work, but they evidently mean for readers to gather that his account of the eucharist gives a theological context for the hymns that follow. One would not know from the Wesleys that the hymns are as deeply indebted to Brevint's work as they are.

Daniel Brevint[40] was born in 1616 on the Isle of Jersey and was educated at the University of Samur on the Continent, later coming to England and becoming MA and Fellow of Jesus College, Oxford. He was an English exile in France during the Protectorate, where he was ordained by Thomas Sydserff, the exiled Scottish Bishop of Galloway. He was presented for ordination by his fellow exile John Cosin, later the influential Bishop of Durham, who became a lifelong friend.

Brevint's contact with Roman Catholicism while he was on the Continent stirred a sharp dissent from its sacramental doctrine. After the Restoration and back in England, he published two argumentative works: a polemic against the 'dangerous enchantment' of transubstantiation called *Missale Romanum, or the Depth and Mystery of Roman Mass: Laid open and explained for the use of both Reformed and Un-reformed Christians*, published in 1672; and *Saul and Samuel at Endor, or the New Waies of Salvation and Service, which usually tempt men to Rome*, published in 1674. He could argue forcefully and satirically, although his tone was not extreme for the period.

However, his work had another side. While he was in France, Brevint served as chaplain to the eminent Huguenot family of Marshall Turenne. Two women, Madame Turenne and the Duchesse de Bouillon, complained to him of the forbidding body of argumentation that had put the Holy Communion at a distance: 'Jerusalem was so flanked about by bastions that one could hardly see the Temple.' They asked him for an approachable, non-polemical account of the Lord's Supper, and it was for them that he wrote his small, elegant book on the eucharist, *The Christian Sacrament and Sacrifice: By Way of Discourse, Meditation, and Prayer upon the Nature, Parts, and Blessings of the Holy Communion.*

When the monarchy and the established church were restored, Brevint returned to England, and with the support of John Cosin he became rector of Brancepeth, near Durham, a prebend of Durham, and eventually Dean of Lincoln. *The Christian Sacrament and Sacrifice* was published in Oxford in 1673, some years after it had been written.

In *The Christian Sacrament and Sacrifice* Brevint does not so much argue as present and celebrate, leaving concealed the learning that gives depth and authority to his exposition. He writes with restraint, ordering his thought clearly and economically, as not all seventeenth-century writers did. Brevint is inwardly engaged with his theme, and at times, prompted by genuine emotion, he slips from exposition into a passionate first-person address to God or to Christ, and each chapter ends with a well-expressed prayer. Wesley, in his hymns, would draw heavily from these prayer passages.

Brevint orders his thought in eight sections. Section I, 'The Importance of well understanding the nature of this Sacrament', which is quite brief, describes the Holy Communion as a place of meeting between God and the people of faith. 'The holy table, or altar, which presents the sacred banquet, may, as well as the old tabernacle, take to itself the title of *meeting*, since there the people must appear to worship God, and there certainly God is present to meet and to bless his people' (I.1). It is a meeting at which the faithful community receives divine graces, an action that Brevint calls *sacrament*, and at which, in return, it gives itself wholly to God, an action of *sacrifice*. This twofold movement of receiving and giving provides the structure of Brevint's thought.

This organising theme of *sacrament* and *sacrifice* was not unique to Brevint. Jeremy Taylor, writing at about the same time as Brevint, had spoken of 'the graces which are conveyed to us in reception and celebration of this holy Sacrament and sacrifice. For as it is a commemoration and representment of Christ's death, so it is a commemorative sacrifice: as we receive the symbols and the mystery, so it is a Sacrament.'[41]

In Sections II to V Brevint considers the eucharist as a divine work that is received by the Church. In speaking of its *sacramental* aspect, Brevint writes:

Section II – Concerning the Sacrament, as it is a memorial of the Sufferings and Death of Christ

Section III – Of the blessed Sacrament, as it stands for a sign of present graces

Section IV – Concerning the Communion, as it is not a Representation only, but a Means of Grace

Section V – Of the blessed Communion, as being a Pledge of the Happiness and Glory to come

Clearly the thought in this portion of the book passes from past (Section II), to present (Sections III–IV), to future (Section V). Brevint explains:

As it is a Sacrament, this great mystery shews three faces, looking directly towards three times, and offering to all worthy receivers three sorts of incomparable blessings, – that of *representing* the true *efficacy* of *Christ's sufferings, which are past, whereof it is a* memorial; that of *exhibiting* the first fruits of these sufferings in real and *present graces*, whereof it is a moral *conveyance* and *communication*; and that of *assuring* me of all other graces and glories to *come*, whereof it is an infallible *pledge*. (II.1)

Brevint turns in his Sections VI to VIII to the eucharist as *sacrifice*:

Section VI – Of the Holy Eucharist, as it implies a Sacrifice; and first, of the Commemorative Sacrifice

Section VII – Concerning the Sacrifice of our own Persons

Section VIII – Concerning the Oblation of our Goods and Alms; or the Sacrifice of Justice

Here he considers the relation of the eucharistic sacrifice to Christ's sacrifice, referring largely to the union of the sacrifice of the Church with that of the heavenly priest (VI), then he turns to a communicant's self-giving in the sacrament (VII), and then (VIII) to the giving to God of all that one has. Brevint's seventh and eighth sections are the longest in his work.

Brevint's argument unfolds clearly; his thought is often original, and in many passages he speaks with unusual grace. More than many books of its period, *The Christian Sacrament and Sacrifice* remains attractive and readable. The *DNB* article on Brevint by Canon Venables speaks of it as 'this beautiful little book'.[42]

The Christian Sacrament and Sacrifice was given two later editions in the seventeenth century, but it was 1847 before the work was again brought into print, and that edition was the last to date. Brevint died in 1695 and was buried in the retrochoir of Lincoln cathedral.

Before Brevint's work slipped from memory, a strong commendation came from Daniel Waterland, who in his essay 'The Christian Sacrifice Explained', 1738, said of Brevint that he 'was well read in the eucharistic sacrifice: no man understood it better'. Of Brevint's essay, Waterland said, 'One shall scarce meet with anything on the subject that can justly be thought to exceed it, or even come up to it.'[43] He expressed a wish that Brevint's book might be reprinted. But not even Waterland's authority could keep Brevint's name from being largely dropped from the record of sacramental thinkers in the Church of England.

John Wesley bought Brevint's book in 1732 and read it during his voyage to Georgia. (Charles left no record of when he read Brevint.) At the time of the preparation of *Hymns on the Lord's Supper*, John drafted his abridgement of Brevint's work. He edited it with some skill. He follows most sections of Brevint's thought quite closely, although he leaves some passages unused, and he occasionally alters Brevint's vocabulary. A great deal that Wesley deleted is not greatly missed by one who simply wants a sketch of Brevint's thought. Wesley's work reads in its own right as a sober, compact essay. Yet his tight eighteenth-century prose loses the relaxed charm of Brevint's seventeenth-century original.

It seems probable that Charles, as he was composing the hymns, worked from Brevint's text rather than from his brother's abbreviated version, which may well have been in preparation at the time the hymns were being written. More than 25 of Charles' *Hymns on the Lord's Supper*, some of them among the more important, are based on passages of Brevint's essay which are omitted in John's précis.

In his hymns, Charles uses Brevint's work extensively, but unevenly. The large sections into which the hymns are organised follow, with some adjustments, the outline of Brevint's book, and more than two-thirds of Wesley's hymns show some indebtedness to Brevint. In some cases, Wesley uses Brevint for only a part of a hymn (although it may be the part from which the hymn originated in his mind). But in other hymns, the central ideas and much of the wording of whole lines or stanzas come directly from Brevint. Some portions of Brevint's work – especially the prayers with which Brevint ends each of his chapters – provide the source for several hymns. Yet at the same time, other long portions of Brevint's work go unused, and substantial groups of Wesley's hymns show no indebtedness to him.[44] (Appendix 2, pp. 239–43, summarises Wesley's use of Brevint.) Moreover, Wesley often makes no use at all of an effective, poetically expressed passage, image or idea of Brevint's that would seem to have an inevitable appeal to a hymn-writer.

It is true, as Frank Baker remarks, that in his hymns Charles Wesley 'made no attempt to write a verse paraphrase of Brevint, or even of John's abridgement', but took his own direction.[45] Yet seldom have two works, each of them of real originality and merit, been as closely related as are Daniel Brevint's *The Christian Sacrament and Sacrifice* and Charles Wesley's *Hymns on the Lord's Supper*.

The Lord's Supper in the Eighteenth-Century Church of England

Sacramental doctrine and practice of the sort the Wesleys represented were widely regarded with suspicion in eighteenth-century England. It was a sceptical age; sermons and theological treatises appealed to 'rational religion'. Intimations of mystery or expressions of strong conviction risked being dismissed as 'enthusiasm', which meant fanaticism.

In most English congregations the Lord's Supper was observed quarterly, although it was held monthly in some places.[46] The sixteenth-century shapers of the Prayer Book had expected that the customary Sunday liturgy would be Morning and Evening Prayer, the Litany, and the Holy Communion. However, as worship developed in the Church of England, Morning Prayer was followed by the Litany; then the Order for the Lord's Supper was begun, but it was ended after the scriptures, creed, the sermon, and the prayer for the church and the realm. This service was known in England as 'Ante-Communion' – the Communion rite, but only up to the point at which the bread and wine were introduced. (The elements were not to be consecrated unless a sufficient number of people had indicated their intention to receive, and through generations of custom, people had come to seek the Holy Communion very infrequently.) Thus Morning Prayer, Litany, and Ante-Communion had grown into a continuous service that was lengthy, clerical, wordy, and static – even though it was ordered, dignified and full of the scriptures and Psalms. This 'accumulated service', as it came to be known, remained the usual Sunday morning liturgy in Anglican congregations well into the nineteenth century.

Liturgical leadership was shared between the vicar and a 'precentor' (or 'clerk'), who lead the people's responses, the Canticles, and the Psalms (in English meter). The precentor 'lined out' the Psalm texts, meaning that he sang each line through, as a rule very slowly, and the congregation then repeated the line. When hymns were introduced, they were at first sung in the same way. In some parishes, the congregation's singing was supported by instrumentalists who played from a west gallery.

On Sacrament Sunday, at the point in the liturgy at which on most Sundays the 'Ante-Communion' ended, the people who intended to receive communion were invited into the fore part of the church. After a general confession of sin and an absolution, bread and wine were consecrated and administered. The communion of the ministers and people was followed either by a thanksgiving or else by the self-offering of the Church, 'And here we offer and present unto thee, O Lord, ourselves, our souls and bodies.' The rite ended with the *Gloria in Excelsis*, and the people were dismissed with a blessing.

The tone both of the Prayer Book rite and of the sacramental spirituality that was associated with it was restrained, even severe. For many generations the eucharist had been thought of as a representation of Christ's passion, to be approached with a sense of one's sinfulness. Severity of tone was appropriate.

Charles Wesley stands in a long tradition when he asks worshippers at the Holy Communion to attend to the crucifixion. But he asks with unusual drama and urgency:

> See the slaughter'd Sacrifice,
>   See the Altar stain'd with Blood!
> Crucified before our Eyes
>   Faith discerns the Dying GOD. (18:2.1–4)

The lines are arresting and vocative. They could be thought excessive – ill-tuned to Wesley's moderate, classically minded period. This stanza (and there are many others like it) suggests the baroque devotion of post-Tridentine Catholicism or the seventeenth-century intensity of Donne or Crashaw more than it does the quieter eighteenth-century poetry of Gray, Young or Cowper. Many of Wesley's lines seem to leap beyond the restraint and formality of his age and speak a piety of the heart, even of the senses.

However, when one looks at the liturgical setting in which Wesley's impassioned words would be sung, one finds unadorned space and only the simplest ministerial gestures and garb. Although Wesley called the communicant to see 'the dying God . . . crucified before our eyes', the usual appearance of the Lord's Table in eighteenth-century churches would have given such a dramatic act of the imagination virtually no support. Rather than the representations of the crucifixion which were associated with the Counter-Reformation spirituality of the Continent, in the liturgical life of Wesley's England, representational art had been all but excluded. The drama of Christians present at Jesus' passion – 'See . . . the Altar stained with blood' – was confined to words and to interior vision: '*Faith* discerns the Dying God', unaided by visual art.

Individual churches had different histories of building and renovation. The waves of iconoclasm that had broken over England (the Puritan wave being only the most recent of them) had left their mark unevenly. City churches differed from village churches, and family chapels from parish churches. From Wesley's own time, one could hardly find a greater contrast than that between the extravagant baroque chapel of St Michael at Great Witley, in Worcestershire, 1735, and the quiet austerity of St John the Baptist at King's Norton, in Leicestershire, 1761.

As a rule English parish churches of the eighteenth century were plain, although many of them were beautiful in their plainness. The interior walls were commonly white or pastel, and windows were often of clear glass, admitting abundant light. The worship space was full of box pews with high sides. The pulpit, with a tester-board over it and a reading desk below it, would be large and conspicuously located, for these were 'auditory churches'. In most churches of the period the holy table was wooden and plain, standing close to but often free from the east wall, and covered with a white linen. There was frequently no cross in the church, and candles would be at the pulpit or the reading desk, but not on the holy table.

At the time of the Communion, the vessels for the sacrament (a silver or pewter chalice, a flagon of wine, and a plate holding a loaf of bread, sometimes with a knife for cutting it) would be at the north end of the table, along with a Prayer Book resting on a cushion. The minister conducted the sacramental portion of the liturgy from the north end, facing across the chancel. In most places he would wear at all seasons of the year either a black gown, or else a white surplice and a black scarf. On the wall over the holy table, rather than anything pictorial, there were tablets inscribed with the Ten Commandments and the Creed. The rood had been replaced with the royal arms. Somewhere a gilded sunburst or some other touch of colour might suggest transcendence. Some London churches and a few family chapels were rich in style. However, in most churches, even in the Wesleys' 'high' tradition, everything would be tidy, proper and cared for, but artistically minimal.

Even though Charles Wesley took little account of ceremony, he does seem to refer, at least indirectly, to one action of the liturgy. Christians in several traditions – both Nonconformist and Church of England, both before Wesley's day and after it – thought that the minister's breaking of the sacramental bread and pouring the wine represented Jesus' crucifixion. As a rule, these were the most visible – perhaps they were the only – *actions* of the presider prior to the distribution of the bread and the wine. When Wesley says '*Thus* the Bread of Life was broke,/ *Thus* the Lamb of God was slain' (18:1.3–4), he refers to these acts of breaking and pouring. Brevint had said, 'Upon the *breaking* the one and *pouring out* the other of these consecrated elements, you see what Christ hath suffered' (III.11).

Wesley calls on communicants to see not a simple table, a few vessels, some bread and wine, and a celebrant plainly garbed, kneeling at the north end; rather, they should be present at Calvary and behold with the eyes of faith Christ 'crucified before our eyes'. When he describes in this way what the communicant may encounter in the sacrament, Charles Wesley is not posturing, but speaking from his own experience. He reports in his *Journal* that at a service of the Holy Communion a few days after his awakening,

> Before communicating I left it to Christ, whether, or in what measure, He would please to manifest Himself to me in the breaking of bread. I had no particular attention to the prayers, but in the prayer of consecration I saw, by the eye of faith, or rather, had a glimpse of, Christ's broken, mangled body as taking down from the cross. (*Journal*, 25 May 1738)

The shocks of 'ritualism' lay a century in the future. Faith had to do its work unsupported by (or, as many persons at the time would have said, 'undistracted by') candles, colours, representational art, brocaded vestments or ceremonial actions – all of which would have seemed to members of the Church of England in the eighteenth century to be the sheerest popery and unsuited to spiritual worship. Among 'pre-ritualist' high-churchmen, the liturgy was carried out with seriousness and decorum, but outward display was unneeded and unwanted.

The Character and Organisation of Hymns on the Lord's Supper

Overall, one would not characterise Wesley's verse in terms of beauty or lyricism. Although Wesley's hymns contain effective phrases, many of his stanzas are rough or angular. Donald Davie finds a quality of 'physicality' or 'carnality' in Wesley's verse.[47] Perhaps Wesley would have thought of a search for musical phrases as a self-conscious distraction, while he went straight to realities and to the plainest words – at least he did until a Latinism came into his mind.

Perhaps the trait that most distinguishes Wesley's lines is the energy of their thought and feeling. Mind speaks directly to mind, emotion to emotion, imagination to imagination. His mind seems to move rapidly, at times almost breathlessly. It is crowded with his own ideas, with suggestions from Brevint, with the rich phraseology of the Bible, with the evangelical anatomising of the soul, with the literature of his language and church. These sources yield, in Wesley's mind, an individual quality. J. R. Watson speaks of 'Wesley's richness, the density of each line and each verse: it is almost as if his hymns have a higher specific gravity than those of other writers. This skilful compression of thought and image, this density, is Charles Wesley's distinctive feature as a hymn-writer.'[48]

As to the organisation of the collection, Wesley presents his *Hymns on the Lord's Supper* in six parts of unequal size. They speak of the Lord's Supper:

Part I. 'As it is a Memorial of the Sufferings and Death of Christ' (27 hymns).
Part II. 'As it is a Sign and a Means of Grace' (65 hymns).
Part III. 'The Sacrament a Pledge of Heaven' (23 hymns).
Part IV. 'The Holy Eucharist as it Implies a Sacrifice' (12 hymns).
Part V. 'Concerning the Sacrifice of our Persons' (30 hymns).
'After the Sacrament' (9 hymns).

Clearly this sequence of themes follows the structure of Brevint's *The Christian Sacrament and Sacrifice*, but with several adaptations.

Even though Wesley has no group of hymns that corresponds with Brevint's brief first section, in several hymns throughout the collection, he makes use of the fundamental idea of Brevint's Section I that the sacrament is a place of divine/human meeting. Brevint, in the Epistle introducing *The Christian Sacrament and Sacrifice*, identified the true aim of the sacrament as 'nothing less than a mutual communion between us and Christ'.

Both Wesley's Part I and Brevint's second section consider the Holy Communion as a representation of the passion of Christ. Brevint devoted his third section to the sacrament as *sign* and his fourth section to the sacrament as a *means* of grace. Wesley, however, combines these themes in his Part II on the sacrament 'as *sign and means*'. He follows Brevint in turning in Part III to the sacrament as a pledge of heaven and in Part IV to eucharist as sacrifice. Wesley devotes his Part V to the theme of Brevint's seventh section, on the sacrifice of our persons. He does not develop Brevint's quite long eighth section, on the sacrifice of our goods and alms, but introduces a few ideas from it into his Part V.

Wesley's collection ends with nine hymns, 'After the Sacrament'. Brevint, who was writing neither hymns for congregations nor a manual for communicants, had no need to conclude with post-communion devotions.

The sequence of themes in Brevint's and Wesley's common outline give a sense of advancing thought. Frank Baker says, 'Charles seems to have had no predetermined order or size in mind, simply following the general movement of Brevint's tractate in five sections.'[49] Baker judges that Wesley prepared the book for the printer in some haste, not pausing to adjust the flow and order of the hymns. Some of the themes of the hymns (such as sacrifice or heaven) are not confined within the named sections. As Rattenbury noticed, the collection contains some brief hymns of general praise that might well have been placed in almost any part of the work.[50] Several of the hymns make no express reference to the sacrament, although their tone and themes suit the eucharistic occasion.

Within Wesley's large units, there are some groups or short sequences in which several hymns in succession or near to one another have a similar theme, or develop the same image, or in a number of cases have the same meter. One hymn seems to have suggested another; they may have been written at nearly the same time, as a sound, an idea, or a rhythm passed from one hymn to the next; and in arranging the hymns for publication Wesley let them stand much as they had come to his mind and been written.

Theological Themes of the Hymns

Wesley encountered the sacrament interpreted by his long practice of his church's liturgy, by his experience as a communicant, and by years of reading and reflection. His passionate engagement had given him a fresh, intense sense that in the sacrament one meets the crucified and living Christ. He asks:

> Visit us in Pard'ning Grace,
>   CHRIST the Crucified appear,
> Come in thy Appointed Ways,
>   Come, and meet, and bless us here. (63:1.3–6)

Devout Christians, longing for this sacramental appointment with God, pray:

> Come to thy House again,
>   Nor let us seek in vain;
> This the Place of meeting be,
>   To thy weeping Flock repair,
> Let us here thy Beauty see,
>   Find Thee in the House of Prayer. (77:2)

> In thine own Appointments bless us,
>   Meet us here, Now appear,
>   Our Almighty JESUS. (78:9)

In speaking of the sacrament as a place of meeting with Christ, Wesley uses the contention-ridden and seemingly unpoetic term 'real presence'. 'Only do Thou my Heart prepare,/ To find thy Real Presence there' (66:2.4–5), and 'To every faithful soul appear,/ And shew thy Real Presence here' (116:5.5–6).

Christ is present actively and forgivingly. The cup and the bread, Wesley says, are 'sacred means to impart/ Our Saviour's blood, with power imprest/ And pardon to the faithful heart' (73:1.2–4). He prays:

> JESU, dear redeeming LORD,
> Magnify thy dying Word,
> In thine Ordinance appear,
> Come, and meet thy Followers here. (33:1)

Speaking of Christ, Wesley says:

> He gives his Flesh to be our Meat,
>   And bids us drink his Blood:
>   Whate'er th' Almighty Can
>   To pardon'd Sinners give,
> The Fulness of our God made Man
>   We here with CHRIST receive. (81:4.3–8)

Although Christ by his promise is really present, the manner of his presence is not known and need not be defined. Wesley exclaims:

> Receiving the Bread
> On JESUS we feed,
> It doth not appear
> His manner of working; but JESUS is here! (92:6)

Wesley often says that Christ, the Incarnate One is present (see 81:4.7–8, above). However, in one hymn which is addressed to the Father, he asks for a showing of 'thy sacramental presence'. He asks:

> Father, thy feeble Children meet,
>   And make thy faithful Mercies known;
> Give us thro' Faith the Flesh to eat,
>   And drink the Blood of CHRIST thy Son;
> Honour thine own mysterious Ways,
>   Thy Sacramental Presence shew,
> And all the Fulness of thy Grace,
>   With JESUS, on our Souls bestow. (153:1)

As Wesley understands the sacrament, the Father is present with Christ.

It is clear also (see Hymn 16, discussed on p. 73, below) that Wesley thinks that the sacrament is effective through the revealing, proclaiming, applying power of the Holy Spirit, the 'Remembrancer Divine'. Thus, as he sees it, the divine presence in the sacrament is the presence of the triune God. Ole Borgen observes, 'The whole Trinity is present and acting, bestowing upon men the benefits of the incarnation, crucifixion, and resurrection.'[51] To put it so implies that Wesley thinks of Christ as present in the eucharist in the way in which the Father and the Spirit are present.

Wesley speaks of the 'virtue' of Christ in the sacrament, as when he says, 'The virtue of thy blood impart' (32:2.3); or, 'Virtue from his body flows' (39:1.6); or, 'These [feeble elements] the virtue did convey' (57:2.7). With changes in language, the word 'virtual' has come to mean 'in effect'. In Wesley's usage, however, it denotes reality. He would have heard in the word the Latin *virtus*, meaning courage, strength, worth, excellence, or goodness.

Brevint too used the term 'virtue', as when he says, 'God . . . gives still the virtue of his [the Saviour's] death to bless and to save every soul that comes unfeignedly to him' (II.5). In another place he says that 'Faithful communicants eat as effectually of the body of Jesus Christ by receiving its strength and virtue, as the saints eat of the tree of life (Revelation 22.2) because they eat of the fruit of that tree' (IV.10).

Both Brevint and Wesley understand the 'virtue' of a thing or person to be the actuality, immediacy and potency of the thing or person. 'The truth is, we really have, or enjoy, the thing itself, when we are within that distance where we may enjoy its virtue' (IV.10). The 'virtue' of Christ's body and blood is the active presence of Christ in his body and blood. Borgen characterises Wesley's view of eucharistic presence: 'Where God acts, there he is. The "objective presence" cannot be thought of as the static presence of an object, but rather as that of a living and acting person *working* through the means.'[52]

The readiest equivalent for 'virtue' would be 'power', an idea which is sometimes present in lines where the term 'virtue' is not used. A prayer to the Holy Spirit asks, 'Thy life infuse into the bread,/ Thy power into the wine' (72:1.3–4). The Saviour's Blood is 'with Power imprest' and imparts pardon to the faithful heart (73:1.3–4). The body and blood are divine instruments which bestow 'thy mercy and thy strength' (28:2.3–4). 'This mysterious rite' draws forth all Christ's promised might (42:3.3).

No doubt for Wesley, whose mind did not run to speculative categories, such 'virtualism' was as high a sacramental doctrine as one could have. Divine power is divine reality. He would not have thought that replacing his personal, active terms by metaphysical terms would make the presence more real, only more abstract.

While Wesley holds that God works through the bread and wine, he shows little interest in what may or may not happen to the elements in the eucharistic ritual. The bread and wine are essential conveyances of divine life, but the wonder is that they are so while remaining bread and wine (57:2.7–8). Such transformation as does take place in the sacrament happens in the vital encounter between Christ and his people. Wesley asks, 'Come and change my Nature' (87:7.3).

The change, however, is not 'spiritual', as though it somehow stood apart from the sacramental elements, which are, for Wesley, 'fit channels to convey thy love' (72:2.2) or a 'sure communicating sign' (73:2.1):

Who shall say how Bread and Wine
    GOD into Man conveys? (57:1.3–4)

Wesley says that the early Christians

    . . . broke the Bread
  Impregnated with Life divine,
And drank the Spirit of their Head
    Transmitted in the sacred Wine. (166:4)

The divine power in the sacrament is, in Wesley's view, indefinitely accessible. Christ invites believers, half-believers, sinners, and the troubled, to his table, where he meets them in grace. This emphasis is significant, for 'fencing the table' was a Puritan principle, and most of the seventeenth- and eighteenth-century guides for communicants

developed at length the worshipper's preparation for the sacrament, offering detailed programmes for self-scrutiny and contrition, all prompted
by the Pauline counsel that self-examination was needed at the Supper
lest one eat and drink unworthily, failing to discern the Lord's body (1
Corinthians 11.28f.). The widely used mid-seventeenth-century work
The Whole Duty of Man, which is not the most severe of such guides,
laid out a discipline of preparation before the Lord's Supper in terms of
'Examination; of Repentance, Faith, Obedience; of Duties to be done at
the Receiving, and Afterwards'.[53] What was required of one who sought
to come to the Supper was sometimes so laborious, formidable and legal-
istic that conscientious Christians must have been more disheartened
than attracted.

The sacramental spirituality of the Wesley hymns belongs to a different
world. Speaking in the spirit of the rich man in Jesus' parable who made
a great feast and bade many, Wesley invites 'Come to the Supper come,/
Sinner there still is Room' (8:1.1–2). In this matter, Wesley parted with
Brevint, who rather defensively set forth (in V.9–11) the 'crime' of failing
to discern the Lord's body. As Brevint saw it, there were two groups who
came to Christ's Supper, (1) 'the faithful communicants [who] do appear
there to receive Christ, and (2) the faithless to abuse him' (V.10). But
for the Wesleys, on the basis of their experience, the Holy Communion
was, or it might be, a 'converting ordinance'. The open invitation to the
Table was an instrument of their evangelism. As Paul Sanders says, 'The
Eucharist bestows grace not only on the justified but on earnest seekers
as well.'[54] John Wesley remarks that in coming to the Lord's table, 'no
previous preparation is indispensably necessary; but a desire to receive
whatsoever He pleases to give' (*Journal*, 28 June 1740). The Wesleys saw
the eucharist as an act fairly bursting with divine mercy.

Rather soon, however, Methodist practice introduced qualifications.
The open invitation to the table was attracting the careless and the
merely curious. At about the time of the publication of *Hymns on the
Lord's Supper*, some of the Societies were requiring that persons coming
to communion show evidence of membership in the Methodist classes.[55]
If some tension was coming to be felt in early Methodism between free
invitation and necessary caution, nothing in these hymns of 1745 says so.
They simply invite.

The hymns say repeatedly that the eucharist brings remission of sins,
for it is a fresh actualisation of the cross, the one great act of forgiveness.
'We see the Blood that seals our Peace,/ Thy Pard'ning Mercy we receive'
(28:3.1–2). Burdened Christians come to the Supper in faith and find
Christ present in grace.

Yet Wesley knows the ambiguities of eucharistic experience – and for him experience is theologically significant. He speaks, particularly in several of the later hymns of Part II, of believers who come to the table seeking or distraught and find the Saviour strangely withheld. There is tension between the affirmation that Christ is, by his own promise, unfailingly present in the sacrament and the undeniable report of experience that the Supper is at times found unrewarding. Wesley does not analyse the matter, but counsels that when sacramental experience seems barren, one in faithfulness should continue to attend the Supper, expecting Christ in the place he has appointed.

Wesley's doctrine of the eucharist is not bound up with Christology nor ecclesiology so much as with soteriology. When he writes of the sacrament, his thought of Christ is specifically of Christ crucified. The eucharist is a 'sacramental passion' (145:5.4; Wesley takes the phrase from Brevint). The eucharist means what the cross means. It is a place in which God, who dealt with sin finally in the event of Calvary, deals with it as Christ's sacrifice, presented eternally in heaven and now made available on earth, touches new occasions of human sin and need.

Wesley concentrates single-mindedly on sin and salvation. His theology and spirituality expressed freshly and in terms of the Evangelical Revival the cross-centred eucharistic piety that had characterised the West from the Middle Ages, through the Reformation and Counter-Reformation.

Perhaps to a reader's surprise, in Wesley's presentation of the redemptive events in these hymns, he does not link the cross and the resurrection.[56] A reader of Wesley's Easter hymns knows how ringingly he proclaimed Christ's triumph over death. Yet in the sacramental hymns his Christological narrative passes directly from the dying figure on the cross to the eternal high priest at the heavenly altar.

> From the Cross where once He died,
> Now He up to Heaven is gone. (118:1.5–6)

This pattern may seem abrupt. It is unlike Paul, in whose mind death is answered by resurrection. But one may remark that Wesley's pattern in *Hymns on the Lord's Supper* reproduces the Christological contour of the New Testament book of Hebrews, which similarly passes from the cross directly to the throne in heaven. It speaks of Jesus who 'endured the cross, despising the shame, and is set down at the right hand of the throne of God' (12.2).

It is to Hebrews that one must trace Wesley's development of the theme of sacrifice, which is a particular emphasis in his Parts IV and V. Like Hebrews, Wesley insists that Jesus, in his life and death, made the one redemptive sacrifice, which cannot be repeated or supplemented. Then, still following Hebrews, Wesley thinks of Jesus' earthly cross as at the same time an event in heaven – his continual presentation of the sacrifice of himself in the holy place at the heavenly Temple. The saving work continues in the heavenly high-priesthood and eternal sacrifice of the living Christ: 'Jesu's Death is ever New' (3:2.2). He who once offered himself on earth for human sin now offers himself continually: 'Thou Lamb that suffer'dst on the Tree,/ And in this dreadful Mystery/ Still offer'st up Thyself to God' (117:1–3). Moreover, Christ does not act alone; the Great High Priest is in his people, and his people in him. As he offers himself in heaven, the Church, in the eucharist, offers on earth: 'Ourselves presenting with our Head' (140:3.6).

Wesley's understanding of eucharistic sacrifice stands in one respect apart from that of other writers who made the same general affirmation. The Non-jurors, echoing the early liturgies, thought that the consecration prayer should include an offering of the eucharistic gifts, and John Johnson had emphasised the materiality of the sacrifice. Wesley, however, never says that the Church offers the bread and wine. While Christ is imparted to the Church in the sacramental bread and wine, the Church does not offer the bread and wine to God. Rather, the Church offers itself in Christ and Christ in itself.

For Wesley (as is made particularly clear in Hymn 116, see pp. 168–71 below) the three sacrifices – the 'once for all' cross in history, the continual heavenly offering by the eternal priest, and the Church's repeated eucharistic sacrifice – are not three, but are aspects of a unitary action. The Church offers in Christ. Indeed, it is so caught up in him that it is joined in his sacrifice, and he is joined in its. It offers the Christ it receives.

To put forward Wesley's thesis on eucharistic sacrifice here in so summary a way may suggest how easily it can be misunderstood. Some cautious thinkers, it must be acknowledged, have not found and do not find Wesley's account of this theme convincing. They think it has misleading tendencies and that it goes beyond anything said or clearly implied in the New Testament. Yet this general way of thinking about sacrament and sacrifice (a way which stands in a long tradition) brings together in a large imaginative construction cross and altar, heaven and earth.

In describing Wesley's understanding of redemption, it should be remarked that for him, salvation and holiness of life – justification and sanctification – are inseparable. If the sacrament conveys the very reality of Christ's atonement, it brings forgiveness of sins; but forgiveness necessarily inaugurates a new creation. If a life of holiness does not follow from faith, it is as though Christ had died in vain.

Wesley's omission of the resurrection as part of his eucharistic spirituality, which has been noted above, is unexpected. But there are other lacunae. In these hymns Wesley expresses no interest in nature and no sense for what today would be called sacramentality. He sees the physical manifestations at the crucifixion – the darkness, the earthquake (Matthew 27.51–3) – as nature's sympathy with and tribute to the dying Jesus: 'All Nature feels th' Important Groan/ Loud-ecchoing thro' the Earth and Skies' (26:1.3f.). However, Wesley finds nothing in the Church's sacral meal that links it to the earth and human dependence on it, or to common meals, or simply to the world of physical things. The Lord's Supper is not expressly set within what William Temple called a 'sacramental universe'.[57]

This omission is unusual, for Christians of the eighteenth century were occupied with finding God in the regularities and order of nature, assigning nature a foundational place in their theism. Many hymns and many theologians said that while nature is not in itself enough, it is good, and it points unmistakably to its divine Maker.[58] Yet Wesley, in writing 166 hymns about an act centring on bread and wine from the earth, gives no essential place to nature; rather, his theological imagination is entirely occupied with the saving person of the biblical witness.

Perhaps a further omission may be identified. Wesley, one observes, expresses virtually no sense of the sacrament as a sign of the Church, a community of persons who share a common life. Although he speaks for the most part in the 'we' voice, giving expression to a collective life which is the object of God's love and which makes communal response to God, yet he gives no sense that in this shared life persons interact with one another, lovingly, caringly, or otherwise. It is only in Hymn 165, the next-to-last, that he says 'Many, and yet but One we are' (165:2.3).

Wesley similarly makes no connection between the eucharist and baptism – about which there was some ambiguity in Wesleyan thought and practice. The society was nominally Christian and largely baptised. While baptism was valued formally, it was not seen as an act foundational to the Christian and the Church. Wesley does not describe it as a sign whose gift and promises are to be renewed regularly in the Holy Communion. One's conversion was more likely to be considered the beginning of the life of God in the soul. The narratives of the evangelistic work of John and Charles seldom speak of converts being led to baptism, and persons who some time after their baptism are brought to conversion are not asked to repossess their baptism and accept its responsibilities freshly. John Wesley, in a *Journal* entry from early in his career (25 January 1739), distinguished between those who are 'born again in the full sense of the word' and those who are 'only born again in a lower sense'. One's conscious inner experience of God was the regeneration that most concerned the evangelists. When John Wesley speaks of 'the means of grace' in his sermon on the subject, he lists prayer, communicating and searching the scriptures, but not baptism.

It should be said that lacunae such as have been identified here are apparent largely from the vantage of thought and experience that has developed since Charles Wesley's day and from perceptions that might well have occurred to hardly anyone in his age. Yet whatever Charles Wesley may have failed to say, he was saying things about the eucharist that were not being said (or at least not being said as vividly) by anyone else in the British Christian world of the eighteenth century. Indeed, some of them have not been said as vividly since.

It may further be observed that in these hymns Wesley shows no interest in eucharistic ritual. He by-passes exteriorities and goes to interiorities. One would gather from these hymns almost nothing of the shape, sequence and character of the eucharistic rite of the Church of England. They give no attention to a special, set-apart class of celebrants or to the act of consecration. The principal minister of the sacrament, as Wesley sees it, is Christ, present and imparting himself to the faithful. He is host, celebrant and substance: 'Jesus appears to sacrifice/ The Flesh and Blood Himself supplies' (46:3.1–2). While Wesley emphasises the agency of the Holy Spirit in the sacrament, he does not specify where, when and how he sees the Spirit figuring in the liturgical act. If the sacramental event has a climactic moment, it would seem for the Wesleys to be the communicants' *taking* and *eating*, actions which Jesus specified at the institution and to which the hymns often refer. All is for the sake of feeding on Christ. Kenneth Stevenson remarks on this liturgical vagueness, saying that these hymns 'do not localize particular liturgical actions, but rather speak by their very medium of the total celebration of the eucharist'.[59]

Wesley's Use of the Scriptures

Charles Wesley read widely, and he had a retentive memory. In his hymns as a whole there are traces of the classics, of Shakespeare, Milton, George Herbert, Dryden, Edward Young and others.[60] In *Hymns on the Lord's Supper* there is a touch of Herbert's 'The Sacrifice' in 133:2.2,[61] and two of Herbert's poems are included, revised as hymns by John (Hymns 9 and 160). While the revisions are effective for their purpose, the regularities of hymn form cannot reproduce the freedom of Herbert's lines.

We have noted Wesley's debt to Brevint and to a much lesser extent to The Book of Common Prayer. But beyond these, in *Hymns on the Lord's Supper* Wesley's overwhelming debt is to the Bible. Some of the hymns develop a single biblical incident or image (the lame man at the pool, Hymn 58; or Lazarus in his grave, Hymn 68), but many of them bring together around a central theme a virtual collage of references to biblical events, people, images and phrases. Evidently Wesley could assume that the congregations for which he wrote could follow his tumble of biblical allusions as he takes into his rhetoric turns of phrase from the Psalms, Isaiah, the gospels, Paul, Hebrews or Revelation, applying them as suits him. Indeed, many hymns or lines would be quite ineffective if one did not catch the biblical allusion. An unusual choice of words may indicate that he is echoing a biblical phrase, and even a casual biblical echo can give authority and nuance to his lines. But Wesley had so internalised the Bible that passing phrases which use biblical speech may often have hardly been conscious quotations. He sometimes interprets the biblical passage he has in mind, intending to show it in a specific light; but often he simply casts his thought in biblical speech.

Wesley's Bible was the King James Version, which since the seventeenth century had become well established in the Church and in the language. For two centuries more it remained the text that was read and quoted in the English-speaking world, informing not only prayer, hymn, comment and preaching, but much poetry, prose, ordinary conversation, and even the cadences of political oratory. The clarity and power of Wesley's hymns are weakened by the weakening in recent generations of the familiarity of the Authorised Version.

In writing on the Lord's Supper, Wesley turns repeatedly to several parts of the Bible, while making no use of others. He refers often to the circumstances of Jesus' crucifixion, particularly in the first section of the hymns. The words 'Forgive them' that Jesus spoke from the cross he speaks now in the sacrament to the penitent sinner. Jesus' parting command, 'Do this in memory of me,' requires Christians to maintain the Supper. The eucharistic theology of the Wesleys and of their tradition was heavily influenced by the letter to the Hebrews, and the hymns sometimes develop a theme from it, but just as often they suggest the context of Hebrews by a telltale word, such as 'once'. Especially in Part III where he speaks of heaven, Wesley uses liberally phrases and imagery from the book of Revelation. Expressions from the gospels and from Paul are taken up into Wesley's lines, for they had become the language in which he thought and spoke.

Several hymns are almost kaleidoscopic as they pass from one biblical image or phrase to another. Hymn 27 in its 32 lines contains at least 30 allusions. (An exact count is impossible, for some phrases could trace to more than one biblical passage, and biblical allusions that seem clear enough to one reader may seem doubtful to another.) But Wesley seems confident that his Bible-intoxicated readers will follow as his mind leads by association from one allusion, image or borrowed phrase to the next.

Wesley concentrates so single-mindedly on faith and conversion that he finds this theme in all parts of the Bible. The healing miracles of the gospels are not stories of Jesus' compassion for the sick and handicapped so much as they are allegories of conversion, the passage from sin to salvation. He uses the story of the exodus in a spiritual sense as material through which to depict the experience of Christians – freed from Egypt and moving through the wilderness to the land of promise, sustained on the way by bread from heaven. (This typological use of the exodus story had a long Christian tradition behind it.) Evidently Wesley's imagination was so impacted by the evangelical experience that he read all of the scriptures through this interpretive key. Francis Frost has said that Wesley's 'Christocentric interpretation of the Scriptures [is] also *stauro-centric* (from *stauros* in Greek, meaning "cross"). Every single word of Scripture has, for him, an inner sacramental orientation towards Jesus bleeding to death for us on the Cross.'[62] Wesley would probably not have thought that his spiritualising way of using the Bible read the Christian gospel and life into passages which were about something else; rather, he would have thought that he was making clear the divinely intended meanings that were really there.

Reading the Bible in terms of Christian experience as he does, Wesley identifies dramatically and immediately with the text. For him the Bible was more than an external authoritative source that he could quote and that congregations would recognise. Rather, he lives in it, and he writes for readers who live in it with him. He is, and other Christians with him are, wandering Israelites brought out of Egypt and pleading for sustenance in the barren wilderness; they are the blind beggar at the wayside when Jesus comes by; they are Lazarus dead in his tomb; they are present at the crucifixion; they are disciples breaking bread with the risen Jesus at Emmaus; they are in heaven, and they stand as witnesses at the final coming of Christ. The Bible was a mythical world, an account of reality, God-given and revelational, which interpreted the existence of Wesley and his congregations. It informed a shared sense of life and destiny.

The heritage of Anglican sacramental theology took on a unique configuration in Charles Wesley's experience, reflection and reading. His use of the Bible and of Brevint shows that his mind absorbed ideas and phrases readily, and he freely turned other people's words to his own use. However, Charles Wesley's achievement cannot be accounted for by tracing literary and theological influences. Rather, it demonstrates the mystery of creativity. Many earlier English writers had spoken of the Holy Communion with theological and religious depth, and other writers of Wesley's time had access to the same sources that he did, but none of Wesley's contemporaries saw in the sacrament the divine–human drama that Wesley saw. The best evidence for Wesley's mind lies in the hymns themselves, as they make their own disclosures and keep their own secrets.

Wesley's Prosody

The *Hymns on the Lord's Supper* communicate their vitality and thought in part through Wesley's skill with words, phrases, rhythm and structure. The energy, passion, and at times the torrent of his ideas, are served by rhetorical skill and craftsmanship.[63] Something Wesley earnestly wants to say is bonded with a vigorous, effective way of saying it. Attention to Wesley's techniques gives access to his meanings.

Structure

In the great mass of Charles Wesley's verse there are some shapeless, overlong hymns, but characteristically Wesley's published hymns exhibit a firm structure. The sacramental hymns are generally well-shaped and economical. (Hymn 166, which runs to 22 stanzas, is a concluding poem rather than a hymn written with a congregation in mind.) As a group *Hymns on the Lord's Supper* shows Wesley at his best. The hymns express passion, yet each one develops with a unifying idea and with direction or shape. Even the hymns that seem overweighted with ideas, images or biblical allusions, have a theme, which they pursue directly, and when they are through, they end.

Wesley's period expected that its artists' work would show 'simplicity, unity of design, proportion, and symmetry'.[64] Readers today often admire poems (from the present or from the pre-eighteenth-century past) which Wesley's age would have regarded as little more than gatherings of material that might be made into poems. The eighteenth century did not think that the poet's task was to set down private thought fragments, but to order one's material into finished, shareable wholes.

Some English hymn-writers of later generations lacked Wesley's sense of structure. When their work is set in modern-day hymnals, stanzas, or indeed whole groups of stanzas, may be (and in fact often are) omitted or rearranged with little loss. But Wesley's best hymns have beginning, middle and end. His opening lines propose something, or ask something, or introduce a theme – usually a theme that plunges the reader at once into some aspect of the relation between God and the human soul. Later stanzas develop the theme, communicating a sense of its urgency or setting possible misunderstandings to rest. And at the end, the theme is brought to a firm close.

Meter and Stanza Form

Wesley's published hymns are all in regular meter and rhymed stanzas. In this matter he was a part of his formal, orderly age. Paul Fussell has said, 'Of all metrical systems in English, the accentual-syllabic is the most hostile by nature to impulse, irregularity, and unrestrained grandiosity. It seems all but impossible to transmit impressions of hysteria or the frantic within a strict accentual-syllabic versification.'[65] Nevertheless, within his rhymed lines and well-formed stanzas Wesley articulates a gospel which breaks out of conventionality or simple rationality. His verse forms are without fail regular and neat, but the thing of which they speak is unpredictable, unconfined – at times only statable in paradox. Wesley's verse is characteristically restless and volatile.

> Father see the Victim slain,
>   JESUS CHRIST the Just, the Good,
> Offer'd up for guilty Man,
>   Pouring out his precious Blood,
> Him, and then the Sinner see,
> Look thro' JESU's Wounds on Me. (120:1.1–6)

He never achieves the tone of quiet serenity that Watts expresses in lines which are in many respects similar to Wesley's in thought and vocabulary:

> O the sweet wonders of that cross
> Where God the Saviour lov'd and dy'd!
> Her noblest life my spirit draws
> From his dear wounds and bleeding side.

I would for ever speak his name
In sounds to mortal ears unknown,
With angels join to praise the Lamb,
And worship at his Father's throne. (10:5–6)

Perhaps the felt tension between Wesley's impassioned message and the regular poetic forms which at times seem to struggle to contain it creates part of the interest of his hymns.

In Wesley, poetic form tends to correspond with idea. Stanzas are often a single sentence, although the sentence may be complex. A high proportion of his lines have some kind of end stop. Run-on lines give flexibility and interest to poetry that is to be read, rather than sung; but in the eighteenth century, hymns were still often 'lined out', making it difficult to hold over an incomplete thought or construction to be resumed and finished in the opening words of the following line, and run-on lines are infrequent in Wesley's work.

Charles Wesley's hymns show a variety of meters and stanza form unmatched by the poets and hymn-writers of his time – and probably by any English hymn-writer of any time. The common verse form of fashionable, serious or satiric eighteenth-century poetry was the five-foot rhymed couplet, as when Alexander Pope counsels moderation:

Be not the first by whom the new are try'd,
Nor yet the last to lay the old aside.

('An Essay on Criticism')

While good poets handled this verse form with skill and some flexibility, it tended inevitably to be talky, instructive, and in time monotonous. Wesley seldom wrote in this form, although several of the *Hymns on the Lord's Supper* (5, 12, 31, 119, 140, 159, 161, 163, 164) are in stanzas (of four or six lines, in four or five metric feet, in iambic or trochaic rhythm) wholly comprised of rhyming couplets. As:

JESU, suffering Deity,
Can we help remembering Thee,
Thee, whose Blood for Us did flow,
Thee, who di'dst to save thy Foe! (12:1)

English hymns before Wesley had depended heavily on the ballad stanza – the principal form of popular poetry. This was the form of many of

the metrical Psalms, New Version, by Tate and Brady, and it was also
the form of most of Watts' hymns. While Tate and Brady's work is often
awkward and amateurish, Isaac Watts, within his steady sequence of
four-line stanzas, achieved a considerable variety of emotional tone and
verbal music. Yet one may justly complain of monotony when hymn
after hymn repeats the same rhythm and stanza form.

Wesley used the ballad stanza – sometimes letting it stand alone, and
occasionally doubling it. However, a high proportion of his stanzas are
of six lines, with a rhymed couplet coming before or following after a
quatrain. The couplet, whether at the opening or the close, usually stands
slightly apart from the other four lines, almost as a concise reflection on
what is being said. As J. R. Watson says, 'The quatrain allows the idea to
expand, the couplet encourages it to contract.'[66]

Some of Wesley's six-line stanzas open with three-foot couplets, as:

Yet come Thou heavenly Guest,
And purify my Breast. (43:3.1–2)

Come in thy Spirit down,
Thine Institution crown. (53:3.1–2)

Longer-lined hymns may open with a four-foot couplet, as:

With Pity, LORD, a Sinner see
Weary of thy Ways and Thee. (80:1.1–2)

In other hymns the stanza concludes with a rhyming four-foot couplet,
giving finality to the ending, and Wesley cares about endings:

Mindful of Thee we still attend,
And this we do, till Time shall end. (90:3.5–6)

There LORD we shall thy Pledge restore,
And live to praise Thee evermore. (111:3.5–6)

For important themes Wesley often turned to the steady long-meter
stanza.

Is not the Hallow'd broken Bread
    A sure Communicating Sign,
An Instrument Ordain'd to feed
    Our Souls with Mystic Flesh Divine? (73:2)

or 8.8.8.8.88:

> The Sav'd and Saviour now agree
> In closest Fellowship combin'd,
> We grieve, and die, and live with Thee,
> To thy great Father's Will resign'd;
> And God doth all thy Members own
> One with Thyself, for ever One. (133:5)

In Wesley's short-meter hymns, when he shifts from the three-foot lines to the four-foot line, the added foot gives interest to the stanza even to readers who are unaware of Wesley's craft.

> Because He saith Do this,
> This I will always do,
> Till JESUS come in glorious Bliss,
> I *thus* his Death will *shew*. (86:8)

In several hymns (92, 142 and 156) Wesley uses lines of very different length, 5.5.5.11, a form which traces to a German model.

> With Bread from above,
> With Comfort and Love
> Our Spirit he fills,
> And all his unspeakable Goodness reveals. (92:7)

Twice in this collection (Hymns 78 and 87) Wesley uses a stanza form that seems light-hearted, even though he uses this jaunty meter for serious themes:

> Lamb of God, for whom we languish,
> Make thy Grief Our Relief,
> Ease us by thine Anguish. (78:1)

While the stanza is printed as three lines of 4, 4 and 3 feet, the second line, as Wesley indicates by internal rhyme and by the use of capital letters, is to be read as two rhyming half-lines, making a stanza of 4, 2, 2, 3 feet (8.33.6 meter).

A similar stanza which seems to play with words and rhymes, but is saved from mere Gilbertian cleverness by serious content, is the 55.55.65.65 stanza of hymns 95, 138 and 159. On the page one sees four four-foot lines rhyming *aabb*:

> With mystical Wine He comforts us here,
> And gladly we join, Till JESUS appear,

With hearty Thanksgiving His Death to record;
The Living, the Living Should sing of their LORD. (95:2)

But each line contains two half-lines, and the half-lines in two successive
lines rhyme, suggesting an eight-line stanza of very short lines, rhyming *ababcdcd*. Each line contains two rhythmic units in anapestic meter.
Wesley handles these fairly intricate forms easily.

Rattenbury speaks of Wesley's 'merry metres' whose high spirits gave
to hymn singing a new tonality. Hymns in this manner, Rattenbury says,
expressed the joy of the Evangelical Revival, and he thinks that if they
have come to be little used, it is 'because no one is ecstatically happy
enough to need them now'.[67]

As to rhythm, Wesley usually writes in iambic, but some of his most
vigorous stanzas are in trochaic rhythm, as:

Shall we let Him die in vain?
    Still to Death pursue our GOD?
Open tear his Wounds again,
    Trample on his pretious Blood?
No; with all our Sins we part,
Saviour, take my broken Heart! (23:3)

At times Wesley's stanzas open with an iambic couplet, but continue with
a trochaic quatrain. Yet the mixture reads smoothly.

He ever lives and prays
    For all the faithful Race;
In the Holiest Place above
    Sinners Advocate He stands,
Pleads for us his Dying Love,
    Shews for us his bleeding Hands. (118:2)

Another pattern of mixed rhythms is in Hymn 21, 'God of unexampled
Grace' (see pp. 68f.), in which lines 1, 3, 5, 6 and 7 are of seven syllables and
trochaic, while lines 2, 4 and 8 are of six syllables and iambic. There are
similar mixtures in other hymns, all of which Wesley handles skilfully.

When his work is compared with that of hymn-writers before him and
after him, Wesley's stanza forms and meters show astonishing variety. In
Hymns on the Lord's Supper 28 meters are used (counting the doubled
forms and the various types of six-eights and four-sevens). The dignified
8.8.8.8.88 meter and the 8.6.8.6 Common Meter are both used 18 times;
77.77 is used 13 times. Two meters, 8.8.8.8 and 88.8.88.8, are each

used 10 times. Three meters – 88.6.88.6, 7.6.7.6.7.7.7.6, and 7.7.7.7.77 – are each used nine times. The remaining 80 hymns show 20 stanza forms, ranging from eight uses to a single use. No one metrical form dominates.

The hymns which fell into quatrain form could be sung to familiar psalm tunes. However, Wesley's more intricate stanzas required new and more sophisticated music. In time Methodists learned to sing fairly complex words in fairly complex musical settings, and to sing with joy, and often without book.

Rhymes and Rhyme Schemes

Wesley's verse always rhymes, as most eighteenth-century verse did. Indeed, when Wesley wrote, rhyme was virtually considered constitutive of poetry. Since he composed these 166 hymns on a single theme and within a fairly short time, inevitably ideas recur and rhyme-words reappear.

Rhyme gives unity to poetic stanzas. When one hears the final rhyme, one knows, with an almost physical relaxation, that a unit of speech and thought has closed. Wesley's rhymes are usually smooth and carry a sense of inevitability. Strained or contrived rhymes, which read as though the poet chose an inadequate word because rhyme required it, are infrequent in Wesley's work.

A fair portion of Wesley's rhymes would be called 'imperfect' – a technical term which does not disparage; much rhymed poetry derives its interest from a sprinkling of imperfect endings. It is difficult to judge rhymes, for one cannot know with certainty how the language was pronounced in all parts of eighteenth-century English society, and equivalences that the ear accepts in one generation may not pass in another.[68]

In a few cases 'imperfect' rhymes run throughout the hymn. In Hymn 3, 'prepared' rhymes with 'the Lord'; 'extinguish'd were' with 'as slain appear'; 'first was made' with 'newly dead'; and 'offering join' with 'for ever Thine'. Was Wesley less exacting about rhyme than he was about some other features of prosody or did he at times deliberately stretch the limits of rhyme?

Repetition

Repeating a word or a phrase is a somewhat obvious, almost oratorical, device to establish emphasis and urgency; it is common in oral address; and used sparingly, it can be effective.

Wesley often uses an important word in one line and then repeats it, in the next, somewhat expanding it. An example would be the accented word 'vesture' in 30:1.3–4:

> Before us in thy Vesture stand,
>   Thy Vesture dipt in blood.

or Wesley's use of 'throne' in 43:1.3–4:

> From thy high and lofty Throne,
>   Throne of everlasting Bliss.

or of 'death' in 143:5.5–6:

> But humbly unto Death obey,
>   The Death of JESU's Cross.

Occasionally Wesley uses the same opening word in three or more lines in succession, as in Hymn 33:3, in which the first three lines all begin with 'Thou', or in Hymn 77, whose last four lines begin with 'Come' (see p. 104), or the insistent and moving repetition of 'Dying' at the opening of five lines of Hymn 120 (see p. 156).

Repeating an important word risks making the verse static. However, it is Wesley's usual way to repeat a word from one complex of thought in such a way as to move the flow of ideas forward into the next phrase or line. Rather than holding the thought back, Wesley's way of repeating words moves his verse ahead.

Lists

Wesley often writes lines that are comprised of a series of nouns, adjectives or verbs. His lists often, but not always, fall in threes. Out of scores of instances one might cite:

> Give us Pardon, Grace and Glory,
>   Peace, and Power, and Heaven in Thee. (15:2.7–8)

Some of these lists indicate the structure of a hymn or an idea, or they may sum up a point. They usually have an emphatic rhythm, and often some of their terms alliterate.

> JESU, Sinner's Friend, receive us
>   Feeble, famishing, and faint. (82:1.1–2)

Isaac Watts used this device, although less frequently than Wesley. In a hymn in his series on the sacrament, he wrote a stanza built around two lists:

> Thy light, and strength, and pardoning grace,
>   And glory shall be mine;
> My life and soul, my heart and flesh,
>   And all my powers are thine. (3:3)

List-making was a habit of Wesley's mind. In his *Journal* for 8 April 1740, he reports returning from a difficult meeting with some persons of the 'stillness' persuasion: 'I got home, weary, wounded, bruised, and faint.' This informal prose passage sounds like scores of lines in his hymns: four adjectives, two of which alliterate; and the last five words fall into a four-foot line in trochaic rhythm.

Shifts of Voice

Within a hymn, and sometimes even within a stanza, Wesley changes the voice in which he speaks. A hymn which begins by addressing God may, in its concluding stanzas or lines, be addressed to Christians. Hymn 56, for example, opens, 'How dreadful is the Mystery/ Which instituted, Lord, by Thee . . .' But it ends, 'And we that eat the Bread of Heaven/ The life of Heaven shall live.' Or a hymn may begin speaking to other Christians and end as a prayer or an act of praise. Hymn 91, whose first two stanzas speak *about Christ* ('What He for us did gain'), turns in its third stanza to speak *to God* ('There Lord we shall thy Pledge restore'). Occasionally there are several such shifts within a single hymn.

Congregations were probably not confused. They sang to the Father, to Christ, to the troubled and the seeking, and to one another, in a collective voice and in an individual voice, all with no felt need for transition. Wesley had the model of the Psalms, which can begin by talking *about* God ('The Lord is my shepherd') and then pass to direct address ('For thou art with me') and return to first-person speech, talking again about God ('And I will dwell in the house of the Lord for ever').

Syncope

When a poet shortens a word by leaving out a sound in order to accommodate the meter of a line, usually indicating the omission by an apostrophe, the device is called *syncope*. Wesley uses it often. Some of his apostrophes which indicate a dropped letter do not influence the pronunciation, as when he says 'promis'd' or 'pardon'd' or 'expos'd' or 'renew'd'. But when he says 'pard'ning', or 't'adore', or 't'infect', or 't'augment', or 'cath'lic', or 'cov'nant', or 'degen'rate', or 'quick'ning', he is omitting a syllable that would ordinarily be sounded. (Wesley often tries to compress the word 'Spirit' into a single syllable.[69]) Instances of syncope occur frequently in the eucharistic hymns, but they do not affect the thought.

Inversion

Wesley often writes lines whose words are not in the order they would have in normal speech or written prose. He frequently sets the verb at the end of a line, following its object, as in

> To us thy Gifts and Graces give;
> With Holy Things our Mouths are fill'd,
> 　O let our Hearts with Joy o'erflow. (112:1.4–6)

When inversion is used sparingly and intentionally, it can throw a poet's emphasis on a closing word effectively, as in the line 'Long we for thy love have waited' (83:2.1). In the first line of Hymn 116, 'Victim Divine, thy grace we claim', the ending 'thy grace we claim' is stronger than 'we claim thy grace' would be, even if it rhymed.

However, at times Wesley's use of the device makes a reader pause to puzzle out the sequence of ideas. The second stanza of Hymn 128 is so extreme an example of this characteristic as to read almost like unconscious self-parody.

> Thy Self our utmost Price hast paid,
> Thou hast for all Atonement made,
> 　For all the Sins of All Mankind;
> GOD doth in Thee Redemption give:
> But how shall we the Grace receive,
> 　But how shall we the Blessing find? (128:2.1–6)

Inversions, many of them rather awkward, appear often in the metrical psalms which Charles Wesley had sung all his life. In his day such inversions would have been more acceptable than they came to be two generations later. (Neither Watts nor Cowper uses inversion nearly as frequently as Wesley does.) Inversion which seems to order the flow of ideas to suit the demands of meter and rhyme is a mark of the 'poetic diction' whose artificiality Wordsworth criticised in his 'Preface' to *Lyrical Ballads*, and it has come to sound affected in a way it would not have in the eighteenth century.[70]

Chiasmus

A device that Wesley would have known from his study of the classics and that he uses occasionally is chiasmus – setting words or ideas in an *abba* pattern. The outer words or elements correspond with one another, and they enclose inner words or elements which also match one another. A conspicuous instance is the opening stanza of Hymn 164:

> Sons of GOD, triumphant rise,
> Shout th' accomplished Sacrifice,
> Shout your Sins in CHRIST forgiven,
> Sons of GOD, and Heirs of Heaven!

Vocabulary and Diction

Wesley generally uses short, accessible, Anglo-Saxon words. Many lines or whole stanzas are comprised almost entirely of words of a single syllable. Of course, many words that stand in the theological tradition are long and Latin-derived, such as *condemnation, immortal, institution, oblation, passion, salvation, sanctified*. When Wesley uses these terms freely, as he does, they give him two-, three-, and four-syllable words which can relieve a tendency to choppiness.

However, often in a line comprised of short words Wesley will set a long, Latinate word that is not part of the Church's theological vocabulary: *antedate, antidote, benignest, consummated, convulsions, exhibited, illustrious, inexorably, meritorious, monumental, rapturous, salutary, satiate, stupendous, sustenance, transporting, tremendous, unsubstantial*, and many others. Often, as he uses the word, it is apparent that he hears in it the sharpness and specificity of its Latin origin. Donald Davie remarks that Wesley 'is splendidly aware of the metaphors hidden in latinate words'.[71] (Wesley in his school years had spent many hours translating Latin texts and composing in Latin, and he had been a Latin tutor at Oxford.) Such words do not jar the meter, but fit the lines smoothly. Frank Baker remarks that Wesley is able to incorporate 'poly-syllabic Latinate words into the texture of his verse in such a manner that they illustrate his theme, introduce modulation into the verbal music, and vary without disrupting the rhythm.'[72] Yet an attentive reader tends to notice these words. They are used in a straightforward way and do not seem to be meant as literary or learned. Yet one suspects that many of them would have been lost on worshippers who lacked schoolboy Latin.

Such latinisms are virtually unknown in the hymns of Isaac Watts, who explained in the 'Preface' to his *Psalms of David* that he would 'neither indulge any bold metaphors, nor admit of hard words' lest he tempt 'the ignorant worshipper to sing without his understanding.'[73]

Wesley's distinctive vocabulary is also marked by compound words, often of his own coinage and used for emphasis – words such as: death-recording (1:1.3); ever-slaughter'd (5:5.4); all-atoning (25:3.3; 68:3.1; 85:3.1; 153:2.6); sin-atoning (31:2.1); all-cleansing (39:3.4); blood-besprinkled (71:1.1); all-bounteous (88:1.1); all-loving (91:1.1); all-redeeming (91:1.1; 162:1.7; 139:1.1); soul-transporting (94:1.1); all-reviving (115:1.6); all-prevalent (116:2.4); heaven-deserving (117:2.4); all-sufficient (124:1.5; 140:1.2); all-involved (134:4.1); all-holy, all-divine (147:2.2); all-gracious (152:2.1). In *Hymns on the Lord's Supper*, more than half of such words are compounds using 'all'.

Alliteration

Many of Wesley's lines or phrases are made memorable and effective by his use of repeated sounds. In Hymn 82 (see p. 116, below) he says in line 1.2, 'Feeble, famishing and faint'. Line 1.4 contains four 'w' sounds: 'Now, or now we die for want.' Later lines of the same hymn include the phrases 'sinking spirits', 'through wandering wearied', and 'feed by faith on Thee'. In another hymn, Wesley prays:

> The Sp'rit's Attesting Seal impart,
> And speak to every Sinner's Heart
>   The Saviour died for Thee! (10:4.3–5)

Describing the crucifixion, he says: 'Silence saddens all the Skies.' Such attention to sounds produces a unity of tone which influences even a reader who does not notice how the writer achieved the effect.

Strong Beginnings and Endings

Wesley does not begin, and he does not end his hymns or his stanzas indecisively. Not all of the hymns in this collection are equally forceful, but Wesley's opening and his closing lines are generally arresting. Moreover, he seems to begin and end each section of the collection with a more than ordinarily substantial hymn.

Many features of Wesley's style locate him in the formal rhetorical tradition of the eighteenth century. Yet the directness, immediacy and emotional energy of Wesley's lines set his work somewhat apart from the verse of his classical age, as do the variety in his stanza forms and his relaxed attitude towards rhyme. Such features of Wesley's style seem to look restlessly beyond his own age. However, the vitality of Wesley's work seems to arise not so much from conscious stylistic innovativeness as from the way in which his well-equipped mind was seized by his theme.

Comment

Wesley organises his *Hymns on the Lord's Supper* in five parts, followed by a short supplement. In Parts I–III he speaks of what God gives or shows in the Supper (the aspect that Brevint calls 'sacrament'). In these hymns Wesley presents the Holy Communion as: an imaginative repossession of the past redemptive event (Part I), a complex encounter with Christ in the present (Part II), and a vivid anticipation of the Christian's future with Christ (Part III). The Lord's Supper sets the communicant within the panorama of divine redemption where one touches immediately the ultimate origins of salvation in the cross, the active presence now of the living Christ, and final destiny in glory.

In Parts IV–V Wesley turns to write of the Lord's Supper in terms of what and how the Church or the communicant offers to God. (Brevint calls this side of the act 'sacrifice'.) In Part IV he relates the sacramental act not so much to Christ's cross, which was the theme of Part I, as to Christ's eternal priesthood and his present heavenly ministry. The Church offers in Christ's great eternal offering. Part V speaks of the sacrifice of life and goods which a Christian makes in union with Christ.

The nine hymns 'After the Sacrament' conclude the volume with the praise of God.

This sequence follows generally the organisation of thought in Brevint's *The Christian Sacrament and Sacrifice*, providing the collection of hymns with structure and movement. The theological argument of both Wesley's hymns and Brevint's essay might be thought of as developing Brevint's thesis of the sacrament as a mutual exchange. The Holy Communion, he says, is a place of meeting, where the people appear to worship God and where God is present to meet and bless the people. At this meeting, Brevint explains, 'the Christian Communicants are in a special manner invited to offer up to God their souls, their bodies, their goods, their vows, their praises, and whatsoever they can *give*; and God, on the other side, offers to us the body and blood of his Son, and all those other blessings, withal, that will surely follow this sacred gift' (I.1).

The following chapters of this book offer comment on the successive portions of Wesley's collection – not on each hymn, but on hymns or lines which express themes that seem to have been important to Wesley. The comments pause occasionally for some close reading, often taking note when Wesley draws salient expressions and ideas from Daniel Brevint. At the end of most chapters there are topical essays, bringing together material that fills out some aspect of Wesley's sacramental thought.

Wesley evidently wrote these hymns in a fairly short time. Only a few of them had appeared in earlier collections, and he returned to the Lord's Supper infrequently in later years. He was deeply caught up in his theme and wrote with seriousness and intensity. These hymns evidence how deeply Wesley cares about the sacrament and about the evangelical reality that the sacrament conveys, and how earnestly he seeks that Christians participate in the Supper understandingly and faithfully.

Part I

As it is a Memorial of the Sufferings and Death of Christ

HYMNS 1–27

Wesley's first unit of hymns develops the connection between the Lord's Supper and 'the sufferings and death of Christ' – a connection that arises out of the very charter of the sacrament. Paul and Luke report Jesus' saying at the Last Supper, 'Do this in memory of me,' and Paul told the Corinthians that by the Supper 'ye do show the Lord's death'. From the beginning, Christians have regarded the Lord's Supper as an instituted sign which holds before them Jesus and his redemptive death. Many writers on the Holy Communion, including both Wesley and Brevint, have remarked a parallel between the Christian eucharist and the Jewish Passover, a rite by which Israel kept the exodus in mind, and, indeed, repossessed it in every generation. Brevint had spoken of our 'holy Communion, which succeeds the Passover, and is undoubtedly no less a blessed and powerful sacrament to set before our eyes *Christ our Passover, who is sacrificed for us*' (II.3).

As the biblical tradition understands memory, formative divine events to which the believing community always stands indebted do not recede in time, becoming more difficult to recall as years pass. Rather, in such events, eternity intersects time, and they are potentially present to any moment. When they are remembered, they become contemporary, or the rememberer's 'now' becomes contemporary with them. Wesley asks that 'the years between' may pass away (5:3.4). He was, in this matter, following Brevint, who had said: 'This Sacrament, duly given and faithfully received, makes the thing which it represents as really present for our use, and as really powerful in order to our salvation, as if the thing itself were newly done, or in doing' (II.3). Borgen comments that these hymns express 'a two-way suspension of time and place'.[1]

Brevint had said that what takes place at the Church's altar sets before the faithful communicant the dreadful (that is, the awe-inspiring) events that took place at Jesus' crucifixion. 'I do observe on this altar somewhat very like the Sacrifice and passion of my Saviour. For thus the *bread of life* was broke, thus the *Lamb of God* was slain, thus his most precious *blood* was shed' (II.5).

Wesley duplicates in his own way this sense of the presentness of the cross in the sacrament and the communicant's involvement in the saviour's passion. 'Jesu's death is ever new' (3:2.4); 'we here [in the sacrament] his Passion shew' (4:2.6; 12:3.2).

The Last Supper

As Wesley opens the collection, he holds off his emphasis on Jesus' crucifixion to speak in his first hymn of the Last Supper:

1   In that sad memorable Night,
        When JESUS was for Us betray'd,
    He left his Death-recording Rite,
        He took, and bless'd, and brake the Bread,
    And gave his Own their last Bequest,
    And thus his LOVE's Intent exprest:

2   Take eat, this is my Body given,
        To purchase Life and Peace for You,
    Pardon and Holiness and Heaven;
        Do this, my dying LOVE to shew,
    Accept your precious Legacy,
    And thus, my Friends, remember me.

3   He took into his Hands the Cup,
        To crown the Sacramental Feast,
    And full of kind Concern look'd up,*
        And gave what He to them had blest,

---

* *He . . . look'd up:* an 'eye-witness' touch that is not in the gospel accounts of the Supper but which appears in the synoptic narratives of the miraculous feeding (Matthew 14.19; Mark 6.41; Luke 9.16) and in the Johannine account of Jesus' intercessory prayer (John 17.1). It entered the liturgical tradition, appearing in the institution narrative of the eucharistic rite as early as the late fourth century *Apostolic Constitutions*, VII.12.35–7: 'He took bread in his holy and undefiled hands, and looking up to you, his God and Father, he broke it . . .' This interpolation was continued in some of the classic liturgies, including the canon of the Latin Mass. The Non-juror Thomas Deacon included it in his *Devotions*, 1734. The Wesleys knew the *Apostolic Constitutions* (and thought it to be earlier than it is), and they knew and used Deacon's work.

And drink ye all of this, He said,
In solemn memory of the Dead.*

4   This is my Blood which seals the New
    Eternal Covenant of my Grace,
My blood so freely shed for You,
    For you and all the Sinfull Race,
My Blood that speaks your Sins forgiven,
And justifies your Claim to Heaven.

5   The Grace which I to all bequeath
    In this Divine Memorial take,
And mindful of your Saviour's Death,
    Do this, my Followers, for my sake,
Whose dying LOVE hath left behind
Eternal Life for all Mankind.

The hymn moves between two voices. The first stanza and the first part
of the third stanza speak in the third person of what Jesus did and said.
However, most of the hymn (stanzas 2, 3b, 4 and 5) represents Jesus
speaking in the first person to 'his own' at the Supper, and through them
to the Church, telling of 'the grace which I to all bequeath'. Stanzas 1 and
2 speak of the bread/the body, and stanzas 3 and 4 of the cup/the blood.

The opening lines emphasise that the Supper was a part of the passion
event. It was instituted 'In that sad memorable night/ When Jesus was
for us betrayed.' The Church's sacrament, as Wesley sees it, is a gesture
in which the departing Jesus showed his 'dying love'. His word 'Do this'
was his final, kindest command, his 'last bequest', his 'precious legacy'.

Isaac Watts' earlier hymns 'Prepared for the Lord's Supper' had similarly begun with a hymn recalling Jesus' act of institution and containing
several lines of scene-setting:

'Twas on the dark, that doleful night
When powers of earth and hell arose
Against the Son of God's delight,
And friends betray'd him to his foes:

Before the mournful scene began
He took the bread, and blest and brake . . . (1:1.1–2.2)

---

* *solemn*: not sad, but dignified, weighty, ceremonial, beyond the ordinary.

Watts' work may have suggested to Wesley that his series of hymns on the Lord's Supper might also begin with Jesus' words and acts at the Last Supper.

In line 1:1.3 Wesley speaks of the sacrament which was left by the departing Jesus as his 'death-recording rite'. Several times in later hymns he again refers to the Supper as a 'recording' act: The sacrament records Jesus' sufferings (4:3.1–2); communicants 'thus record the passion of that Lamb Divine' (89:1.1, also 88:1.3, 95:2.3). Wesley calls, 'Come we that record the death of our Lord' (142:1.1–2). (Watts in his first hymn for the Supper had said, 'Meet at the table, and record/ The love of your departed Lord' (1:6.3–4); and in a later hymn he says, 'Here . . . we his death record' (4:8.2).) But Wesley thinks of the record of Jesus as maintained by divine agency as well as human, for in a later hymn he says to God, 'Thou here [in the sacrament] record'st thy name' (63:1.2). He speaks of the Holy Spirit as the 'true Recorder of his passion' (16:1.5). In a print culture one records something by writing it down and placing the written text where it can later be referred to. In a pre-print culture, an event would be held in mind by a repeated solemn act and a frequently told story more than by writing.

As Jesus mentions his blood, he elaborates, 'My Blood that speaks your sins forgiven' (1:4.5). The living, heavenly Christ intercedes, as Wesley will often say, not by spoken words, but by his blood – the sacrificial act he carried out on earth and which now pleads in heaven for sinners. Rattenbury makes the point: 'What is his intercession? He does not speak, his wounded humanity, which He has taken into Heaven does.'[2]

Wesley's words, the 'blood that speaks', allude to Hebrews 12.24, which says that Jesus' blood of the new covenant 'speaketh better things than that of Abel'. Hebrews in turn refers to the story of Cain and Abel in which God says to Cain, the murderous brother, 'What hast thou done? The voice of thy brother's blood crieth unto me from the ground' (Genesis 4.10). Abel's blood cried from the ground for retribution, but Jesus' blood 'speaketh better things'; it asks for the forgiveness of sinners. Wesley uses the image often, in one place saying, 'Still his blood cries out "Forgive them,/ All their sins were purged by me"' (14:2.3–4). In the same hymn, Wesley extends the figure, not only saying that Jesus' blood speaks in behalf of sinners, but asking the Father to hear it, 'Father, hear the blood of Jesus,/ Speaking in thine ears above' (14:1.1–2).

Past and Present

After this opening hymn, Wesley moves between the cross and the Church's present act of sacramental recalling: 'By faith his flesh we eat,/ Who here his passion show' (4:2.5–6).

Reflecting on the bread and wine, he says:

In this expressive Bread I see
The Wheat by Man cut down for me,
    And beat, and bruis'd, and ground:
The heavy Plagues and Pains and Blows
Which JESUS suffer'd from his Foes,
    Are in this Emblem found. (2:1)*

When Wesley says that the bread is 'expressive' he has in mind the actions of harvesting wheat and baking it to make it into bread – actions which destroy the form of the grain and which therefore, as he sees them, suggest Jesus' passion. In the next lines, he speaks in the same way of 'the bread dried up and burnt with fire' (2:2.1). Wesley takes this idea from Brevint, who in the prayer that ends his Section II proposes that the making of bread suggests Jesus' suffering and death:

My Lord and my God! I behold here in this bread, made of a substance that was cut down, beaten, ground and bruised by men, all the heavy blows, and plagues and pains, which my Saviour did suffer from the hands of his murderers; I behold the bread, dried up, and baked, and burnt in fire, the fiery wrath also which he suffered for me. (II.1)

In the following hymn Wesley sets Jesus' cruel death firmly in the past by remarking that the tools by which it was brought about have vanished.

The Instruments that bruis'd Him so
Were broke and scatter'd long ago,
    The Flames extinguish'd were,

Yet, he goes on to say, the reality of his sacrifice remains as fresh as when it was made. Jesus appears in the sacrament as one who was slain.

---

* *this Emblem:* In the seventeenth century, 'emblem books' presented religious ideas in both pictures and words. The sacramental bread is God's 'emblem' of the passion.

But JESU's Death is ever New,
He whom in Ages past they slew
　　Doth still as slain appear.

Th' Oblation sends as sweet a Smell,
Ev'n now it pleases GOD as well
　　As when it first was made. (3:2.1–3.3)

Wesley takes these unusual ideas from Brevint, who had said:

> Though the instruments that bruised Him be broken to pieces, and
> the direful flames that burned Him be quite put out, yet this bread,
> which is the body of the Lord, continues new. The spears and swords
> that slew, and the burnings that completed the Sacrifice, are, many
> years since, scattered and spent; but the strength and sweet smell of the
> oblation is still fragrant. (II.11)

When both Brevint and Wesley refer to 'flames' and 'burnings', they are
not thinking literally of the passion events, in which fire played no part,
but they are thinking metaphorically both of the baking of the bread
of the Supper and of Jesus' death on the analogy of a levitical burnt
sacrifice. The writers both use the biblical anthropomorphism that God
is pleased with the smell of sacrifices that are made in obedience (Genesis
8.21; Leviticus 26.31).

The sacrament brings the past saving act into the Church's present.
Christ's sacrifice appears to Christians as 'ever new', and it continues to
be pleasing to God. But the passion is not made present in newness and
power by a strenuous act of human imagination. Rather, Wesley asks
Jesus, the living Saviour, to take the initiative:

Thou bidst us call thy Death to mind,
　　But Thou must give the Solemn Power,
Come then, thou Saviour of Mankind,
　　Bring back that last tremendous Hour,*
And stand in all thy Wounds confest. (25:2.1–5)

---

* *tremendous hour:* the hour that makes one tremble.

Wesley's Graphic Presentism

By faith, the sacrament is an enactment of Calvary, and through it communicants are made bystanders at the redemptive event itself. Wesley expresses the hereness and nowness of the cross in seven hymns at the beginning of Part I (Hymns 2–8) and again in a group toward the end (Hymns 18, 21, 22, 24, 26), and it is at least suggested in several others.[3] Wesley regarded the sacrament as an occasion for an especially vivid, almost physiological, remembering of the saving act. He repeatedly places the faithful communicant at the crucifixion, where one can see, hear and feel the events as they unfold.

> CHRIST revives his Sufferings here,
>   Still exposes them to View,
> See the Crucified appear. (8:2.3–5)

Wesley seeks immediate vision, 'Now let it pass the years between,/ And view Thee bleeding on the Tree' (5:3.4–5). The communicants lie 'humbly at thy Cross' (15:1.2). They ask, 'Place us near th' accursed wood' (22:2.1). The line 'I see him bound and bruis'd and slain' (2:4.2) sets the writer at Jesus' very cross as a witness of his suffering; and through him the worshipper at the Holy Communion stands there as well.

Several times Wesley speaks of 'yonder tree' or 'yon Cross', as though the sacrament had transported the worshipper to the passion scene, where one can see or point to Jesus' cross standing close by, 'Hangs our Hope on yonder tree' (22:3.5, and see 2:3.5).

Communicants ask to stand at the cross as Mary did and feel what she felt:

> Near as once thy Mother stood;
>   Partners of the Pangs divine,
> Bid us feel her sacred Smart,
> Feel the Sword that pierc'd her Heart. (22:2.3–6)

The thought had been suggested by Brevint's remark that the worthy receivers should 'elevate their faith, and stretch their very souls up to the *Mount*, with the blessed Virgin, who stood nearest the Sacrifice' (II.9).

The prayer of the longing communicant is answered. Christ crucified appears:

Surely now the Prayer He hears:
    Faith presents the Crucified!
Lo! the wounded Lamb appears
    Pierc'd his Feet, his Hands his Side. (22:3.1–4)*

Wesley bids the communicant *see* in the sacrament Jesus' very passion:

Lift your Eyes of Faith, and look,
    On the Signs He did ordain!
Thus the Bread of Life was broke,**
    Thus the Lamb of GOD was slain,
Thus was shed on *Calvary*
His last Drop of Blood for me!

See the slaughter'd Sacrifice,
    See the Altar stain'd with Blood!
Crucified before our Eyes
    Faith discerns the Dying GOD. (18:1.1–2.4)

See his Body mangled, rent,
    Cover'd with a gore of Blood! (23:1.3–4)

He hangs! – adown his mournful Face,
    See trickling fast the Tears and Blood! (24:1.3–4)

Wesley's conviction that the act of remembering places a believer at Jesus' very cross, where its sights and sounds are present to faith, was not original with him, but had roots in Western spirituality, both catholic and evangelical. John and Charles included in several of their collections a hymn on the crucifixion written by their father, Samuel Wesley, which contained a strong appeal to see and hear:

Behold, the Saviour of mankind
    Nailed to the shameful tree:***
How vast the love that him inclined
    To bleed and die for thee!

---

* *his Feet, his Hands his Side*: the *five wounds* of Jesus.
** *was broke*: Wesley occasionally uses a simple past tense where present day usage would call for a participle with a form of 'to be'. Here he is influenced by Brevint, see the quotation on p. 54.
*** *the shameful tree*: The poetic use of 'the tree' for Jesus' cross is very old. See Acts 5.30; 10.39; 13.29; Galatians 3.13; 1 Peter 2.24.

Hark, how he groans, while nature shakes,
  And earth's strong pillars bend!
The temple's veil in sunder breaks,
  The solid marbles rend.

. . . See where he bows his sacred head!
  He bows his head and dies.

(1780 *Collection*, Hymn 22)[4]

Western eucharistic spirituality, Catholic and Protestant, has been cross-centred. Sacramental piety has meant piety of the passion. However, this passion-centred realism came to expression differently. At the same time that Baroque Catholic devotion had its crucifixes, stations, and sacred hearts, the eminently rational seventeenth-century Cambridge mathematician and theologian Isaac Barrow explained that the Lord's Supper is 'a solemn and sensible representation' of Christ's redemptive suffering. In it 'we behold him crucified, as it were *in effigy*, his body broken, his blood poured out for us; it being, in a sort, a putting us into the circumstances of those who did behold our Saviour for us hanging upon the cross'.[5]

British non-conformity is usually thought of as almost aggressively non-visual, but sight is such a presiding sense that it cannot be denied, even if one intends only an inward seeing. The early eighteenth-century Presbyterian Matthew Henry, writing some years before the Wesley hymns, expressed vividly what the devout communicant is to *see* at the sacrament. In *The Communicant's Companion*, 1704, Henry describes 'the affecting sights that are to be seen by faith in this ordinance', saying:

> The wounds of this Lamb are here open before us. Come, see in Christ's hands the very print of the nails, see in his side the very marks of the spear. Behold him in his agony, sweating as if it had been 'great drops of blood falling to the ground'. . . Behold him upon the cross, enduring the pain, and despising the shame of the cursed tree. Here is his body broken, his blood shed, his soul poured out unto death; all his sufferings, with all their aggravations, are here, in such a manner as the divine wisdom saw fit, by an instituted ordinance, represented to us, and set before us.[6]

Isaac Watts' communion hymn 'When I survey the wondrous cross' similarly asks the communicant to visualise the crucifixion:

> See from his head, his hands, his feet,
> Sorrow and love flow mingled down;
> Did e'er such love and sorrow meet?
> Or thorns compose so rich a crown?

His dying crimson like a robe
Spreads o'er his body on the tree. (7:3.1–4.2)

What Wesley did when he depicted the Lord's Table as a vivid representation of Jesus' passion and the communicant as a first-hand witness of
the saving event had been done by others. Yet no one else in England in
Wesley's time, Church of England or Dissenter, developed this sacramental drama of the senses with such circumstantiality and immediacy as he
did. It is in this section that one may observe what Donald Davie has
called the 'physicality' or the 'carnality' of Wesley's hymns.[7]

A Deeply Involved Beholder

A believer cannot look at the cross and remain a disinterested observer;
one is drawn into the event and is impelled to worship. Brevint had
spoken of the involvement of the Christian observer: 'As soon as I see
[these Sacraments] used in the church . . . I will not fail both to remember
my Saviour who consecrated these Sacraments, and to worship also my
Saviour whom these sacraments do represent' (II.6). The sacrament, he
says, elicits 'a vigorous and intense act of faith'. The eucharistic memorial is enriched 'with such an effectual and real presence of continuing
atonement and strength, as may *both evidently set forth Christ Himself
crucified before our eyes* (Galatians 3.1) and invite us to his sacrifice,
not as done and gone many years since, but, as to expiating grace and
mercy, still lasting, still new, still the same that it was when it was first
offered for us' (II.7). The sacrifice of Christ, Brevint says, 'is as effectual
now, at this holy *table*, as it was then at the very cross . . . The worthy
Communicant is prostrated at the Lord's table, as at the very foot of his
cross' (II.9, 10).

Many of Wesley's hymns on the Supper as memorial express such a
'vigorous and intense act of faith'. As Borgen put it, 'The "memorial"
Wesley presents is a dynamic drama of worship in which both the believer
and the Holy Spirit are actively involved.'[8]

The communicants identify with the Saviour:

Prince of Life, for Sinners slain,
    Grant us Fellowship with Thee,
Fain we would partake thy Pain,
    Share thy mortal Agony. (22:1.1–4)

In Hymn 4 Wesley carries the worshipper into something like a passion play, placing the present-day believer at the cross itself, where by an almost physiological immediacy, one not only sees and hears, but feels as well:

> Ev'n now we mournfully enjoy*
> Communion with our LORD,
> As tho' we every one
> Beneath his Cross had stood,
> And seen him heave, and heard him groan,
> And felt his gushing Blood. (4:3.3–8)

And in the next lines, Jesus dies:

> O GOD! tis finish'd now!
> The Mortal Pang is past!
> By Faith his Head we see Him bow,
> And hear him breathe his last! (4:4.1–4)

But Wesley cannot depict Jesus' death without linking it to the believer:

> We too with Him are Dead,
> And shall with him arise,
> The Cross on which He bows his Head,
> Shall lift us to the skies. (4:4.5–8)

The devout communicant, personally involved in the cross, acknowledges with a broken heart that one's own sins have brought Jesus to such agony (see 23:1–2, p. 70 below).

> Ah, give me, LORD, my Sins to mourn,
> My Sins which have thy Body torn,
> Give me with broken Heart to see
> Thy last tremendous Agony,
> To weep o'er an expiring GOD,
> And mix my Sorrow with thy Blood. (6:1)

---

* *mournfully enjoy:* an oxymoron; here, and usually in *Hymns on the Lord's Supper*, 'to mourn' means 'to mourn one's sins'.

The Sympathy of Nature

The communicant, present at the cross, sees and feels the manifestations in the physical world that accompanied Jesus' death, as described in Matthew's passion account (Matthew 27.51–3). Speaking in present tense, Wesley says that Jesus' death is felt in nature, as his final groan is heard throughout earth and skies. The earth trembles, and heaven becomes as dark as hell. The veil of the Temple is torn; the rocks are broken; the graves give up their dead and the bodies of the saints arise.

> 1   'Tis done! th' Atoning Work is done:
>   JESUS the World's Redeemer dies!
>   All Nature feels th' Important Groan
>   Loud-echoing thro' the Earth and Skies,
>   The Earth doth to her Centre quake,
>   And Heaven as Hell's deep Gloom is black!
>
> 2   The Temple's Veil is rent in twain,
>   While JESUS meekly bows his Head,
>   The Rocks resent his mortal Pain,*
>   The yawning Graves give up their Dead,
>   The Bodies of the Saints arise,
>   Reviving as their Saviour dies.

Having mentioned these dramatic signs, Wesley spiritualises them, praying that Jesus' passion may shake our earth, break up our hearts of stone, and rouse us from the grave to life that does not end:

> 3   And shall not We his Death partake,
>   In sympathetic Anguish groan?
>   O Saviour, let thy Passion shake
>   Our Earth, and rent our Hearts of Stone,
>   To second Life our Souls restore,
>   And wake us that we sleep no more. (26)

In Wesley's long and complex Hymn 21, the communicants are deeply engaged by Jesus' passion. They see him 'crucified before our eyes' (2.3) and 'stretch'd on yonder Cross' (3.3). In the terrible scene, they 'discern the Deity' (3.5) and cry out in recognition ''Tis He, 'tis He,/ My God that suffers there!' (3.7–8).

---

* *resent:* in an old sense of 'feel sympathetically with'.

Nature is caught up in the suffering and death of nature's Lord.

> Endless Scenes of Wonder rise
>   With that mysterious Tree,
> Crucified before our Eyes
>   Where we our Maker see. (21:2.1–4)

Jesus' death 'tears the graves and mountains up . . . Nature in convulsions lies' (21:4.3, 5). Wesley uses a philosophical term in paradox, saying that the First Cause dies (21:5.1). Then, dipping into classical mythology, he speaks of Christ as 'the true eternal Pan' who 'falls to raise us from our fall' (21:5.2–3).[9] Wesley describes the darkness at the crucifixion as the sympathetic withdrawal of the sun.

> Well may *Sol* withdraw his Light,*
>   With the Sufferer sympathise,
> Leave the World in sudden Night,
>   While his Creator dies.

> Well may Heaven be cloath'd with black
>   And solemn Sackcloath wear,
> JESU'S agony partake
>   The Hour of Darkness share. (21:5.5–6.4)

Even the hosts of heaven fall silent:

> Mourn th' astonied Hosts above,
>   Silence saddens all the Skies,
> Kindler of Seraphick Love
>   The God of Angels dies. (21:6.5–8)

All of this cosmic display is beheld by the deeply moved communicant. J. R. Watson says that 'even more than most of Wesley's hymns', Hymn 21 'is dramatic, impassioned, and densely allusive. In it he exclaims, cries out, feels the mortal smart, shares the hour of darkness, breaks his heart, weeps, blesses, and worships.'[10]

---

* Latin, *Sol*, the sun, widely taken in Roman times to be divine.

Grace for Sinners

The sacrament represents Christ's sufferings, bringing back his dying hour. 'Thus the Lamb of God was slain' (18:1.4). But Christ's terrible death is an extension of grace, which is effective for sinners.

> Let Thy blood, by faith applied,
>   The sinner's pardon seal. (20:3.1–2)

And it speaks freshly to the Father:

> 'To thy pard'ning grace receive them,'
>   Once he prayed upon the tree;
> Still his blood cries out, 'Forgive them,
>   All their sins were purged by me.' (14:2.1–4)

In one of his most dramatic hymns, Wesley implores an obdurate heart to recognise that sin – one's own sin – has brought Christ to the cross, 'Murdered God's eternal Son':

> 1   Hearts of Stone, relent, relent,
>   Break by JESU's Cross subdued,
>   See his Body, mangled, rent,
>   Cover'd with a gore of Blood!
>   Sinful Soul, what hast Thou done?
>   Murther'd GOD's eternal Son!
>
> 2   Yes, our Sins have done the Deed,
>   Drove the Nails that fix Him here,
>   Crown'd with Thorns his sacred Head,
>   Pierc'd Him with the Soldier's Spear.
>   Made his Soul a Sacrifice;
>   For a sinful World He dies.
>
> 3   Shall we let Him die in vain?
>   Still to Death pursue our GOD?
>   Open tear his Wounds again,
>   Trample on his pretious Blood?

After these intense, repeated questions, the plea has its effect.

> No; with all our Sins we part,
> Saviour, take my broken heart! (23)

The hymn which began 'Hearts of stone, relent, relent' ends with the chastened sinner saying, 'Saviour, take my broken heart!'

Heightening the contemporaneity of the cross, Wesley speaks in the present tense, saying 'dies', and he personalises, 'My God, who dies for Me, for Me!' (5:3.6). Jesus' prayer for his tormentors, 'Forgive them', is, as Wesley sees it, timeless; in the sacrament, Jesus still asks it in behalf of sinners, 'Forgive, the Saviour cries,/ They know not what they do' (19:1–2). The adoring communicants identify with Jesus' crucifixion and seek to become participants in his 'great offering', even sharing his pain (a theme which Wesley will develop in Part IV). Yet, knowing that his death was for them, in this shattering encounter they find grace and occasion for thankfulness. The sacrament yields 'Rivers to refresh and heal/ The fainting sinsick Soul' (27:3.3–4). Communicants ask:

> Receive us then, Thou Pard'ning GOD,
> Partakers of his Flesh and Blood
>   Grant that we now may be. (10:4.1–3)

Since the Wesleys were convinced that the Holy Communion might be 'a converting ordinance', they invited sinners and seekers to the table, persuaded that it was a place where one might find the Saviour. The Wesleys' conviction was supported by their experience as evangelists. John once said in a sermon, 'Ye are witnesses. For many now present know, the very beginning of your conversion to God (perhaps, in some, the first deep conviction) was wrought at the Lord's Supper,' (*Journal*, 27 June 1740).

The invitation is particularly expressed in Hymn 8, which opens:

> Come to the Supper come,
> Sinners there still is Room;
> Every Soul may be his Guest,
>   JESUS gives the general Word;
> Share the Monumental Feast,*
>   Eat the Supper of your LORD. (8:1.1–6)

The sacrament is a meal prepared for sinners to which Jesus has given a

---

* *the monumental feast*: the memorial feast; Latin *monumentum*, memorial.

general invitation, but each person must respond. Many of the manuals of sacramental devotion of the period offered heavy emphasis on inward and often laboured preparation for the sacrament, and they gave warnings against eating and drinking unworthily. Wesley, by contrast, does not commend that one first prepare and then come when one is qualified; rather, 'come' is his first word. The sacrament overflows with 'Gushing Streams of Life' (27:2.7).

The Holy Spirit in the Sacrament

In two hymns of Part I, Hymns 7 and 16, Wesley establishes that the connection between the cross, the sacrament and the heart of the believer is made by the Holy Spirit. Both of these hymns open with an address to the Spirit, echoing the Latin hymn *Veni Creator Spiritus*.

Not all sacramental doctrine and spirituality and not all eucharistic texts have made an express connection between the eucharist and the work of the Holy Spirit. Wesley, however, asks the Holy Spirit to interpret the sacrament to the believer. The 'internal testimony of the Spirit' was an important Methodist emphasis; God bears witness to God, no other witness being adequate. It is by the Holy Spirit that the communicant is enabled to grasp inwardly the meaning of the saving events. The divine witness reveals the death of Christ as paradoxically 'the death by which we live' (7:1.4). It would be quite possible to see in the Holy Communion only the signs, the bread and wine. However, by the inward working of the Spirit the communicant 'discerns' Jesus' passion in 'the sacred sign' (7:2.3).

1   Come Holy Ghost, set to thy Seal,
         Thine inward Witness give,
     To all our waiting Souls reveal
         The Death by which we live.

2   Spectators of the Pangs Divine
         O that we Now may be,
     Discerning in the Sacred Sign
         His Passion on the Tree.

Even more powerfully, by the Spirit one is made contemporaneous with the redemptive event; the communicant sees the crucifixion, hears Jesus' cry, feels the earthquake, and sees the opened graves – referring to Jesus' cry of dereliction on the cross and to the physical manifestations which accompanied his death in the account in Matthew 27:45–53.

3   Give us to hear the dreadful Sound*
    Which told his Mortal Pain,
Tore up the Graves, and shook the Ground,
    And rent the Rocks in twain.

The Spirit is asked to 'repeat' Jesus' cry of abandonment so authoritatively that 'every heart' echoes, with wonder, the centurion's confession, 'This was the Son of God!' (Matthew 27.54; Mark 15.39).

4   Repeat the Saviour's dying Cry
    In every Heart so loud,
That every Heart may now reply
    This was the Son of GOD! (7)

Wesley returns to the theme of the Holy Spirit in Hymn 16, again speaking in the vocative:

1   Come, Thou everlasting Spirit,
    Bring to every thankful Mind
All the Saviour's dying Merit
    All his suffering for Mankind:
True Recorder of his Passion,
    Now the living Faith impart,
Now reveal his great Salvation,
    Preach his Gospel to our Heart,

2   Come, Thou Witness of his Dying,
    Come Remembrancer Divine,
Let us feel thy Power applying
    CHRIST to every Soul and mine;
Let us groan thine inward Groaning,
    Look on Him we pierc'd, and grieve.
All receive the Grace Atoning,
    All the sprinkled Blood receive. (16)

Both stanzas ask the Spirit to come to the communicants in the Supper to do an inward work, for what has been done by Christ and what is made

---

* *dreadful*: awe-inspiring, terrible, fearful.

accessible in the sacrament can only be truly apprehended through the
Spirit. As Wesley sees it, the appreciation of the gospel, as much as the
gospel itself, is divinely given. The Spirit is the prompter of the Christian's
mind who now brings to memory Christ's sufferings – imparting living
faith and preaching the gospel freshly in the Supper. The Supper is a
'vivid preaching', and the Spirit is the first preacher.

Wesley describes the Spirit as the Divine Witness of Christ's dying[11]
and a remembrancer who 'groans' within (Romans 8.26f.), applying
Christ to every soul; while the communicants in sympathetic response
'groan' with the Spirit's inward groaning.

The English missiologist M. A. C. Warren, writing on the Holy
Communion rite of the 1662 Prayer Book, remarked that this hymn of
Wesley's seemed to him to have its model in the well-known preparatory
prayer: 'Almighty God, unto whom all hearts be open, all desires known,
and from whom no secrets are hid; Cleanse the thoughts of our hearts
by the inspiration of thy Holy Spirit, that we may perfectly love thee and
worthily magnify thy holy Name.' Both the hymn and the collect are
about the interior work of the Holy Spirit; they both say that it is only
through God that the Church can worship God. Warren suggests that if
this parallel between Wesley's hymn and Cranmer's collect is granted,
the Church of England's eucharistic liturgy, which contains no *epiclesis*
in the consecration prayer, 'puts the invocation of the Holy Spirit . . . at
the very beginning of the worship, and his power is invoked directly upon
the worshippers themselves'.[12]

The Mysterious Traveller

Hymn 17 (which does not mention the sacrament) engages the imagination. A mysterious Traveller is encountered. The poem asks two
questions and receives two replies: The first stanza asks 'Who is this?'
and the third stanza asks 'Why are your garments red?' These questions
are answered by the Traveller, who is obviously Jesus, who speaks for
himself in stanzas 2 and 4.[13]

  1 Who is This, that comes from far
      Clad in Garments dipt in Blood?
    Strong triumphant Traveller,
      Is he Man, or is he GOD?

2   I that speak in Righteousness,
      Son of GOD and Man I am,
   Mighty to redeem your Race;
      JESUS is your Saviour's Name.

3   Wherefore are thy Garments red,
      Died as in a crimson Sea?
   They that in the Wine-fat tread*
      Are not stain'd so much as Thee.

4   I the Father's fav'rite Son,
      Have the dreadful Wine-press trod,
   Borne the vengeful Wrath alone,
      All the fiercest Wrath of GOD.

Wesley weaves through his hymn the questions to an earlier traveller and the traveller's replies, which he found in Isaiah 63.1–3a:

Q. Who is this that cometh from Edom, with dyed garments from Bozrah? this that is glorious in his apparel, travelling in the greatness of his strength?
A. I that speak in righteousness, mighty to save.
Q. Wherefore art thou red in thine apparel, and thy garments like him that treadeth in the winefat?
A. I have trodden the winepress alone, and of all the people there was none with me.

Wesley, following a long tradition of interpretation, thinks that these words of Isaiah spoke beforehand of Christ, and he appropriates them for his hymn accordingly. (This passage from Isaiah 63 was read in the liturgy of the Church of England for the epistle on Monday of Holy Week.)

When the questioner asks concerning the unknown figure, 'Is he Man, or is he God?' Jesus replies that to redeem he had to be both 'Son of God and [son of] Man'. The Redeemer had to be divine in order to save ('Mighty to redeem your Race'). But at the same time he had to be one with those he undertook to redeem. Answering the question about his stained garments, Jesus says of his solitary sufferings: 'I . . . have the dreadful Wine-press trod,' which is again interpreted to say that Christ in his passion bore the wrath of God.

---

* *the Wine-fat*: the vat where the grapes are pressed.

Remembering

Hymn 20, a particularly effective hymn, is an act of Christian remembering, spoken from within the sacramental occasion. Prayer arises as the
communicants, recalling the Saviour's 'bleeding love', plead for Christ,
the Lamb of God, to extend mercy – to respond to their remembering him
by his remembering them: 'Think on us who think on Thee.'

1   Lamb of GOD, whose Bleeding Love
    We thus recall to mind,
Send the Answer from above,
    And let us Mercy find;
Think on us, who think on Thee
And every struggling Soul release:
O remember *Calvary*,
    And bid us go in Peace.

2   By thine Agonizing Pain,
    And Bloody Sweat, we pray,
By thy Dying Love to Man,
    Take all our Sins away;
Burst our Bonds, and set us free,
From all iniquity release:
O remember *Calvary*,
    And bid us go in Peace.

3   Let thy Blood, by Faith applied
    The Sinner's Pardon seal,
Speak us freely Justified,
    And all our sickness heal:
By thy passion on the Tree
Let all our Griefs and Troubles cease:
O remember *Calvary*,
    And bid us go in peace.

4   Never will we hence depart,
    Till Thou our Wants relieve,
Write Forgiveness on our Heart,
    And all thine Image give:
Still our Souls shall cry to Thee
Till perfected in Holiness:
O remember *Calvary*,
    And bid us go in peace.

The hymn uses a collage of images to describe the human condition and to ask for remedy. Humanity is held in bondage, guilty, sick, full of griefs and troubles. A series of petitions for deliverance arises: send us the answer, let us find mercy, think on us, release every struggling soul, take away our sins, burst our bonds and set us free, release us from all iniquity, seal us by your blood, declare us justified, heal our sickness, and let our troubles cease. The hymn begins by asking for pardon; it ends by yearning for the restored image of God and the perfection of holiness.

Each stanza ends with the haunting refrain, 'O remember *Calvary*, and bid us go in peace.' (Refrains are uncommon in Wesley.) The line 'O remember *Calvary*' asks Christ to remember his own death, as though the eucharist were a memorial for the Saviour as well as for Christians. Wesley may have had in mind biblical passages which ask God to remember former acts and promises. Isaiah 62.6–7, for example, speaks of watchmen who are 'the Lord's remembrancers' (AV margin) who give God no rest until Jerusalem is made a praise in the earth.

This idea had appeared in one of Isaac Watts' hymns for the Lord's Supper, where, having spoken of the Saviour's compassionate act, he says:

> Now tho' he reigns exalted high,
>   His love is still as great:
> Well he remembers Calvary,
>   Nor lets his saints forget. (4:5.1–4)

Watts says that Jesus, who experienced Calvary, now in his heavenly life remembers Calvary, and his recalling is an act of love. When Wesley wrote the refrain of Hymn 20, Watts' line may have been, at least at some level, in his mind.

The form of stanza 2, with its repeated expression 'By thy . . .' suggests the obsecrations of the Prayer Book Litany, echoing specifically Cranmer's lines, 'By thine Agony and Bloody Sweat; by thy Cross and Passion . . . Good Lord, deliver us.' The same form appears in 15:2.1–4, where Wesley says, 'By thy meritorious dying/ Save us from this death of sin,/ By thy pretious blood's applying/ Make our inmost nature clean.' In such prayer, the Church asks something for itself, basing its request on a specific event in the Saviour's work. In virtually all Church of England congregations in Wesley's time the Litany would have been said every Sunday; its phrases and rhythms would have been in Wesley's ears and in the ears of many communicants.

Hymn 20 is one of Wesley's more technically accomplished hymns. The meter is 7.6.7.6.7.8.7.6. The seven-syllable lines are trochaic, while the lines with an even number of syllables are iambic. The fifth and sixth lines of every stanza rhyme with the words 'Calvary' and 'peace' which conclude lines 7 and 8 of the refrain.[14]

This hymn is associated with an incident in early Methodist history. In 1748 John Lancaster, a petty thief who was converted but then lapsed and returned to his former way of life, was arrested and sentenced to execution. He and nine others were visited in prison daily by the devout Methodist Sarah Peter, who led them back to faith. It proved impossible to secure a pardon for them, and as Lancaster and the others were led to Tyburn they sang: 'Lamb of God, whose bleeding love/ We still recall to mind,/ Send the answer from above,/ And let us mercy find.'[15]

The 'Evangelical Paradox'

Wesley develops throughout these hymns a theme that might be termed the 'evangelical paradox'. The theme occurs with special frequency in Part I, in which Wesley is speaking of the saving cross.

The paradox may be described as *a divine reversal*: Out of Jesus' dying comes life for believers; from his diminishment others are exalted. Wesley makes the point in many ways: 'Whose dying Love hath left behind/ Eternal Life for all Mankind' (1:5.5–6). 'He suffers to reverse our doom' (2:5.4). 'Still we by his Death are blest' (4:2.3). 'The cross on which He bows His head/ Shall lift us to the skies' (4:4.7–8). 'The Death by which we live' (7:1.4, and 27:1.8). 'True Love . . . whose dying breath gave life to us' (9:3.4f.). 'Let us by thy dying live' (14:1.8). 'By thy meritorious dying, save us from the death of sin' (15:2.1–2). 'Dying that our souls might live' (18:2.5). 'Matter of eternal praise/ We in thy passion find' (21:1.3–4). 'Falls to raise us from our fall' (21:5.3). 'Revive us by thy dying cries' (25:3.4). 'Reviving as their Saviour dies' (26:2.6; that is to say, others come to life just as the One who brings about their revival dies himself). 'Made a curse our souls to bless' (27:2.3). In Part II, hymns 78 and 87 are organised very largely as statements of the paradox: 'Make thy grief our relief,/ Ease us by thine anguish', or 'By thy bonds release us' (78:1.2–3; 3.3).

Jesus' death, Wesley says, is a death that saves from death. 'Grant us . . . by thy death to live' (27:1.8). In the ordinary course of things, death is final, unproductive, a negation; it leads to nothing beyond itself. But in the redemptive work of Christ the ordinary course of things is overturned. This death of one leads to life for many. It is cause, not for lament, but for grateful praise.

No doubt the material of this paradox can be found in the fundamental prophetic message that God's favour is set on insignificant people, and in the Pauline gospel of life out of death and strength made perfect in weakness, and in the tradition of Christian preaching and devotion. The gospel holds together apparent opposites and plays with unexpectedness. (Many Christian thinkers have found paradox congenial. It is a preacher's theme.) Brevint had said, 'O blessed Jesus! this my life comes out of thy death, and the salvation which I hope for, is purchased with all the pain and agonies which thou didst suffer' (III.11). Isaac Watts expressed the reconciled oppositions of the gospel when he said in his sacramental hymns that Christ 'sunk beneath our heavy woes/ To raise us to his throne' (4:3.3–4), and in a later hymn he said:

> Thy cruel thorns, thy shameful cross
>   Procure us heavenly crowns;
> Our highest gain springs from thy loss,
>   Our healing from thy wounds. (23:3)

Donald Davie has said that 'paradoxes are at the heart of Wesley's writing, as of any writing in the centrally Christian tradition; and time and again the laborious clarity of Wesley's verse takes on rhetorical splendour and intensity when paradox is concentrated into its appropriate rhetorical figure, oxymoron.'[16]

Convinced Christians of the eighteenth century, such as Watts and Wesley, used shock rhetoric to challenge the orderly, common-sense world of their time. The paradox of life out of death and glory through sacrifice is just the sort of overturning of the expectations of nature and reason whose statement would have helped the Evangelical movement define itself and its message against the rationalism and moralism that were setting the cultural tone. Wesley never seeks to explain how the death of one is life for many. He simply states it, always in speech full of biblical resonance. His call was as a proclaimer, rather than an explainer.

The Holy Communion, as interpreted in the hymns of Part I, has brought seeking, deeply self-aware Christians to the crucified Saviour.

* * *

ESSAYS

The 'Crucified God' Theme

A reader of *Hymns on the Lord's Supper* frequently encounters Wesley's affirmation that human redemption came through the suffering and death of God – surely one of the most striking features of his thought. Wesley expresses the paradoxical idea that since the one who was crucified was divine, Jesus' passion somehow belongs, if one may put it so, to the 'experience' of God.

What may have suggested this unusual theme to Wesley? There are several possibilities. A strain of late medieval piety, which was expressed in written texts and in devotional art, saw the cross as sign of the grief and compassion of God.[17] The Wesleys in their period of interest in mystical writers may have encountered such works. Another possible source is the early liturgical text *The Apostolic Constitutions*, which the Wesleys knew and which influenced Charles at several points in his sacramental hymns. In this ancient rite, the *anamnesis* of the eucharistic prayer develops a series of paradoxes: 'The Saviour of Mankind [was] condemned; although impassible, he was nailed to the Cross; and, although Immortal, died: The Giver of Life was laid in the Grave' (*Apostolic Constitutions*, VIII.12.33).[18] The Non-juror Thomas Deacon was known to the Wesleys, and his *Devotions*, 1734, contains a passage that follows these words closely. A close-at-hand source may have been Brevint, who had said, as hardly more than a hint, that the worthy communicant 'shall fall amazed at that stroke of Divine Justice, that, being offended but by *men*, could not be satisfied nor appeased but by the sufferings and death of God' (II.10).

However, the writer who before Wesley most memorably developed the theme was Isaac Watts. In his communion hymn, 'When I survey the wondrous Cross,' he describes the cross as 'the death of Christ my God' (7:2.2). In one of Watts' best sacramental hymns he says, 'O the sweet wonders of that cross/ Where God the Saviour lov'd and dy'd' (10:5.1–2). He describes Jesus as 'the God that fought and bled/ And conquered when he fell' (21:2.2). He exclaims, 'Blest fountain! springing from the veins/ Of Jesus our incarnate God' (22:5.3–4). Before Wesley made the theme his own, Isaac Watts had articulated it in 1707.

Wesley developed the motif, making it a running theme of *Hymns on the Lord's Supper*. The theme appears frequently in Part I:

O Thou eternal Victim slain (5:1.1)
My God, who dies for me, for me! (5:3.6)
To weep o'er an expiring God (6:1.5)

... the Pangs Divine (7:2.1 and 22:2.3)
Jesu, suffering Deity (12:1.1)
Faith discerns the dying God (18:2.4)
We see our Maker ... crucified before our eyes (21:2.3–4)
Publish we the Death Divine (21:2.6)
My God, that suffers there! (21:3.8)
The great *Jehovah* dies! (21:4.8)
Dies the glorious Cause of All (21:5.1)
... while his [the sun's] Creator dies (21:5.8)
The God of angels dies (21:6.8)
O my God, He dies for me (21:7.1)
Sinful Soul, what hast Thou done?
Murther'd God's eternal Son! (23:1.5–6)
Still to death pursue our God? (23:3.2)
The death of God, the death of sin (24:2.4)

There are several occurrences in Part II:

[God] ... died a victim for mankind (36:2.4)
God doth for his creature die (45:1.6)
The man that suffer'd in my place,
   The God that groan'd and dyed (55:2.3–4)
Here I view the God that died (59:3.3)
In memory of your dying God (73:5.1)
Made our God a man of grief (83:1.6)

The theme returns in Part III:

Followers of the dying God (106:1.8)

See there the quickning cause of all
   Who live the life of grace beneath!
God caus'd on Him the sleep to fall,
   And lo, his eyes are clos'd in death. (114:1.1–4)

Glory to God who reigns above,
But suffer'd once for man below. (115:2.1–2)

Part IV opens with the paradox, 'Victim Divine' (116:1.1). And the theme appears several times in Part V when Wesley is again dealing with sacrifice:

Sharers with the dying God,
And crucified below. (131:3.7–8)

By faith ev'n now we see
The suffering deity. (132:2.1–2)

Our sins which murder'd God shall die! (133:3.6)

The sinless body of our God
Was fasten'd to the tree. (135:1.2–3)

Shall we let our God groan
And suffer alone? (142:2.1–2)

    All Glory and Praise
    To the Antient of Days,
Who was born and was slain to redeem a lost Race.

    Salvation to God,
    Who carried our Load,
And purchas'd our lives with the price of his blood. (156:1–2)

These more than thirty instances will indicate the prominence of the motif of the suffering and dying God in *Hymns on the Lord's Supper*. (A few less clear instances might be added.) The theme was established in Wesley's mind as early as his 1738 hymn, 'And can it be, that I should gain/ An interest in the Saviour's blood?' which contains the lines, 'Amazing love! How can it be/ That thou, my God, shouldst die for me?/ 'Tis myst'ry all: th' Immortal dies!' (the 1780 *Collection*, 193:5–7).

Although Wesley in his hymns on the Supper states the theme often, he does little to develop it. Yet it carries revolutionary implications. The common theological/metaphysical tradition had held that God, being beyond time and change, is beyond suffering. The God of the Bible is 'the living God', who is not subject to pain or death. God is eternally God; no emotions can be attributed to the divine, for emotion would mean that God could be acted upon. The expressions of divine emotion in the Jewish scriptures were taken to be instances of naive, harmless anthropomorphism. The first of the Thirty-Nine Articles of the Church of England (to which Wesley had subscribed) expresses this traditional doctrine, saying that the one living and true God is 'without body, parts, or passions'.

Yet the Bible and the tradition that stems from it are mixed. Alongside the sense of divine unchangeableness, affirmations in the prophetic scriptures, in Christian art, and in spirituality, entertained the idea of an afflicted God. Even Richard Hooker (not one inclined to trifle with the character and attributes of God) once said, 'It is our comfort, and our wisdom; we care for no knowledge in the world but this, that man hath sinned, and God hath suffered' (*Of Justification*, sec. 6).

Clearly, from whatever influences, the Wesleys had come to qualify in their own minds the tradition of divine 'impassibility'. When John edited the Thirty-Nine Articles for use in Methodist congregations in the American colonies, he omitted the words 'or passions' from Article I.

When Charles Wesley says that in Christ God suffers and dies (as when he affirms 'the evangelical paradox') he almost throws defiance at the Age of Reason. The God of Wesley's gospel is not the disengaged God of deism, not a First Cause, nor an Unmoved Mover. Rather, when Wesley speaks of the 'suffering Deity' he is saying that human redemption had a cost for God. He takes with utter seriousness the incarnation. The hymns which speak of a dying God should be held alongside the hymns of the nativity in which Wesley speaks of God being born – as 'Being's source begins to be,/ And God himself is born!' (*Hymns for the Nativity*, 1745, 4:2.7–8).

Wesley's point, which was also Brevint's and Watts' point, was largely disregarded in their time and, indeed, it was for the most part ignored by academic theologians in the century that followed. However, the long tradition of a God beyond suffering has come to seem to many late nineteenth- and twentieth-century theologians to owe more to speculative philosophy than to the high personalisation of the Bible. The God of Abraham, Isaac and Jacob is a God who is open to the pain of the creation, who listens, cares and responds. 'In all their affliction, he was afflicted' (Isaiah 63.9). Many able present-day Christian thinkers, speaking in different idioms and bringing different experience, have envisioned a God who suffers, and suffers passionately, in and with the suffering creation.[19]

Indeed, it may have become possible, at least in some places, to speak so easily of the suffering of God that the scandal is removed. Wesley, for his part, does not solve the issue by a philosophical thesis of a limited and finite God. The force of the paradox lies in his juxtaposing two unqualified affirmations. In a hymn in the 1749 collection he wrote the striking line: 'Impassive, He suffers; immortal, He dies.'[20] (Clearly the line is based on the *Apostolic Constitutions* – perhaps mediated by Deacon's *Devotions*.) It was the glory of Wesley's gospel that what could not be was. The one who was incapable of suffering suffered; the one who could not die died.

*   *   *

The Atonement and the Sacrament

In Wesley's mind, sacramental theology is closely bound into atonement theology.[21] The eucharist holds before God, before believers and before the world the redemptive death of Christ. The rite means what the cross means.

The Wesleyan eucharistic hymns, being hymns, do not (or at least they usually do not) argue or theorise; rather, they affirm, picture or present. Even though they set forth no developed account of the atonement, in speaking of the eucharist, they must speak of that of which the eucharist speaks. As they do so, they put forward a coherent body of affirmations concerning Christ's redemptive work. Wesley adopts the elemental images of redemption that appear in the New Testament where they express the Church's immediate grasp of an act that had come from God's initiative and had transformed human existence, giving 'pardon, grace and glory, peace and power and heaven' (15:2.7f.). The primal images present an act in which persons enslaved are ransomed; parties estranged are reconciled; an insurmountable debt has been paid; persons inwardly soiled are cleansed; those who are diseased in spirit are made whole; guilty parties are declared righteous; persons living in darkness are brought into the light; death yields to life. These images are not sharply distinct; rather, since all are images and all refer to a single divine saving act, they tend to mingle and pass into one another. In *Hymns on the Lord's Supper* Wesley uses these biblical images repeatedly, often moving rapidly from one of them to another. To a great extent, these images do not so much speak descriptively about the atonement as they speak from the inside, confessing what Christ's work means for a believer.

In referring to the atonement, the hymns of Part I have several emphases, most of which return in later hymns:

1. *Christ in his passion stood and stands with and for believers:* 'He bears my sins on yonder tree, and pays my debt in blood' (2:3.5). 'He bears the universal load/ Of guilt and misery' (2:5.2–3). 'My God, who dies for me!' (5:3.6). 'Now believe he died for you' (8:2.6). 'We . . . long to feel applied/ The blood for our redemption given' (11:3.4–5). 'Thee, whose blood for us did flow,/ Thee who diedst to save Thy foe' (12:1.4). 'The purchase of his blood' (13:2.6). 'Expiring in the sinner's place' (24:1.1; cf. 27:1.2).

2. *Christ is source of forgiveness and freedom:* Christ says, 'My body, given to purchase life and peace to you, pardon and holiness and heaven' (1:2.2f.). 'My blood that speaks your sins forgiven' (1:4.5). The communicants say, 'His life to ransom ours is given' (2:4.4).

3. *The atonement is for all:* Wesley challenges, usually somewhat in passing, the Calvinist doctrine that the effect of the atonement is limited to the elect, insisting that Christ's death was for all: 'My blood shed . . . for all the sinful race' (1:4.4 and see 5.5–6). Hymn 9, which is John Wesley's adaptation of George Herbert's 'The Invitation', opens six stanzas with 'Come hither all', and the final stanza plays on the word 'all'. 'Thy well-belov'd hath died/ For all Mankind t'atone' (10:2.5–6 and see 3.1). Redemption is 'open'd that all may enter in' (24:2.2). The Rock of Israel was cleft 'For us, for all mankind' (27:1.1–2).

4. *Christ and his cross exhibit divine love:* Jesus says concerning the Holy Communion, 'Do this my dying love to show' (1:2.4). God is asked to love 'the dearly ransom'd race in the Redeemer's love' (10:3). Regarding the cross, a communicant exclaims, 'Was never love like thine!' (21:2.8). The sacrament calls to mind the 'bleeding love' of the saviour. 'By thy dying love to man, take all our sins away' (20:2, and Hymn 20, *passim*). The eucharist communicates the 'pardoning love' of God (Hymn 14, *passim*). The saving work traces to 'Love, meer causeless love' (36:2.2).

5. *The atoning work is continued in Christ's present life of intercession:* 'Jesu's death is ever new,/ He whom in ages past they slew/ Doth still as slain appear' (3:2f.); 'Father, hear the blood of Jesus/ Speaking in thine ears above' (14:1.1–2). It asks, 'Forgive them'.

O Thou eternal Victim, slain
A Sacrifice for guilty Man,
By the Eternal Spirit made
An Offering in the Sinner's stead,
Our everlasting Priest art Thou,
And plead'st thy Death for Sinners now.

Thy Offering still continues New,
Thy Vesture keeps its Bloody Hue,
Thou stand'st the ever-slaughter'd Lamb,
Thy Priesthood still remains the same. (5:1.1–2.4)

Wesley's *theologia crucis* is balanced with a *theologia gloriae* as Christ's work culminates at the right hand of God (Hebrews 10.11–14; 12.2). Indeed, the work continues as Christ lives, deeply and forever bonded both with God and with humanity. The Eternal Word who became one with humankind – bone of its bone and flesh of its flesh – never reversed the act, but in glory he remains one with the race, bearing the wounds he received in his earthly life and carrying before the Father the names of forgiven sinners.

6.   *The atonement is completed as Christ's people die and live in him:*
The cross is an act of God which intended a human response. While
Christians are beneficiaries of Christ's saving work, which they can only
receive in gratitude, in some sense they are also participants in it: Let
us 'in thy great offering join' (3:4.3). Like Mary, Christians, identifying
with the crucified Jesus, are 'Partners in the pangs divine' (22:2.4; cf.
26:3). 'We share . . . his sacrifice' (4:2.4); 'we too with him are dead, and
shall with him arise' (4:4.5–6); 'fain we would partake thy pain,/ Share
thy mortal agony' (22:1.3f.).

7.   *The work of redemption culminates in a believer's life of purity.* In
Wesley's mind, 'pardon and holiness' are linked (1:2.3). At the sacrament
we are 'Resolved to lead our lives anew,/ Thine only glory to pursue,/
And only thee obey' (10:1.4–6). Christ is asked, through the application
of his blood, to 'make our inmost nature clean' (15:2.4). We shall cry out
to Christ 'till [we are] perfected in holiness' (20:4.5).

> Shall we let him die in vain?
>   Still to death pursue our GOD?
> Open tear his wounds again,
>   Trample on his precious blood?
> No; with all our sins we part,
>   Saviour, take my broken heart! (23:3)

8.   *Christ dies as the object of divine wrath or judgement:* Wesley
holds that the crucified Christ, because he was the representative of sinners and the bearer of human sin, was made the object of God's wrath.
When Wesley says to the Father, 'Jesus thy wrath hath pacified' (10:2.4)
he is only repeating what would have been an accepted part of much
atonement theology of the time.

Wesley follows the 'satisfaction' theory of the atonement which had
been put forward in the eleventh century by Anselm of Canterbury
and had dominated subsequent Western discussion of the subject. By
Wesley's time, Anselm's idea had been to a great extent combined with
the doctrine of penal substitution – the sinless Jesus received the penalty
that should have fallen to sinful humanity; his death was payment owed
by humanity to offended divine righteousness. Many Christian thinkers were convinced that this doctrine was that of the Bible. Wesley says
that 'Christ's blood procured our life and peace,/ And quenched the
wrath of hostile heaven;/ Justice gave way to our release' (36:12.1–3).
He later addresses Christ, saying, 'Thou only hast for sinners died./ By

one oblation satisfied/ Th' inexorably righteous God' (128:1.4–6). In another hymn Wesley has Jesus say, 'I, the Father's fav'rite Son,/ Have the dreadful wine-press trod,/ Borne the vengeful wrath alone,/ All the fiercest wrath of God' (17:4).

Brevint, who holds the same doctrine (but mentions it less), thinks that the making of wheat into bread symbolises Christ's suffering at the hands of God. The fire in which the wheat is 'dried up, and baked and burnt' represents 'the fiery wrath which he [Jesus] suffered from above, and from the hand of his own Father'. Then Brevint breaks into an address to God, adapting Jesus' cry of dereliction into a believer's question, 'My God, my God, why hast thou forsaken Him?' (II.11). Wesley (particularly in Hymn 2) adopts Brevint's image: 'The Bread dried up and burnt with fire/ Presents the Father's vengeful ire.' Following Brevint, he turns Jesus' anguished cry to the Father into the writer's question to God, 'Why hast thou, Lord, forsook thine own?/ Alas, what evil hath he done?' A few lines later he says, 'Lo! the fiercest fire of heaven/ consumes the sacrifice' and, 'He suffers both from man and God' (2:2.1–2; 3.1–2; 4.5–5.1).

This harsh streak in Wesley's theology of the cross appears often in the sacramental hymns, especially in Part I. He speaks of divine love for sinners, expressed in Jesus' cross, and he speaks of divine wrath against sin, also expressed in Jesus' cross. And he sets the two emphases alongside one another, not reconciling them, but letting them stand together evidencing the tensiveness of Christian doctrine.

Part II

As it is a Sign and a Means of Grace

HYMNS 28–92

In the hymns of Part II, which is the longest unit in *Hymns on the Lord's Supper*, Wesley describes the sacrament as a present act of God – 'the sacred, true, effectual sign', 'the glorious instrument divine' (28:2.1, 3). He combines the emphasis of Brevint's Section III, 'Of the blessed Sacrament, as it stands for a *sign* of present Graces', with his Section IV, 'Concerning the Communion, as it is not a Representation only, but a *Means* of Grace'. Wesley will say in these hymns that the sacrament does, indeed, represent, but at the same time it conveys what it represents. It is 'figure and means of saving grace' (28:1.4).

The earlier hymns of Wesley's Part II (28–53) largely speak of the sacrament as sign, and they follow Brevint's Section III, while the later hymns (from 54 to 68) emphasise the instrumental aspect of the sacrament, and they follow Brevint's Section IV. The two themes cannot, however, be sharply distinguished. Rattenbury conjectured that Wesley intended to write two groups of hymns, but 'when he read those that he had written, he discovered that his symbolical hymns were really instrumental', and in preparing his hymns for publication, he did not seek to keep the subjects distinct.[1]

In the last portion of Part II (Hymns 69–92) Wesley drops his consecutive following of Brevint and pursues independent lines – drawing on Brevint randomly, when he draws on him at all. This is the largest section in this collection which shows so little dependence on Brevint.

Sign and Means

As Wesley has set forth in Part I, the Holy Communion is a 'picture of thy [Jesus'] passion' (87:1.1). But it is more. It not only recalls a past redemptive act, but is itself a present act of grace. Brevint too had spoken of the holy eucharist as 'a mystery, wherein, one way or other, true Christians shall find, not a commemoration or representation only, but a communion also with the blood so represented and remembered' (IV.4). Wesley could not think of the Lord's Supper as only a memorial, a drama in the mind, a 'vivid preaching' of a past event. Rather, in the sacrament believers encounter the living Christ. Brevint had said that the blessed Communion yields present graces, for it is 'first, a *figure*, whereby God represents; secondly, a moral *instrument*, whereby he is pleased to convey them unto the Church' (III.1).

Wesley sees the sacrament as a sign which shows Christ's body and blood, but it is an effective sign – a sign that enacts what it signifies, a bestowal of God's mercy and strength. The blood imparts pardon, the bread gives sustenance.

> The sacred true effectual Sign
>   Thy Body and thy Blood it shews,
> The glorious Instrument Divine
>   Thy Mercy and thy Strength bestows.
>
> We see the Blood that seals our Peace,
>   Thy Pard'ning Mercy we receive:
> The Bread doth visibly express
>   The Strength thro' which our Spirits live. (28:2–3)
>
> Is not the Hallow'd broken Bread
>   A sure Communicating Sign,
> An Instrument Ordain'd to feed
>   Our Souls with Mystic Flesh Divine? (73:2)*
>
> JESU, my LORD and GOD, bestow
> All which thy sacrament doth show,
>   And make the real sign
> A sure effectual means of grace. (66:1.1–4)

Wesley invites Christians to the meal of faith, which is both sign and means:

> 1   Draw near ye blood-besprinkled Race,
>   And take what GOD vouchsafes to give,

---

* *mystic(k):* The term is not biblical, and it has no specific theological meaning; it refers to something that points to or seems to carry divine reality. Samuel Johnson's first meaning is 'sacredly obscure'.

The Outward Sign of Inward Grace,
  Ordain'd by CHRIST Himself, receive:
The Sign transmits the Signified,
The Grace is by the Means applied.

Communicants are asked to 'draw near', to 'receive', to 'feel', to 'eat',
'drink', and 'feast' – to take what God is pleased to give, indeed, to feed
on God. These terms all emphasise the reception of the communion, as
did Jesus' words at the Last Supper, 'take and eat . . . drink this'. By divine
promise, there is in the sacrament something to be taken: 'sure pledges of
his dying love'. The communicant must, however, be receptive.

Lines 1.3–4 utilise the description of a sacrament which had since
1604 been in the Prayer Book Catechism: 'An outward and visible sign
of an inward and invisible grace given unto us; ordained by Christ himself, as a means whereby we receive the same, and a pledge to assure us
thereof.'[2] Grace is not only signified; it is actualised: 'The sign transmits
the signified,/ The grace is by the means applied.'

  2 Sure Pledges of his Dying Love
       Receive the Sacramental Meat,
     And feel the Virtue from above,
       The Mystic Flesh of JESUS eat,
     Drink with the Wine his healing Blood,
     And feast on th' Incarnate GOD.

Lest the high claim that by the Supper we 'feast on th' Incarnate God'
sound like magic, Wesley cautions in stanza 3, 'Gross misconceit [grave
misunderstanding] be far away!' Then he clarifies. While the sacrament
is an act of divine self-imparting, it is through 'faith only' that it conveys
the Spirit and fills communicants with the very life of God.

  3 Gross Misconceit be far away!
       Thro' Faith we on his Body feed,
     Faith only doth the Spi'rit convey,
       And fills our Souls with living Bread,
     Th' Effects of JESU's Death imparts,
     And pours his Blood into our Hearts. (71)

Wesley is convinced that, while there are many means of grace, the Holy
Communion is Christ's 'choicest instrument' for imparting his blessings
(42:1.3). He does not argue the supremacy of the eucharist. (One does

not argue in hymns, unless one is willing to risk writing poor hymns.)
He simply says that, while other means, such as fasting and prayer,
'can much avail', none can give Christ's mercy and might as does 'this
mysterious rite'.

> But none like this Mysterious Rite*
>   Which dying Mercy gave
> Can draw forth all his promis'd Might
>   And all his Will to save.
>
> This is the richest Legacy
>   Thou hast on Man bestow'd,
> Here chiefly, LORD, we feed on Thee,
>   And drink thy precious Blood. (42:3–4)

Presence

Repeatedly and in varied ways Wesley affirms that Christ is truly present,
met and received in the sacrament:

> In thine own Appointments bless us,
>   Meet us here, Now appear,
>   Our Almighty JESUS. (78:9)

The Saviour is self-revealed; the tokens of his dying love are received, and
the quickening Spirit moves (30:3–4). 'Thy flesh becomes our food,/ Thy
life is to our souls conveyed/ In sacramental blood' (65:3.2–4). Speaking
positively, then negatively, Wesley says:

> Great is thy Faithfulness and Love,
> Thine Ordinance can never prove
>   Of none Effect and vain,
> Only do Thou my heart prepare,
> To find thy Real Presence there,
>   And all thy Fullness gain. (66:2.1–6)

Theologians of a scholastic mind had developed the doctrine of sacramental presence in metaphysical terms. Wesley, however, gives the theme

---

* *Mysterious Rite:* an act which holds an unfathomable depth.

of presence new vitality, as in Part I he had the theme of memorial. Speaking in interpersonal terms, Wesley says that at the Table, Christ imparts himself, engaging each believer.

> JESU, dear redeeming Lord,
> Magnify thy dying Word,
> In thine Ordinance appear,
> Come, and meet thy Followers here.

> In the Rite Thou hast enjoyn'd
> Let us now our Saviour find,
> Drink thy Blood for Sinners shed,
> Taste Thee in the broken Bread. (33:1–2)

Christ is asked to show himself in the sacrament, 'Now, Saviour, now thyself reveal,/ And make thy nature known' (30:3.1–2). 'We come with confidence to find/ Thy special presence here' (81:1.7–8). 'This the Place of meeting be' (77:2.3). The Lord's Supper is, for the faithful receiver, virtually a Christophany:

> Our Hearts we open wide
> To make the Saviour room:
> And lo! the Lamb, the Crucified,
> The Sinner's Friend is come! (81:2.1–4)

Brevint, stating the matter in his own way, had said that as the Lord, who is present everywhere, was present in a particular way in the ancient tabernacle, so Christ is present in the sacrament 'to meet and to bless his people' (I.1). His blessings are dispersed, sometimes more, sometimes less richly; and persons are not always equally receptive. However, 'In those places and ordinances which He hath in an especial manner set out to record his passion, and to renew the sacrifice of his body, He will certainly come with such fullness of blessing as attend this sacred body, which is the proper seat of blessings' (IV.12).

Wesley similarly identifies the sacrament as a particular *locus* of personal divine presence. He sees communicants as the two disciples who were met by the risen Jesus on the road to Emmaus (Luke 24.13–35):

> 1   O Thou who this Mysterious Bread
>   Didst in *Emmaus* break,
>   Return herewith our Souls to feed
>   And to thy Followers speak.

2 Unseal the Volume of thy Grace,
     Apply the Gospel-word,
   Open our Eyes to see thy Face,
     Our hearts to know the LORD.

3 Of Thee we commune still, and mourn
     Till Thou the Veil remove,
   Talk with us, and our hearts shall burn
     With Flames of fervent Love. (29)

Jesus who once met his disciples and spoke and ate with them, is asked to speak the 'gospel-word' again, to break the bread, to open his followers' eyes and their hearts to see and know him, to talk with them until their hearts burn within them. The eucharistic parallel was suggested by Brevint's prayer in which he asks Christ, 'Let not my heart burn with less zeal to follow thee and serve thee now, when this bread is broken at this table, than did the hearts of thy disciples, when thou didst break it at Emmaus' (II.11). Indeed, when Wesley and Brevint speak of the bread that is broken at this table as 'this mysterious bread', they seem to identify it with the bread of the table at Emmaus.

   In describing the sacramental encounter with Christ, experience is part of Wesley's evidence. He asks devout but often struggling Christians, 'Is the memorial of your Lord/ An useless form, an empty sign? Or doth He here His life impart?' adding, 'What saith the witness of your heart?' (89:1.3–5). The *doctrine* of the sacrament is validated (or else it is not validated) in the *experience* of the sacrament. The communicant may put demands to the Church and its rite:

1 'Tis not a dead external Sign
     Which here my Hopes require,
   The living Power of Love Divine
     In JESUS I desire.

2 I want the dear Redeemer's Grace,
     I seek the Crucified,
   The Man that suffer'd in my Place,
     The GOD that groan'd and dyed.

3 Swift, as their rising LORD to find
     The two Disciples ran,
   I seek the Saviour of Mankind,
     Nor shall I seek in vain. (55)

The comparison of the seeking communicant with the two disciples running to Jesus' tomb (John 20:3–10) was suggested by Brevint's effective sentence: 'I want and seek my Saviour Himself, and I watch for all the opportunities of coming to his Sacrament, for the same purpose that once made St. Peter and St. John run so fast to his sepulchre, – because I hope to find him there' (IV.4).

The communicants come eagerly, seeking meeting and blessing: 'Expect we then the quickening word,/ Who at his altar bow' (60:6.1–2). Although in a sense the initiative is with Christ, more than 25 times in the hymns of Part II the communicants ask God or Christ or the Spirit to 'come': 'Come, and meet thy followers here' (33:1.4). 'Come quickly from above' (75:4.2). 'Meet us all at thy own feast' (76:4.2). 'This the place of meeting be' (77:2.3). 'Meet us here, now appear' (78:9.2).[3]

When Wesley implores Christ to 'come', he uses the deeply engaged language of the Bible, addressing a God who is present, but incognito, in ordinary life, and who meets persons in their here-and-now particularity at moments of epiphany. God is all-pervading, but is personal and personally known. God *is* where God is encountered.

> In thine Ordinance appear,
> Come, and meet thy Followers here. (33:1.3–4)

> O GOD, thy Word we claim,
>   Thou here record'st thy Name,
> Visit us in Pard'ning Grace,
>   CHRIST the Crucified appear,
> Come in thy Appointed Ways,
>   Come, and meet, and bless us here. (63:1–6)

The presence of Christ, because it is personal, is not static. Wesley describes the sacrament in exodus images, reading Christ and the Christian into the story of God and Israel. The people cry to God to come down and free them from Egypt (meaning their sins); God delivers the 'Israelites' (the Christians), protecting them by the blood of the Paschal sacrifice (40:1–2). Now as in the deep past, God feeds the people in the wilderness. 'By Jesus out of Egypt led/ Still on the Pascal Lamb we feed,/ And keep the Sacramental Feast' (44:1.4–6). The pilgrims' wants are supplied 'by constant miracle' (44:2.6).

Hymn 51 is influenced by Brevint's prayer, 'Father of everlasting compassions, forsake not in the wilderness a feeble Israelite whom thou hast brought a little way out of Egypt' (III.13).

1   Thou very Pascal Lamb,
    Whose Blood for us was shed,
Thro' whom we out of *Egypt* came;
    Thy ransom'd People lead.

2   Angel of Gospel-Grace,
    Fulfil thy Character,
To guard and feed the Chosen Race,
    In *Israel's* Camp appear.

3   Throughout the Desart-way
    Conduct us by thy Light,
Be Thou a cooling Cloud by Day,
    A chearing Fire by Night.

4   Our Fainting Souls sustain
    With blessings from above,
And ever on thy People rain
    The Manna of thy Love. (51)

Wesley's imagery here does not speak of beginnings or endings, but of a people on the way (supported by having a somewhat domestic-sounding fire in the grate). The mention of manna (4.4) is the hymn's only reference to the sacrament, and it is indirect.

The efficacy of the sacrament is rooted not in a believer's faith or perception, but in the promise of Christ. Wesley describes the sacrament as a 'sure pledge of his dying love' which imparts the effects of Jesus' death (71:2.1; 3.5). It is 'a sure communicating sign' (73:2.2). Sinners may 'believe, and find him here' (73:4.3). 'We come', he says, 'with confidence to find/ Thy special presence here' (81:1.7–8).

Out of the meeting of Christ and Christian in the sacrament there issues a life of blessedness, of *shalom*:

Surely if Thou the Symbols bless,
The Cov'nant Blood shall seal my Peace,
Thy Flesh e'en Now shall be my Food,
And all my Soul be fill'd with GOD. (58:7)

Even though life in and with God is deeply satisfying, one cannot encounter the holy love of Christ without interior renovation – a renewal of which God is the enabler: 'Searcher of hearts, in ours appear' (76:1.1).

'O Eternal Priest, come in,/ And cleanse thy mean abode' (67:2.2–3). The communicants ask, 'melt us', and 'work in us faith, or faith's increase' (76:3.2–3).

Forgiveness

Wesley says repeatedly in Part II that the sacrament yields the forgiveness of sins. At the Holy Communion something happens. The rite is not a 'useless form, an empty sign', but an imparting of divine life (89:1.4–5). It is a fresh bestowal of that which was won at the cross.

> Th' Effects of his Atoning Blood,
>   His Body offer'd on the Tree
> Are with the awful Types bestow'd. (73:3.1–3)*

The sacrament of the table, received in faith, is an ever-renewed absolution. 'Thy pard'ning mercy we receive' (28:3.2). 'Thou [in the sacrament] thy pardoning grace declare' (33:3.2). 'Jesu, our Pardon we receive,/ The Purchase of that Blood of thine' (36:4.1–2). 'Pardon into my soul convey' (47:1.4). 'Communion closer far I feel,/ And deeper drink th' atoning blood' (54:5.1–2). 'Pardon and power and perfect peace/ We shall herewith receive' (56:4.2–3). 'Now pronounce my sins forgiven' (68:3.3). The sacrament gives anew what the cross gave.

> Yes, thy Sacrament extends
>   All the Blessings of thy Death
> To the Soul that here attends. (64:2.1–3)

> Is not the Cup of Blessing, blest
>   By Us, the Sacred Means t'impart
> Our Saviour's Blood, with Power imprest
>   And Pardon to the Faithful Heart? (73:1)

Wesley uses healing stories from the gospels to express the transforming power of Christ in the sacrament. He tells in Hymn 39 of the woman who came to Jesus seeking healing (Mark 5.25–34), thinking that if she could only touch his garments she would be cured. The evangelist says that when she touched his robe and was healed, Jesus perceived that 'virtue

---

* *the awful Types: awful*, inspiring awe or reverence; the interpreting, images or *types* of Christ, largely biblical in origin, carry impressive power.

had gone out of him'. Wesley refers to the Supper as Christ's 'sacramental clothes', saying:

> Sinner with Awe draw near,
>   And find thy Saviour here,
> In his Ordinances still,*
>   Touch his Sacramental Cloathes,
> Present in his Power to heal,
>   Virtue from his Body flows. (39:1)

Later, in Hymn 69, Wesley similarly spiritualises the story of the blind beggar who sat by the roadside and, hearing that Jesus was passing by, called out to him. Jesus summoned him and healed his blindness (Mark 10.46–52). The speaker of the hymn says, '[I am] sinful, and blind, and poor . . . Begging I sit by the wayside.' The blind man's cry, 'Jesus, Son of David, have mercy on me!' becomes a sinner's appeal for the removal of 'the darkness of my heart'.

> JESU, attend my Cry,
>   Thou Son of David hear,
> If now Thou passest by,
>   Stand still and call me near,
> The Darkness from my Heart remove,
> And shew me now thy pard'ning Love. (69:2)

In Brevint's prayer at the end of his Section III, he had cried to Christ for salvation in the sacrament in words taken from this gospel incident, 'O Son of David! save and preserve' (III.13). Perhaps Brevint's brief allusion suggested the hymn to Wesley.

Reality and Theory

Wesley makes clear that the reality of the sacrament does not depend on one's ability to explain the manner of the presence.

---

* *his Ordinances*: from Latin *ordo*, regular series; *ordine*, duly, regularly; a term used widely to refer to the sacraments, speaking of them as actions done in obedience. 'Ordinance' was a preferred term among Christian groups that were suspicious of 'sacrament', but it was widely acceptable and it is used freely by Brevint, Watts and the Wesleys.

> Who shall say how Bread and Wine
>   GOD into Man conveys?
> *How* the Bread transmits his Blood,
>   Fills his Faithful Peoples Hearts
> With all the Life of GOD! . . .
>
> Sure and real is the Grace,
>   The Manner be unknown. (57:1.3–7, 4.1–2)
>
> Receiving the Bread
> On JESUS we feed,
> It doth not appear
> His manner of working; but JESUS is here! (92:6)

Anglican theologians since the sixteenth century had argued that while the eucharist challenges the mind and must be thought about, its efficacy does not require that a receiver hold a true account of its meaning. Richard Hooker had asked, 'What moveth us to argue of the manner how life should come by bread, our duty being here but to take what is offered, and most assuredly to rest persuaded of this, that can we but eat we are safe?' (*Ecclesiastical Polity*, V.lxvii.12). The immediate source of Welsey's thought is Brevint, who had said, 'The manner of this real communication and conveyance is the great unfathomable mystery which the holy fathers have ever admired, and which therefore we neither need nor do take it upon ourselves to explain' (IV.6).

Along with previous Anglican thinkers, Wesley held that, as an account of the meaning of the Holy Communion, Roman doctrine of transubstantiation, as it had come to be defined, was mistaken, for it qualified the integrity of the bread and wine, separating the accidents of the elements from their substance. Wesley says of the bread and wine, 'These the virtue did convey,/ Yet still remain the same' (57:2.7–8). The power of Christ, he insists, is given through the elements, while they remain bread and wine. The Christians' role is, through the earthly bread and wine, to 'taste the heavenly powers'. 'Thine [God's it is] to bless, 'Tis only ours/ To wonder, and adore' (57:4.7–8). Wesley concurs with Brevint, who had said, 'How these mysteries become in my behalf the supernatural instruments of such blessings, it is enough for me to admire' (IV.8).

Moreover, the Roman Church's account of Christ's presence in the sacrament, as Wesley saw it, localised God. This seems to have been in his mind when he wrote:

> No local Deity
> We worship, LORD, in Thee:
> Free Thy grace and unconfined,
> Yet it here doth freest move. (63:2.1–4)

Yet he strongly affirms presence, using terms of divine 'power' or 'virtue': 'Thy Power into the Means infuse' (58:4.3). 'The virtue of thy blood impart;/ O let it reach to all below' (32:2.3–4). The blessed cup is the sacred means to impart 'Our Saviour's Blood, with Power imprest' (73:1.3). 'The Spirit and Power/ Of Jesus our God' is found in 'this Life-giving Food' (92:1.2–4). God's power is God present and self-demonstrated. As Borgen put it, 'Where God acts, there he is.'[4] The presence is not something that inheres in the sacramental elements, but is a sharing of life. The sacrament is an actualisation of the 'virtue' – the character and potency – of God.

Continued Life and Union

The relationship with Christ in faith must continue and grow. Free exchange in trust and love leads to deeper disclosure and sharing: 'Talk with us, and our hearts shall burn/ With flames of fervent love./ Enkindle now the heavenly zeal,/ And make thy mercy known' (29:3.3–4.2). 'Now, Saviour, now thyself reveal,/ And make thy nature known' (30:3.1–2). 'We long thy open face to see' (38.5.2). 'Thy promised grace vouchsafe to give,/ As each is able to receive' (76:22.1–2).

> [We] now begin by Grace to live,
> And breathe the Breath of Love Divine. (36:4.3–4)

> Saviour, Thou didst the Mystery give
> That I thy Nature might partake,
> Thou bidst me outward Signs receive,
> One with Thyself my Soul to make,
> My Body, Soul and Spi'rit to join
> Inseparably one with Thine. (54:3)

As the life with God is begun in grace, so, Wesley is certain, it continues by grace:

> Saviour of my Soul from Sin,
> Thou my kind Preserver be,

Stablish what Thou dost begin,
　Carry on thy Work in me,
All thy Faithful Mercies shew,
Hold, and never let me go . . .

Save me, and persist to save. (48:1.1–6, 2.4)

Brevint had spoken of the benefits of Christ's sufferings (benefits that are given 'both at the holy table and upon all other occasions') as 'maintenance and improvement of life'. As natural life decays without food, so Christ supplies strength and grace to 'improve and set forward that spiritual life and new being which he hath procured us by his cross' (III.6). Wesley too understands that the devout communicant is called into a relationship which promises its own continuance:

Quicken our dead Souls again,
Then our living Souls sustain. (35:2.1–2).

1　　　Author of Life Divine,
　　　　Who hast a Table spread,
　　　　Furnish'd with Mystick Wine
　　　　And everlasting Bread,
　　Preserve the Life Thyself hast given,
　　And feed, and train us up for Heaven.

2　　　Our needy Souls sustain
　　　　With fresh Supplies of Love,
　　　　Till all thy Life we gain,
　　　　And all thy Fulness prove,
　　And strength'ned by thy perfect Grace,
　　Behold without a Veil thy Face. (40)[5]

Pardon into my Soul convey,
Strength in thy Pard'ning Love to stay,
　And to the End endure. (47:1.4–6)

Tenderest Branch alas am I,
Wither without Thee and die;
Weak as helpless Infancy,
O confirm my Soul in Thee.

Unsustain'd by Thee I fall,
Send the Strength for which I call;
Weaker than a bruised Reed,
Help I every Moment need.

All my Hopes on Thee depend,
Love me, save me to the End,
Give me the Continuing Grace,
Take the Everlasting Praise. (49:2–4)

Wesley is confident that God works actively to hold a wayward person, 'Thou wouldst not let me go away;/ Still thou forcest me to stay' (80:3.1– 2). He asks, 'Ah, do not, Lord, Thine own forsake' (50:2.1).

Forgiveness and Holiness

In Wesley's mind, justification and sanctification, forgiveness and holiness, together comprise full salvation. Forgiveness enables holiness; holiness completes what forgiveness begins. Unless forgiveness leads to a life of sanctity, it is as though Christ had died to no purpose:

The Blood remov'd our Guilt in vain
    If Sin in us must always stay. (37:2.1–2)

Purge we all our Sin away,
    That old accursed Leaven;
Sin in us no longer stay,
    In us thro' CHRIST forgiven. (84:2.1–4)

Holiness of life, however, cannot be thought of as a human achievement. It is a gift of God working inwardly. Along with the language of Christian resolve, Wesley uses that of humble prayer:

To thy foul and helpless Creature,
    Come, and cleanse All my Sins,
Come and change my Nature. (87:7)

In several hymns (31, 37, 38, 74 and 75) Wesley speaks of salvation and the continued life of holiness using the image of the water and blood that flowed together from Jesus' pierced side. The water and blood are mentioned in the New Testament only in the Johannine passion account, where they are not explained (John 19.34). The terms are highly evocative, and over the centuries they have often been interpreted symbolically.

As Wesley understands them, the 'blood' signifies atonement for sin, while 'water' stands for sanctification, holiness or purification. The blood has satisfied justice, removed punishment and secured pardon, while the water, after pardon is granted, washes and sanctifies. The two are inseparable.

> By Water and by Blood redeem,
> And wash us in the mingled Stream.
>
> The Sin-atoning Blood apply,
> And let the Water sanctify,
> Pardon and Holiness impart,
> Sprinkle and purify our Heart. (31:1.5–2.4)
>
> The Stream that from thy wounded Side
>   In blended Blood and Water flow'd,
> Shall cleanse whom first it justified,
>   And fill us with the Life of GOD.
>
> Proceeds from Thee the double Grace;
>   Two effluxes with life Divine. (37:3.1–4.2)

Charles Wesley's interpretation of the water and blood in terms of the 'double life' of 'pardoning and hallowing grace' (38:1.2–3) was shared with his brother John, who on Good Friday, 1740, preached from John 19.34, reporting in his *Journal*: 'I was enabled to speak strong words, both concerning the atoning blood, and the living, sanctifying water.'

This interpretation (which may now be thought somewhat strained) can be found in Brevint, who had described divine grace as 'the first irradiation of God's mercy,' which is represented by 'the blood that hath satisfied divine justice'. Then he adds, 'But, alas! how soon would this first life vanish away were it not presently followed and supported by a second!' (III.8). This second life, which delivers from stupid and senseless falling into sin, 'relates properly to the *water*, that after propitiation and pardon, washes and sanctifies the sinner' (III.8).

Isaac Watts, in one of his hymns for the Supper, writing a generation before Wesley, said somewhat in passing

> My Saviour's pierced side,
> Pour'd out a double flood;
> By water we are purify'd,
> And pardon'd by the blood. (9:4)

A spiritualising interpretation along these lines is very old, appearing as early as Ambrose of Milan (c. 339–97), who asked, 'Why water? Why blood?' and answered, 'Water to cleanse, blood to redeem.'[6] Many links, most of them now beyond recovery, must have connected fourth-century Milan and eighteenth-century England.

If this idea appears in Brevint, writing in the later seventeenth century, and then in Watts in 1707, and in John Wesley in 1740, and in Charles Wesley in 1745 (and it recurs in Toplady's 'Rock of Ages', 1776)[7] – all of them seeming confident that this interpretation of the passion story will be understood and accepted – one can be quite sure that it was said by many others in the seventeenth- and eighteenth-century tradition of evangelical preaching and biblical interpretation.

Blessing and Transformation

Wesley sometimes speaks of Christ in the eucharist with quiet joy:

1   Searcher of Hearts, in Ours appear,
    And make, and keep them all sincere,
    Or draw us burthen'd to thy Son,
    Or make Him to his Mourners known.

2   Thy promis'd Grace vouchsafe to give
    As each is able to receive,
    The blessed Grief to All impart;
    Or joy; or Purity of Heart.

3   Our helpless Unbelief remove,
    And melt us by thy pard'ning Love,
    Work in us Faith, or Faith's Increase,
    The Dawning, or the Perfect Peace.

4   Give each to Thee as seemeth best,
    But meet us all at thy own Feast,
    Thy Blessing in thy Means convey,
    Nor empty send One Soul away. (76)

The 'Searcher of hearts' (the Holy Spirit, 1 Corinthians 2.10) is asked to do an inward work – to 'appear in our hearts', and make them sincere (without pretence), to draw us to the Son, to make himself known to 'mourners' (those who grieve for their sins), to give the promised grace, to impart either 'the blessed grief', which is penitence, or else joy or purity of heart, to remove 'our helpless unbelief' and 'melt us by pard'ning love', to give us faith and its increase, and to grant us perfect peace. When Wesley asks God to give according to each one's ability to receive and as God knows to be best, he follows Brevint, who had said, 'Of these blessings, Christ from above is pleased to dispense sometimes more, sometimes less, into these inferior courts of the people, either according to the several degrees of their faith, or according to the several ways and times which He hath appointed to them for presenting themselves nearer to Him' (IV.12). Wesley is saying that the inward response of even the most devout communicant is given by God, and he prays for its bestowal.

The divine self-imparting and the drawing of persons to Christ is understood to be the ministry of the Spirit (1 Corinthians 2.10). The hymn emphasises repentance, faith, joy, love and peace – all of which are spoken of by St Paul as fruits of the Spirit (Galatians 5.2f.). Yet the expression 'thy Son' in 1.3 seems to indicate that the hymn is addressed to the Father, and the words 'thy feast' (4.2) suggest an address to Christ. Speaking in a manner that is more suggestive than specific, the hymn seems to ask God to do the sort of work in the human heart that only the triune God can do.

The tone of appeal continues in the next hymn:

2   Come to thy House again,
        Nor let us seek in vain:
This the place of meeting be,
    To thy weeping Flock repair,
Let us here thy Beauty see,
    Find Thee in the House of Prayer.

3   Let us with solemn Awe
        Nigh to thine Altar draw,
Taste Thee in the Broken Bread,
    Drink Thee in the Mystic Wine;
Now the Gracious Spirit shed,
    Fill us now with Love Divine.

4   Into our Minds recall
        Thy Death endur'd for All:
Come in this Accepted Day,
    Come, and all our Souls restore,
Come, and take our Sins away,
    Come, and never leave us more. (77)

And again:

9   In thine own Appointments bless us,
         Meet us here, Now appear,
             Our Almighty JESUS.

10   Let the Ordinance be sealing,
         Enter Now, Claim us Thou
             For thy Constant Dwelling.

11   Fill the Heart of Each Believer,
         We are Thine, Love Divine,
             Reign in Us for ever. (78)

Jesus, through the Spirit and the sacrament, effects a transformation in believers. Wesley again takes images from Jesus' healing miracles. Hymn 59 speaks in the voice of the blind man in John 9 who was healed by Jesus. He did not know how he had been healed, but only that he had been blind, but now could see. Wesley begins the hymn reflecting on the incomprehensible ways of God, specifically on how the sacrament imparts God: '*How* the means transmit the power –/ Here he leaves our thoughts behind.' Then he realises that the enquiry into *how* is not necessary: 'I cannot the way descry,/ Need not know the mystery;/ Only this I know – that I/ Was blind, but now I see' (59:2.5–8). (Brevint had previously used this gospel story to represent sacramental experience.) In Wesley's final stanza, the lines pass between features from the Johannine story and the enquiring but baffled communicant whose 'eyes are opened wide'.

Now mine Eyes are open'd wide,
    To see his Pard'ning Love,
Here I view the GOD that died
    My Ruin to remove;
Clay upon mine Eyes he laid,
    (I at once my Sight receiv'd,)
Bless'd, and bid me eat the Bread,
    And lo! my Soul believ'd. (59:3)

The most dramatic of these hymns of transformation, Hymn 68, speaks in the voice of Lazarus (John 11.1–44), who calls from the grave to Jesus, asking him to hurry to the tomb and restore him to life.

1   JESU, Son of God draw near,
         Hasten to my Sepulchre,
         Help, where dead in Sin I lie,
         Save, or I forever die.

2 Let no Savour of the Grave
   Stop thy Power to help and save,
   Call me forth to Life restor'd
   Quicken'd by my dying Lord.

3 By thine all-atoning Blood
   Raise and bring me near to GOD,
   Now pronounce my Sins forgiven,
   Loose, and let me go to Heaven. (68)

To be in sin is to be in death; Jesus is asked to call 'me' from the grave, to pronounce forgiveness through his blood, to raise me and bring me to God. The opening lines of stanza 2, 'Let no savour of the grave/ Stop thy power to help and save,' refer to the point in the gospel story when Jesus ordered the removal of the stone from the mouth of the grave, and Lazarus' sister Martha objected that since her brother had been dead for four days there would be an offensive odour (John 11.9). Jesus disregarded Martha's objection and brought Lazarus forth, restored to life. The eucharist, as Wesley presents it, is a sign, indeed, the actuality of coming to life out of death.

Feeding, Banqueting

Many of the hymns of Part II breathe joy and confidence: 'Thee we approach with heart sincere,/ Thy power we joy to feel./ To thee our humblest thanks we pay,/ To thee our souls we bow' (85:1.3–6). Wesley often speaks in terms of bread and wine, of eating, feeding, tasting, feasting, banqueting and satisfaction.
   He asks:

1 LORD of Life, thy Followers see
   Hungring, thirsting after Thee,
   At thy Sacred Table feed,
   Nourish us with Living Bread.

2 Chear us with Immortal Wine,
   Heavenly Sustenance Divine,
   Grant us now a fresh Supply,
   Now relieve us, or we die. (34)

He gratefully says:

> Thou in this Sacramental Bread
> Dost now our hungry Spirits feed,
>   And cheer us with the hallow'd Wine. (61:3.7–9)

> Now on the sacred Table laid
>   Thy Flesh becomes our Food,
> Thy Life is to our Souls convey'd
>   In Sacramental Blood.

> We eat the Offerings of our Peace,
>   The hidden Manna prove,
> And only live t'adore and bless
>   Thine all-sufficient Love. (65:3–4)

> The Banquet by thy Presence crown. (75:3.3)

The terms of feeding, which mark these hymns, draw on an elemental human mystery. Human beings take into themselves something that is not themselves – something from the world around them, something that has lived, but no longer lives, yet which, in a repeated physiological marvel, becomes a life-sustaining part of themselves. Eating is a repeated demonstration of dependence, of grace. Brevint had remarked the fitness of bread and wine, 'which are the ordinary means of preserving our life and strength' (III.3), for their sacramental significance. Wesley uses such terms repeatedly:

> Satiate the Hungry with good Things,
>   The Hidden Manna give.

> The Living Bread sent down from Heaven
>   In us vouchsafe to be. (30:6.3–7.2)

> Now, LORD, on Us Thy Flesh bestow,
>   And let us drink Thy Blood,
> Till all our Souls are fill'd below
>   With all the Life of GOD. (30:8.1–4)

Wesley prays, 'Nourish us with living bread./ Chear us with immortal wine' (34:1.4–2.1). And, 'O Thou pascal Lamb of God,/ Feed us with thy flesh and blood,/ Life and strength thy death supplys,/ Feast us on thy sacrifice' (35:1.1–4). 'Let us feed by faith on Thee' (82:2.8). (And see Hymn 40, quoted on p. 100.)

In Hymn 46 Wesley says – in a point that might be thought somewhat recondite, but that he thought was within the grasp of the congregations for which he wrote – that the priesthood of Christ was prefigured by Aaron (whose priestly work involved the slaying of a victim and the shedding of blood) and by Melchizedek (whose priesthood, bringing offerings of bread and wine, stood for nourishment, Genesis 14.17–20). The two priesthoods are united in Christ's priesthood:

> *Aaron* for us the Blood hath shed,
> *Melchizedec* bestows the Bread,
> To nourish this, and that t'atone;
> And both the Priests in CHRIST are One. (46:2)

In another hymn Wesley speaks of feeding, with allusions to the exodus:

> In this barren Wilderness
>   Thou hast a Table spread,
> Furnish'd out with richest Grace,
>   Whate'er our Souls can need. (84:4.1–4)

Often his lines simply express satisfaction and plenty:

> Our Spirits drink a fresh Supply,
>   And eat the Bread so freely given,
> Till borne on Eagle's Wings we fly,
>   And banquet with our LORD in Heaven. (28:4.1–4)

>   The Mystic Flesh of JESUS eat,
> Drink with the Wine his healing Blood,
> And feast on th' Incarnate GOD. (71:2.4–6)

In the sacrament, hungry and thirsty communicants are filled with heavenly food and drink – renewed, refreshed and satisfied. Brevint, writing earlier, had said, 'Our life in general is the time of this festival, and the blessed Communion is the bread and wine of the banquet' (III.13). Wesley exults: 'We banquet on immortal food,/ And drink the streams of life divine' (61:3.11–12).

With pure celestial Bliss
   He doth our Spirits chear,
His House of Banqueting is This,
   And He hath brought us here. (81:3.1–4)

What is sought through the sacrament is oneness with Christ, for this is
the food of the believer.

Thou bidst me outward Signs receive,
   One with Thyself my Soul to make;
My Body, Soul and Spi'rit to join
Inseparably one with Thine. (54:3.3–6)

The presence and self-imparting of Christ brings the communicant to a
point of virtual ecstasy:

The Joy is more unspeakable,
   And yields me larger Draughts of GOD,
'Till Nature faints beneath the Power,
And Faith fill'd up can hold no more. (54:5.3–6)

Later Wesley says:

And now our Bosoms feel
The Glory not to be exprest,
   The Joy unspeakable. (81:2.6–8).

And again:

In rapturous Bliss
He bids us do This,
   The joy it imparts
Hath witness'd his gracious Design in our Hearts. (92:4)

The Stillness Controversy

In five important hymns in Part II (Hymns 54, 86 and 90–92) Wesley
speaks to the 'stillness controversy' which troubled Methodism in its
earliest days. The Society at Fetter Lane with which the Wesleys met
after their return to London came under the influence of Philip Molther,

recently come from Germany, who taught that the inward relation of the Christian with God made external things unnecessary – in fact such things may distract one from God or subvert a relation that was properly constituted purely in faith. He questioned whether one could use any 'means' without coming to trust in them. One's spiritual task was to 'be still' before God and wait for grace, which, when it came, would be ministered directly by God with no need of 'means'. This inner self-imparting of God was so immediate and authoritative that it could take priority over ministers, preaching, prayer, sacraments, or even written Scripture. The movement reached the height of its influence in the Fetter Lane Society in the early 1740s.

This questioning, on spiritual grounds, of the Sacrament of the Table was not a simple issue, for the inward witness of God was important to the Wesleys and their followers. The quiet waiting commended by those of the 'stillness' persuasion could seem to be only an advanced expression of something to which in principle the Wesleys were also committed.

Yet rather quickly the Wesleys rejected the 'stillness' emphasis. They thought that introspection was making the quietist group too individualistic. As John had said in the preface to his 1739 collection, *Hymns and Sacred Poems*, 'The Gospel of Christ knows of no religion, but social; no holiness, but social holiness.' But more importantly, the anti-sacramental counsel seemed to the Wesleys to be outright disobedience to Jesus' command 'do this'. In John's sermon on 'The Means of Grace', 1746, he said, 'According to the decision of Holy Writ, all who desire the grace of God are to wait for it in the means which he hath ordained; in using, not in laying them aside' (*Sermons*, III.1, p. 162). All argument had to yield before the fact that Jesus had commanded, and 'Whoe'er rejects the kind command,/ The word of God shall ever stand' (61:9.3–4). In July 1740 the Wesleys led a group out of the Fetter Lane Society over the issue.

In addressing the matter in his hymns, Charles entertains his opponents' question: Could not faith, independent of any 'means', bring forgiveness and holiness?

> Why did my dying LORD ordain
>   This dear Memorial of his Love!
> Might we not all by Faith obtain,
>   By Faith the Mountain-sin remove,
> Enjoy the Sence of Sins forgiven,
>   And Holiness the Taste of Heaven? (54:1)

He replies simply that the sacrament and its blessing were appointed by Jesus:

> It seem'd to my Redeemer good
>   That Faith should *here* his Coming wait,
> Should here receive Immortal Food,
>   Grow up in Him divinely great,
> And fill'd with Holy Violence seize
> The Glorious Crown of Righteousness. (54:2)

The Saviour, Wesley says, has given this 'dear memorial' to bring believers into union with himself. His language of 'seizing' the crown of righteousness by 'holy violence' contrasts with the passivity of the 'stillness' group. The final stanza describes satiety with a suggestion of ecstasy – virtually intoxication!

> Communion closer far I feel,
>   And deeper drink th' Atoning Blood,
> The Joy is more unspeakable,
>   And yields me larger Draughts of GOD,
> 'Till Nature faints beneath the Power,
> And Faith fill'd up can hold no more. (54:5)

Wesley is telling those of the 'stillness' persuasion that by their 'spiritual' veto on the sacraments they are excluding themselves from something that not merely is commanded, but is supremely rewarding.

The 'stillness' theme returns in Hymn 86:

> 1   And shall I let Him go?
>   If now I do not *feel*
>   The Streams of Living Water flow
>   Shall I forsake the Well?
>
> 2   Because He hides his Face,
>   Shall I no longer stay,
>   But leave the Channels of his Grace,
>   And cast the Means away?
>
> 3   Get Thee behind me Fiend,
>   On Others try thy Skill,
>   Here let thy hellish Whispers end,
>   To Thee I say *Be still!*

Wesley adopts the voice of a person who has come to find no inward, felt reward in the Supper and considers letting go of Christ. But he quickly hears this proposal as the voice of the Tempter, and he says to the Fiend, 'Here let thy hellish whispers end,/ To Thee I say *Be still!*' (When he says 'be still', he uses the language of the 'stillness' teachers against them.) The one voice he will hear is that of Jesus.

4　JESUS hath spoke the Word,
　　His Will my Reason is,
　Do *this* in Memory of thy LORD,
　　JESUS hath said, *Do this!*

5　He bids me eat the Bread,
　　He bids me drink the Wine,
　No other Motive, LORD, I need
　　No other Word than Thine.

6　I chearfully comply
　　With what my LORD doth say,
　Let Others ask a Reason why,
　　My Glory is T'obey.

7　His will is good and just:
　　Shall I his Will withstand?
　If JESUS bid me lick the Dust
　　I bow at his Command:

8　Because He saith Do this,
　　This I will always do,
　Till JESUS come in glorious Bliss
　　I *thus* his Death will *shew*. (86)

One partakes of the Holy Communion not on the basis of one's feelings or of perceived reward, but because one is obeying Jesus' word, 'do this'. 'His will my reason is.' 'No other motive, Lord, I need.'

The hymn evidences a somewhat conflicted experience of the sacrament. The Wesleys taught their followers to be attentive to and in some ways to trust their experience in divine matters. But when experience in itself yielded little reason for attending the Supper, they had to bring in the scriptures as a check on experience. Wesley sets his argument quite simply as a matter of obedience. 'Let others ask the reason why,/ My glory is t'obey' (86:6.3–4).

Hymn 90 deals with the contention by the 'stillness' group that Jesus' directions 'do this' and 'take, eat' were given to his immediate followers and do not bind the later Church. Wesley replies that such arguments subvert the letter of Scripture. The disciples in the Upper Room were the Church; what Jesus said to them he still says to his people. His words were commandments given with the Supper, his 'dear bequest'. They endure, and to them Christians will remain obedient. While those who oppose the sacrament claim freedom and a clearer spiritual light, Wesley thinks they only are setting themselves free to disobey. They 'insist that a part of the Christian calling is liberty *from* obeying, not liberty *to* obey' (*Journal*, 25 April 1740). Wesley does not dismiss the 'stillness' Christians, but ends this hymn with a prayer that the faithful witness of those who continue in 'the ancient paths' will eventually win over the misguided quietists.

> Our wandring Brethren's Hearts to gain
> > We will not let our Saviour go,
> But in thine ancient Paths remain,
> > But thus persist thy Death to shew. (90:5.1–4)

In the following hymn Wesley speaks of the 'stillness' Christians in 'we–they' terms. Yet he does not condemn, but asks God to look with pity on the 'wandering sheep'. Despite serious differences, 'we' remain bound in faith with 'them'. Indeed we cannot fully enjoy sacramental life, knowing that those of the stillness persuasion exclude themselves from it. 'Can we enjoy thy richest Love,/ Nor long that They the Grace may share?' (91:2.1–2). Christ is asked to bring them to the sacrament: 'O let their joys like ours abound,/ Invite them to the Royal Cheer' (3.3–4). Wesley concludes with a prayer that both 'we' and 'they' will find unity in 'One hallow'd undivided bread,/ One body knit to thee our head' and be gathered into 'one fold'.

The next hymn, 92, opens with a rebuke to the contention of the 'stillness' group that the Lord's Supper is not for Christians of all time. But the hymn ends, not with polemic, but with a celebration of the sacrament:

> In rapturous Bliss
> He bids us do This,
> The Joy it imparts
> Hath witness'd his gracious Design in our Hearts. (92.4.1–4)

Negative Experience

Despite the vital experience of the sacrament that Wesley has presented, he acknowledges that the Holy Communion is caught up in the human mixture of faith and doubt, in the reality of sin and obtuseness, and in the sheer mystery of the ways of God. (The hymns that carry this tone fall towards the end of Part II where Wesley has stopped following *The Christian Sacrament and Sacrifice*. The description of the ambiguity of sacramental life is Wesley's own; nothing of the sort appears in Brevint.) Communicants, he knows, can attend the sacrament repeatedly with little or no perceived inner reward. Christ is not found to be present, but absent. When Charles Wesley describes a troubled communicant, he speaks from his own experience. At the time of his awakening, he wrote in his *Journal*, 'I received the sacrament, but not Christ' (19 May 1738); and a few days later, he wrote, 'Being to receive the sacrament today, I was assaulted by the fear of my old accustomed deadness' (24 May).

The hymns express a communicant's hesitancy and misgiving: 'I am a frail sinful man,/ All my nature cries, Depart!' (43:2.5–6). Troubled believers call out in yearning, 'Jesus, regard . . . the groaning [the cry for assurance] of thy prisoners here' (79:1.2). They evidence periods, perhaps years, of waiting and frustration: 'Long we for thy love have waited' (83:2.1). 'Long have I groan'd thy grace to gain,/ Suffer'd on, but all in vain' (80:2.1f.).

Hymn 80 cries out to Christ with weariness or near-despair and yearning – a state of mind that might well come to a devout person at the Holy Communion, where expectation is high and disappointment may be keenly felt. For a long time ('an age of mournful years') devotional practices have been found barren, and the speaker has grown weary of Christ's way and even of Christ. The communicant, identifying with the man begging at the wayside in Matthew 20.29–34, and speaking throughout in the 'I' voice, says that years of waiting, suffering, prayers and tears have brought no relief.

> 1   With Pity, LORD, a Sinner see
>   Weary of thy Ways and Thee:
>   Forgive my fond Despair*
>   A Blessing in the Means to find,
>   My Struggling to throw off the Care
>   And cast them all behind.

---

* *fond*: foolish, usually spoken with affection, rather than in blame.

2   Long have I groan'd thy Grace to gain,
       Suffer'd on but all in vain:
         An Age of mournful Years
     I waited for thy passing by,
     And lost my Prayers, and Sighs, and Tears,
       And never found Thee nigh.

3   Thou wouldst not let me go away;
       Still thou forcest me to stay.
         O might the Secret Power
     Which will not with its Captive part,
     Nail to the Posts of Mercy's Door
       My poor unstable Heart.

Christ engages in a benign but passionate struggle with the discouraged communicant: 'Thou would'st not let me go away' (3.1). Only your love can bring a cure (4.5).

4   The Nails that fixt Thee to the Tree
       Only They can fasten me:
         The Death thou didst endure
     For me let it effectual prove:
     Thy Love alone my Soul can cure,
       Thy dear expiring Love.

The final stanza pleads for a direct relation to Christ through the sacrament, 'Now the means of grace impart'.

5   Now the Means of Grace impart,
       Whisper Peace into my Heart;
         Appear the Justifier
     Of all who to thy Wounds would fly,
     And let me have my One Desire
       And see thy Face, and die. (80)

This hymn, which ends still asking, seems to address indirectly yet compassionately an experience of futility that had been expressed by devout people who had gone repeatedly to the sacrament with little interior reward. The hymn is full of expressive, well-crafted phrases: 'Weary of thy ways and thee' (1.2); 'Long have I groaned thy grace to gain' (2.1); 'An age of mournful years/ I waited for thy passing by' (2.3f.); 'And lost

my prayers and sighs and tears' (2.5); 'the secret power/ Which will not
with its captive part' (3.3f.); 'Thy love alone my soul can cure' (4.5);
'Whisper peace into my heart' (5.2).

Still in an urgent tone, Hymn 82, speaking for tired, hungry, helpless
people, pleads to Jesus for nourishment.

> JESU, Sinner's Friend, receive us
>   Feeble, famishing, and faint,
> O thou Bread of Life relieve us,
>   Now, or now we die for want
> Least we faint, and die for ever
>   Thou our sinking Spirits stay,
> Give some Token of thy Favour,
>   Empty send us not away.
>
> We have in the Desart tarried
>   Long, and nothing have to eat,
> Comfort us thro' wandring wearied,
>   Feed our Souls with Living Meat,
> Still with Bowels of Compassion*
>   See thy helpless People see,
> Let us taste thy great Salvation,
>   Let us feed by Faith on Thee. (82:1–2)

Christians plead that they have been long in the desert with nothing to eat.
'Receive us . . . relieve us . . . now, or now we die for want.' The biblical
allusions pass between Israel hungry in the wilderness and the people in
the feeding stories of the gospels who followed Jesus until they became
hungry. Wesley refers these biblical incidents to the longing Christian at
the Lord's Table.

Devout persons come to the Table, but the Christ they come to meet
might be wonderfully self-given or strangely withheld. They ask that he
not be indifferent, but see them with compassion – that he receive and
relieve them with 'some token of thy favour' (1.7). Believers who sometimes went from the sacrament confident and buoyant at other times left
with their longing and uncertainty unrelieved.

The cries of these hymns of negative experience come almost to

---

* *Bowels of Compassion:* In an archaic meaning, the term *bowels* refers to the seat of pity
or sympathy; Watts, the AV Bible and many other writers also used the term; 'feelings' is an
approximate equivalent, but lacks the physiological realism of the old word; 'heart' is hopelessly
shopworn.

desperation: 'Now relieve us, or we die' (34:2.4). Grace is needed because peril is near: 'Save out of the destroyer's hand/ This helpless soul of mine' (47:2–3). 'Hasten to my sepulchre;/ Help, where dead in sin I lie,/ Save, or I for ever die' (68:1.2–4). 'Lost without thy grace,/ Thy mercy I implore,/ And wait to see thy face' (69:1.2–4). 'O thou bread of life, relieve us,/ Now, or now we die for want' (82:1.3–4).

In times of clouded faith, one considers discarding Christ himself:

> And shall I let him go?
> If now I do not *feel*
> The Streams of Living Water flow
> Shall I forsake the Well?
>
> Because He hides his Face,
> Shall I no longer stay,
> But leave the Channels of his Grace,
> And cast the Means away? (86:1–2)

Wesley counsels the seeking, confused, disappointed communicant not to stop coming to the sacrament, for it is at the sacrament that the inner rewards will again be found. Earnest Christians should come to the place of divine appointment and 'humbly at thy Altar wait' (112:2.3).

Ultimately, Wesley is sure, Christ's promise will be vindicated:

> Is it the dying Master's Will
>   That we should This persist to do?
> Then let him here Himself reveal,
>   The Tokens of his Presence shew,
> Descend in Blessings from above,
> And answer by the Fire of Love.
>
> In Confidence we ask the Grace,
>   Faithful and True appear, appear. (89:2.1–6, 3.3–4)

After struggle and unfulfilled longing, the final stanza of Hymn 89 comes as an emotional, mental and almost physiological relief:

> 'Tis done; the Lord sets to his Seal,
>   The Prayer is heard, the Grace is given,
> With Joy unspeakable we feel
>   The Holy Ghost sent down from Heaven,
> The Altar streams with sacred Blood,
> And all the Temple flames with GOD! (89:4)

Christ makes himself known in the sacrament, 'The Lord sets to his seal.'
The inward validation which was sought is granted: 'The prayer is heard,
the grace is given.' The communicants feel, with Pentecostal joy, 'the
Holy Ghost sent down from Heaven'. In ecstatic final lines that suggest the baroque spirit of Richard Crashaw, the plain Holy Table of an
eighteenth-century English church 'streams with sacred blood, and all
the Temple flames with God!'

There is, however, a further dimension in Wesley's record of the
ambiguity of eucharistic experience. When he describes the struggle and
at times the unsatisfactory character of Christian experience of the sacrament, he sometimes seems to say that the pain, bafflement and unfulfilled
longing are not due entirely to the obstinacy or dullness of the communicant's heart, but in some measure to the mystery of the one they come
to meet. Like Job, Jeremiah, Jesus in Gethsemane and on the cross; and
like St John of the Cross and Gerard Manley Hopkins in his 'terrible son-
nets', Wesley, out of confusion and pain (his own, and that of believers
he knows and for whom he speaks), questions the ways of God. If communicants struggle with themselves and with God, Wesley draws bold,
but largely undeveloped hints that God, as known in the uncertain life of
faith, is unpredictable – not capricious, but at times strangely self-given
and at other times strangely self-withheld. God on occasions 'hides his
face' (86:2.1), meanwhile holding believers to the task of faithful waiting.

This honest report of negative experience may be unexpected. This
extraordinary collection of hymns has helped communicants to structure
their experience of the sacrament, allowing them to discover through
Wesley's words what they might expect of the rite and of themselves.
Although the hymns hold before the communicant a richly rewarding
experience, they do not idealise sacramental participation as though it
brought nothing but joyful encounter with Christ or as though its inward
blessing were unfailing. While the devout communicant is sometimes carried into ecstasy, at other times the Supper fails to lift one's dullness and
despair. Such descriptions of the complexity of sacramental experience in
effect gave devout persons permission to have frustrating, barren periods
at the Table of the Lord. Persons who encounter an unrewarding period
need not blame themselves. They are simply entering into the ambiguity
of the human relation to God.

These hymns of Wesley's Part II express, as hardly anything else in
post-Reformation English spirituality does, the intense relation between
Christ and the troubled and confident, despairing and exultant Christian
communicant. Longing and entreaty – even abandonment – stand alongside union, assurance and soul-transporting joy. If these hymns, by their

honesty, permit a believer to acknowledge times of dryness, disappointment and anxiety at the very table of the Lord, yet, beyond the barren
occasions, they also put before the devout communicant a deep, fulfilling
encounter with Christ.

> Then let him here Himself reveal,
>   The Tokens of his Presence shew,
> Descend in Blessings from above,
> And answer by the Fire of Love. (39.2.3–6)

Since Christ's presence is grasped by faith, in all its confidence and its
frailty, the experience of the Holy Communion is elusive. Christ as known
in the actuality of the sacrament is present and yet absent, shown and yet
hidden, here and yet longed for. These hymns are a tumult of emotions
as Christ is passionately engaged with a communicant and each communicant is passionately engaged with Christ. Wesley's *Hymns on the
Lord's Supper*, and particularly those of Part II, bring to articulateness
each Christian's rejoicing, fighting, praying, watching, working, suffering, and groaning for full redemption.

* * *

ESSAYS

The 'I' of the Hymns

In most of the sacramental hymns, Wesley speaks in the 'we' voice – the
'we' of the believing community declaring itself to God, to Christ, to the
impercipient world, or to itself. Of course, the 'we' is always at the same
time Charles Wesley, in the community, speaking for it the secrets of its
heart.

Other hymns, however, speak in the singular 'I' voice and can seem to
express individual experience:

> Raise, and enable me to stand,
> Save out of the Destroyer's Hand
>   This helpless Soul of mine. (47:2.1–3)

> And shall I let Him go?
> If now I do not *feel*
> The Streams of Living Water flow
>   Shall I forsake the Well? (86:1)

In several hymns Wesley passes between the singular 'I' and the communal 'we' and the extended 'all' – sometimes widening to 'for all', and sometimes narrowing to a final 'for me'. Twenty-five hymns in the collection are largely or entirely in first person singular, plus stanzas or lines of a few others.

One must ask: When a hymn says 'I', is the voice that of Charles Wesley speaking for himself, or is Wesley's 'I' a dramatic 'personation' in which he speaks as a confident, a troubled or a longing believer?[8] There is no clear indication, even in the hymns that seem most self-revealing, that Wesley is writing confessionally. In his *Journal* and elsewhere he does record the intense dealings of his soul with God. At times he expresses deep feelings of unworthiness and at other times spiritual elation. But in the passing of voices and moods in these sacramental hymns – singular and collective, despairing and exultant – whom may we hear? Did Charles Wesley himself pass through all the things that the hymns express, so that he is reporting out of his own experience? Or is he speaking representatively, recording things which as pastor and friend he had known from others?

It was characteristic of the eighteenth century to prefer the general and the abstract to the particular and the personal. Unlike their counterparts in the previous century or in the next century, eighteenth-century writers seldom put their personalities or their unique interiority on display. Wesley's work is given authority by his own experience, but his experience is interpreted, even to himself, by the expectations and the shared rhetoric of the community for which he writes.

At the time of his evangelical awakening, Charles Wesley was reading Luther on Galatians, and he sought the personalisation of the apostle Paul (Galatians 2.20). He records, 'I laboured waited and prayed to feel "who loved ME, and gave himself for ME"' (*Journal*, 17 May 1738). The gospel, as Wesley often said, is for all. Yet at the same time it presents a personal self-imparting by God, to be personally received by a believer – although each believer stands in a community. The communal and the individual are not opposed to one another; the salvation which is for each is at the same time for all. When Wesley, speaking of matters of the spirit, says 'for me', what is most particular may at the same time be most sharable.

In estimating the first-person voice in the sacramental hymns, a reader, rather than looking for autobiography, may consider Wesley's principal literary source. It is commonly observed that Wesley makes heavy use of the well-expressed summary prayers with which Brevint ends each section of *The Christian Sacrament and Sacrifice*. Approximately 40 of the hymns in *Hymns on the Lord's Supper* trace specifically to these prayer passages. Eighteen of the 25 'I' hymns in the collection have their source in Brevint's prayers in which he is necessarily speaking in first person singular. In a great portion of his 'I' hymns, Wesley is simply catching and reproducing the rhetoric of his source, saying, like Brevint, 'I', 'me' and 'my'.

In these hymns, as throughout his thousands of hymns, Wesley articulates varied aspects of Christian interior life. It would seem fair to judge that when he does so, he had experienced, either first-hand or by empathy, the states of mind of which he wrote. He could identify with believers who were in a period of barrenness or at a peak of exultation because he had at one time or another stood where they stood. But the 'I' of the hymns seems to be a representative 'I'. Always one knows that whether the hymns say 'I' or 'we', they are the work of a single writer, Charles Wesley. But Wesley is speaking in and for the community of believers. And over the generations, the readers of his hymns have ratified his work, acknowledging that they discover their voices through him.

* * *

The Holy Spirit and the Supper

The Methodists – like the Puritans and much of the Nonconformist tradition, and like the central Anglican, Jeremy Taylor – saw the Holy Spirit as God in immediate, personal engagement with the human spirit. What God does in human life, God does by the Spirit. If God is known, it is by God's own witness within the believer. The Spirit struggles and pleads – teaching, correcting, awakening, strengthening and assuring each devout Christian.

This emphasis on the Spirit in Christian life, and more particularly in the eucharist, was a recovery by the Methodists (and by some other groups at the time and before) of an emphasis which had an early history, but had to a great extent gone into eclipse.

The book of Acts and the Pauline epistles portray the earliest Church as a community of the Spirit, growing and innovating and possessing the gifts required to sustain its life and mission. The Spirit was active in worship through charisms of prophecy and utterance. As liturgical life developed in the early centuries, some Christian traditions continued to accord the Spirit a place in their eucharistic liturgies and theologies, commonly asking in the prayer of consecration that the Spirit would bless the sacramental elements so that they would be to the receivers the Body and Blood of Christ. Other liturgical traditions, however, developed with no invocation of the Spirit in the consecratory prayer. In general, a prayer for the Spirit has been included in the historic eucharistic liturgies of the East, but not in those of the West.

The presence or absence of a prayer for the Spirit in the eucharistic consecration has, since the sixteenth century, divided the Anglican liturgical tradition. Thomas Cranmer introduced a prayer for the Holy Spirit in the consecration prayer of the first English Prayer Book of 1549, even though there had been none in the Latin Mass.[9] However, in the second Prayer Book of 1552 Cranmer dropped this prayer – an omission that was followed in the Prayer Book of 1662, which was the Prayer Book of the Wesleys (and which, indeed, remains the Prayer Book of many Anglicans). Later Anglican Prayer Books have fallen, in the matter, into two general 'families', following either Cranmer's 1549 model or his 1552 model.

The differences in liturgical wording represent different theological emphases. Generally speaking, Reformed thought, which became influential in England through the Puritans, tended to set natural *things* outside the holy. Spirit bears witness with spirit, but not through material things. While all parties might agree that the Holy Spirit is active in the eucharist, some judged that the Spirit is active in the hearts of communicants, while the bread and wine were almost incidental – something of a crutch, provided because weak human faith needs external help. The remarkably full epiclesis of Richard Baxter's 'Savoy Liturgy', 1661, spoke of the action of the Holy Spirit in the communicants' hearts, but made no mention of the eucharistic action or elements.

However, other English theologians, who were more incarnational or sacramental, had no difficulty in thinking of the Spirit working in and through material things. At issue was the relation of nature to grace, of matter to spirit. In seventeenth-century England, Jeremy Taylor, the Non-jurors and others used their position of independence to create liturgies which implied a criticism of the spareness of the Prayer Book of the Church of England and returned an *epiclesis* to the central liturgical thanksgiving.

The Wesleys knew and in their early years sympathised with the Non-jurors. The eucharistic rite of Thomas Deacon contained an epiclesis. The Wesleys would have heard the case for the essential place of the Holy Spirit in the eucharistic community, action and elements.

Anglican theologians over the generations had affirmed the Holy Spirit as part of their creed and their trinitarian doctrine. But only a few writers and preachers (notably Jeremy Taylor) had developed the theme in 'experimental' terms; and hardly any of the previous writers (again with the exception of Taylor) described the Spirit as in vital association with the sacraments.

(Wesley's emphasis on the Holy Spirit, interestingly, owes nothing to Brevint, who hardly mentions the Spirit.)

The Evangelical Revival brought the sense of the Spirit of God, in life and sacrament, to the foreground. The divine redemptive work is actualised or 'realised', in the sacramental sign by the Spirit, who is God and who imparts God. Writing at the time when *Hymns on the Lord's Supper* was being prepared, John Wesley said, 'All true faith, and the whole work of salvation, every good thought, word, and work, is altogether by the operation of the Spirit of God.'[10] While God may use means (the terms of the human condition require it), yet the divine engagement with humanity is immediate – life imparting life; Spirit bearing witness with spirit. Wesley emphasises that the power comes from God:

In Presence of the meanest Things,
(While all from Thee the Virtue springs,)
　Thy most stupendous Works are wrought. (61:1.4–6)

Several of the *Hymns on the Lord's Supper* focus on the relation of the Holy Spirit to the communicant and to the sacrament. Three are addressed to the Holy Spirit and open in the tone of the *Veni Creator*: 'Come Holy Ghost' (7, 72) and 'Come, Thou everlasting Spirit' (16).

Two of these hymns were discussed in comments on Part I: Hymn 7 (pp. 72f.) makes no mention of the sacramental bread and wine, but speaks of the Holy Spirit witnessing in the souls of believers. By the Spirit, the communicant, kneeling at the altar, sees and hears Christ on his cross. Hymn 16 (pp. 73f.) also speaks of the Holy Spirit working inwardly – bringing Christ's death to the thankful receiver's mind, imparting living faith, revealing salvation, and preaching the gospel to the believing heart. The Spirit is true recorder, witness and reminder of Jesus' passion. By the Spirit, Christ is applied to the soul, and believers sorrow with the dying Christ and receive his atoning grace.

The quite brief Hymn 72, located in Part II, speaks of the eucharistic elements, as Hymns 7 and 16 had not, asking the Holy Spirit to actualise the sign, bringing divine life and power into the bread and the wine, making them channels of divine life and love.

Come, Holy Ghost, thine Influence shed,
　　And realize the Sign,*
Thy Life infuse into the Bread,
　　Thy Power into the Wine.

Effectual let the Tokens prove,
　　And made by Heavenly Art
Fit Channels to convey thy Love
　　To every Faithful Heart.

These three hymns suggest what is sometimes called a 'double epiclesis' – a prayer for the action of the Holy Spirit on the sacramental elements and on the people – 'Bless these gifts, and bless us also.'

Several other hymns in the collection speak briefly of the Spirit:

• In 10:4.4–6, God is asked that the Spirit's attesting seal may speak of the Saviour to every sinner's heart. This interior speaking is described with only indirect reference to the sacrament.

• 30:4 prays that upon receiving the sacramental tokens, the quickening movement of the Spirit may be felt.

• In 53:3.1–2, God is asked, 'Come in thy Spirit down' and 'crown' (fulfil) Jesus' instituting act. *Anamnesis* leads to *epiclesis*.

• The couplet which ends the first stanza of Hymn 64 summarises the divine–human relation that is brought about by Christ and the Spirit and enacted in the sacrament: 'God for Jesu's Sake forgives/ Man by Jesu's Spirit lives.'

• In Hymn 71, Wesley says that the sacrament does not act automatically, but 'Thro' Faith we on his Body feed;/ Faith only doth the Spirit convey.' The Spirit is given only through faith; but through faith the Spirit is given.

• In Hymn 76 the Holy Spirit is not expressly named, and some verbal touches suggest that the hymn is addressed to the Father or to Christ. It describes God doing an inward work, and it mentions functions and gifts of the Spirit: faith, repentance, joy, purity of heart, peace. 'Thy blessing in thy means convey.'

• Lines 77:3.5–6, 'Now [now, in the sacrament] the Gracious Spirit shed,/ Fill us now with Love Divine' are a prayed version of Romans 5.5, 'The love of God is shed abroad in our hearts by the holy Ghost, which is given unto us.'

• In the prayer of 88:3, God is asked at the Holy Communion to

---

* *realize:* in an objective sense: 'make real', 'actualise'.

'breathe the loving filial Spirit into my waiting heart'. Wesley follows Paul's thought about 'the Spirit of adoption' from Romans 8.5, 'For ye have not received the spirit of bondage again to fear: but ye have received the spirit of adoption, whereby we cry, Abba, father.' It is by the Spirit acting inwardly that believers are made to know that they are children of God.

• Hymn 150 asks the Father that the Spirit through which the Son offered himself may be bestowed on waiting communicants so that they may present themselves to God and obey God's will completely. As the saving action was through the Spirit, the human response too is by the Spirit.

• Hymn 151, which speaks of the Christian's self-sacrifice at the Holy Communion, says that only by the divine 'Spirit of contrition' can communicants recognise their own sins and bring them to die on Jesus' cross.

Even though Wesleyan eucharistic theology and these sacramental hymns give a substantial presentation of the Holy Spirit, curiously, in the Prayer Book that John Wesley prepared for the American Methodists in 1784, he repeated the eucharistic prayer of the 1662 Prayer Book, taking no advantage of the occasion to reintroduce an epiclesis into the consecration prayer.

*   *   *

Love and Sacramental Experience

Love is a repeated emphasis in the doctrine and spirituality of *Hymns on the Lord's Supper*. The word 'love' appears more than 120 times, falling especially in Part II, where it occurs 61 times and in 43 of the 65 hymns.

The reality of love occupies a strategic place in the structure of the hymns, suggesting its place in Wesley's thought. 'Love' often falls in the first or the last stanza, and in more than a dozen hymns it is the final word, suggesting the ultimacy of love. All arises from love, communicates love and culminates in love.

The Lord's Supper is a place where love meets love, and Wesley does speak, albeit infrequently, of human love for God. Sinners, he says, may come to love Jesus (21:2.6). He speaks of the believer's 'tears of humblest love' (21:8.2), of 'fervent love' (29:3.4), and of a communicant's 'rapturous joy and love and praise' (93:1.10).

However, the love of which Wesley principally speaks in *Hymns on the Lord's Supper* is God's or Christ's love. God is the 'God of truth and love' (53:1.1). The saving divine actions bespeak the 'amazing mystery of love' (36:1.1; 83:1.5). Faith is to be as firm as God's 'unshaken love' (5:3.2). Wesley identifies the sacrament as the place in which, amidst the ambiguities of ordinary life, believers, with wonder, encounter 'Love, unbounded Love' (36:2.2). The eucharistic elements are 'tokens of his [Christ's] love' (12:2.3). The sacrament is a 'memorial of his love' (54:1.2). Communicants feed on Christ's 'forgiving Love' (70.4). Wesley seeks in the sacrament a disclosure of Christ: 'Now, Saviour, now thyself reveal,/ And make thy Nature known' (30:3.1–2); and through this sacrament of mercy, it is made clear that 'God and love are one' (29:4.4). The sacrament brings 'thy love into our hearts' (31:3.2). In the Supper, an inner witness attests 'that God is perfect Love' (75:4.4). Wesley is confident that in the Lord's Supper the seeker can find assurance that God loves and is love. 'In the means thy love enjoined/ Look we for thy richest love' (63:2.5–6).

While the word 'love' can be a noun or the verb 'to love', in the sacramental hymns, in all but a very few instances, Wesley uses 'love' as a noun. However, 'love', as a substantive, does not define itself. Wesley sets the term in phrases which associate it with qualifiers. The love that is demonstrated in the gospel is shown too in the sacrament of 'love divine' (36:4.4; 55:1.3; 57:1.1; 58:3.4; 77:3.6; 78:11.2; 92:8.4). It is 'unexampled love' (21:1.1), 'love ever new' (21:1.8), 'seraphic love' (21:6.7), 'glorious love' (21:9.6), 'sanctifying love' (32:2.1), 'love, unbounded love' (36:2.2), 'tremendous love' (45:1.1), 'everlasting love' (50:1.1; 81:3.8; 102:3.8), 'his closest love' (60:1.3), 'all-sufficient love' (65:4.4), 'thy faithfulness and love' (66:2.1), 'holy love' (85:2.3), 'amazing love' (135:1.1), God's 'bounteous love' (153:2.4). It is free, unlimited, and it comes from the other side. Christians are embraced with the arms of divine love (47:2.5). Divine love cannot be accounted for by something more ultimate than itself; it is 'Love, mere causeless Love' (36:2.2). It is the way of love to impart itself, and Christians can by grace begin to live 'and breathe the Breath of Love Divine' (36:4.4).

Love, as Wesley sees it, is centrally demonstrated or defined by the cross. He emphasises the sacrificial character of love by speaking of Christ's (or sometimes he has Christ speak of 'my') 'dying love', as: 'O the length, and breadth, and height,/ And depth of dying love!' (102:1.1–2). (The expression 'dying love' is also used in: 1:2.4, 5.5; 13:1.17; 20:2.3; 45:2.12; 71:2.1; 118:2.5; 137:2.4; 158:1.3; 165:4.20.) Similarly, Wesley speaks twice of Christ's 'expiring love' (80:4.6; 166:2.4), and he mentions

Jesus' (or has Jesus speak of 'my') 'bleeding love' (20:1.1; 90:1.2; 162:1.6).

The love of which Wesley speaks is active; it transforms flawed and otherwise hopeless human life. He describes its redemptive power, speaking of 'pardoning love' (14:1.4; 47:1.6; 59:3.2; 69:2.6; 76:3.2; 112:1.7), 'thy healing love' (58:5.4), 'thy forgiving love' (70:1.4; 119:3.2), 'thy quickening love' (44:3.5), or 'sanctifying love' (32:2.1). The love of which he sings brings sight to the blind and life to those who had been closed in death. The communicant confesses, 'Thy Love alone my Soul can cure' (80:4.5).

Wesley mentions 'perfect love' seven times (31:3.6; 33:4.2; 35:3.4; 38:1.4; 64:2.6; 75:4.4; 164:8.4), often asking that we may 'prove' (demonstrate) God's perfect love. The expression 'perfect love', as it was used by the Wesleys and their followers, spoke of both forgiveness and sanctification. This divine 'perfect love' is self-imparting or shared. The Wesleys' understanding of Christian perfection or entire sanctification was only developing when these hymns were written. (In fact, it never came to a clear formulation. There seem to have been differences between John and Charles on the matter; John appears to have expressed himself differently about it at different times; and the later Methodist movement interpreted the theme variously.) In these hymns, one should probably not look for a specific meaning for the phrase, but rather understand it through overtones of gift and ideal. Perfect love is given in grace. The Wesleys thought of sanctification more as gift than as achievement; thus perfect love is or can be demonstrated in human lives which are captured by it and drawn by it into holiness.

While Wesley speaks often of love, it seems noteworthy that he speaks of it as sparingly as he does. (He seldom uses the word more than once in a single hymn.) The reality of love is the final, irreducible cause of both divine redemption and human response. It is the central reality of the cross and of the sacrament of the cross. 'Love' is a word of one syllable, and Wesley's verse is heavily comprised of short words. These hymns are occasioned by a banquet of love, and references to love could easily have become facile or predictable. Yet Wesley does not overuse the word nor overwork the theme.

Part III

The Sacrament a Pledge of Heaven

In the Holy Communion, faithful Christians are engaged with the decisive redemptive moment in the past, and they are engaged now with the living Christ – the themes of Parts I and II. Wesley turns in Part III to say that the sacrament also puts believers in touch with their promised future. He will speak of the Lord's Supper as 'a pledge of heaven'.

The orientation of the Lord's Supper to the future traces to its very institution. The thought world of Jesus and the gospels was pervaded by eschatology; in Jesus the Christ, final things had intersected history. His mission was the inauguration of the age to come. He often described the kingdom of God as a banquet or a marriage feast, an image which Christians from the first generations connected naturally with the Church's sacral meal. In the synoptic accounts of the Last Supper, Jesus pointed from his final meal with his disciples to the ultimate meal in the kingdom of God (Matthew 26.29; Mark 14.25; Luke 22.14–18). Writing in the earliest Christian decades, Paul says that the Supper which looks to a past death looks also to a future coming; it proclaims 'the Lord's death *until he comes*' (1 Corinthians 11.26). Alan Richardson says of the sacrament as it is presented in the New Testament, 'It makes not only the past but also the future a present reality. That is to say, it is not a mere looking forward to something which shall be, any more than it is a mere looking back to events long ago. It is the holding of past and future in the 'now' of faith.'[1] In some early and Eastern liturgies, in the *anamnesis* of the eucharistic prayer the Church 'remembers' Christ's future coming in glory.

However, as sacramental doctrine, liturgy and spirituality developed in the West, the eschatological aspect of the eucharist received diminished attention. Discussion of the Holy Communion came to centre around questions of presence and sacrifice. What happens in the sacrament now? At what point and by what instrumentality does it happen? And how does what happens now in the eucharist relate to the event of the cross? These are questions on which both Brevint and Wesley have something to say. But when each of them devotes a substantial section of his work to the sacrament as a pledge of heaven – a present act which claims the future – they enter in their thought structure a largely original emphasis. Paul Sanders remarked that 'The Wesleyan Eucharistic hymns . . . revived the eschatological note that had been missing in Western liturgies from earliest centuries.'[2]

As the eucharist looks back to an accomplished salvation, it also looks forward to an ultimate salvation promised, but waiting to be achieved. Behind the hymns of Wesley's Part III as well as the corresponding pages of Brevint's Section V, there stands the biblical conviction that, through the Holy Spirit, the powers of the age to come impinge on a believer's present. A 'now' stands in tension with a 'not yet' (1 John 3.2), and the sacrament is a place of waiting. 'We now are at his table fed,/ But wait to see our Heavenly King' (93.1.5–6).

The Sacrament as Pledge

Wesley had already suggested that the sacrament is a foretaste of heaven, but in Part III he develops the theme specifically and fully. The Holy Communion, he says, gives us all that our souls can hold in this life, but it promises more. Its present joy bears us on to glory and bliss:

1   Whither should our full Souls aspire
          At this transporting Feast?*
    They never can on Earth be higher,
          Or more completely blest.

2   Our Cup of Blessing from above
          Delightfully runs o'er,
    Till from these Bodies they remove
          Our Souls can hold no more.

3   To Heav'n the Mystic Banquet leads,
          Let us to Heaven ascend,
    And bear this Joy upon our Heads
          Till it in Glory end:

---

* *this transporting Feast:* a feast which carries one beyond ordinary life and to another realm.

4   Till all who truly join in This,
     The Marriage-Supper share,
Enter into their Master's Bliss
     And feast for ever there. (99)

Wesley here draws on Brevint, who had said that the rich blessings of the
sacrament anticipate future blessings which exceed those of the present
'as the glory we hope for exceeds the small degree of grace which we
possess' (V.1).

Brevint develops the ideas of 'earnest' and of 'pledge'. An *earnest*, he
says, is a part payment of things which will be held permanently – as
zeal, charity and holiness, which are gained through the sacrament, will
be forever retained. A *pledge* too, he says, points forward, but it is taken
back when the reality to which it leads is gained – as the sacraments will
end when the reality of which they speak is attained. 'But till that day' he
says, 'the holy Communion [stands as] . . . a pledge and assurance from
the Lord, that in his good time he will crown us with everlasting happiness' (V.2). 'The body and blood of Jesus, is in *full value*, and heaven
with all its fullness is, in *sure title*, instated on true Christians by those
small portions which they receive at the blessed Communion' (V.8). The
past, present and future references of the sacrament are to 'one and the
same glory' (V.6).

Wesley develops his thought along Brevint's lines, saying that the
departed Saviour has left behind a 'sacramental pledge', which the
Church will cherish, showing forth his death until he returns in the clouds.
Christians plead 'Come quickly.' The anticipatory pledge will be ended
when Christ receives his people into heaven:

1   Returning to his Throne above
         The Friend of Sinners cried,
     Do this in Mem'ry of my Love;
         He spoke the Word, and died.

2   He tasted Death for every One,
         The Saviour of Mankind
     Out of our Sight to Heaven is gone,
         But left his Pledge behind.

3   His Sacramental Pledge we take,
         Nor will we let it go;
     Till in the Clouds our Lord comes back
         We thus his Death will show. (100)

Wesley often describes the sacrament as a *pledge* (95:3.2; 101:4.1; 103:2.3; 107:1.5) and as an *earnest* (94:3.3, 4.1; 97:1.7; 103:2.3; 103:2.2). He uses less often the terms *title* (103:2.1), *type* (107:1.5), *emblem* (108:2.1) and *token* (100:5.2; 111:3.1; 114:7.2). These images are not distinct, and this vocabulary often falls together.

> *Title* to Eternal Bliss
>   Here his precious Death we find,
> This the *Pledge* the *Earnest* This
>   Of the purchas'd Joys behind. (103:2.1–4)*

> Communion of thy Flesh and Blood,
>   Sure *Instrument* thy Grace to gain,
> *Type* of the Heavenly Marriage-Feast,
>   *Pledge* of our Everlasting Rest. (107:1.3–6)

> For all that Joy which now we taste
>   Our happy *hallow'd* Souls prepare,
> O let us hold the *Earnest* fast,
>   This *Pledge* that we thy Heaven shall share,
> Shall drink it New with Thee above
> The Wine of thy Eternal Love. (108:2)

Hymn 94 describes with quiet expressiveness the combination of past, present and future in the life of faith.

> 1   O What a Soul-transporting Feast
>   Doth this Communion yield!
>   Remembering here thy Passion past   .
>   We with thy Love are fill'd.

> 2   Sure Instrument of present Grace
>   Thy Sacrament we find,
>   Yet higher blessings it displays,
>   And Raptures still behind.

The third stanza describes a two-way movement; the sacrament carries communicants upward, and at the same time it brings God to communicants.

---

* *Joys behind:* the joys to follow.

3   It bears us now on Eagles Wings,
      If Thou the Power impart,
    And Thee our glorious Earnest brings
      Into our Faithful Heart.

4   O let us still the Earnest feel,
      Th' unutterable Peace,
    This Loving Spirit be the Seal,
      Of our Eternal Bliss! (94)

The present love and peace which the Spirit gives are the earnest of
promised eternal joy.

In another brief hymn, Wesley begins by saying that the Holy
Communion gives now all the benefits of Jesus' passion:

1   Take, and eat, the Saviour saith.
      This my sacred Body is!
    Him we take and eat by Faith,
      Feed upon that Flesh of his.
    All the Benefits we receive
      Which his Passion did procure,
    Pardon'd by his Grace we live,
      Grace which makes Salvation sure.

A second stanza advances the thought, saying that the sacrament is also a
promise. What it gives now is a taste of what will be given:

2   Title to Eternal Bliss
      Here his precious Death we find,
    This the Pledge the Earnest This
      Of the purchas'd Joys behind:
    Here He gives our Souls a Taste,
      Heaven into our Hearts He pours;
    Still believe, and hold him fast,
      GOD and CHRIST and All is Ours! (103)*

---

* One notes the alliteration in this hymn: the 's' sounds in lines 1.1–2; the 'f' sounds in
1.3–4; the 'p's in 1.6–7; the 'p's in 2.2–4; the 'h's in 2.5–6; these sounds tend to fall on accented
syllables.

Support for the Journey

The Supper of the Lord, Wesley emphasises, not only promises a heavenly destination, it also provides support as one moves towards it: 'Strengthen'd by this immortal food,/ O let us reach the Mount of God' (113:2.1–2, also 110). The bliss, the joy, the rapture, the weight of glory are too much for our natural capacities, 'Flesh and blood shall not receive/ The vast inheritance.' But here, in their childhood, believers grow up into Christ, and are made 'ripe for heaven' and 'strong to bear the joys above' (102). Wesley found this emphasis in Brevint, who had said: 'Till we grow to that stature as may fit us to bear up that weight of eternal glory, we are neither of age to enjoy our inheritance, nor of ability to manage well that great estate' (V.5).

Thinking along these lines, Wesley prays:

> Give us, O LORD, the Children's Bread,
> By Ministerial Angels fed,
>   (The Angels of thy Church below)
> Nourish us with preserving Grace
> Our forty Years or forty Days,
>   And lead us thro' the Vale of Woe. (113:1.1–6)

Christians need food suited to their immaturity. Wesley's lines follow Brevint, who had asked:

> O that in the strength of this [sacramental] meat, I may walk, as Elijah did, my forty days, or as Israel, my forty years, and come at last to that holy mountain, where, without the help of any bread, or the ministry of any angels, I shall see my God face to face. Eternal, and blessed, and blessing Spirit of God! bless me now, and help me to drink so worthily of this fruit of the vine, that I may drink it new in the kingdom of my Father. (V.11)

Wesley is drawn to the theme of the continuity between earth and heaven:

> The Holy to the Holiest leads,
>   From hence our Spirits rise,
> And He that in thy Statutes treads
>   Shall meet Thee in the skies. (96:4)

Wesley's line 'The Holy to the Holiest leads' is clarified by the passage from Brevint which suggested it, 'In the real purpose of God, his Church and Heaven go both together: that being the way that leads to this, as the Holy Place [leads] to the Holiest' (V.3). Brevint observes that one could not enter the Holy of Holies except through the Holy Place; the holiest place and the way to it were both holy.

Symbols of Heaven

In seeking to depict any life other than the familiar life of place, time and circumstance, a poet or visionary must use symbolic speech. Wesley takes his symbols of heaven almost exclusively from the Bible – from Jesus' eschatological sayings in the gospels, from Paul's apocalyptic passages, and from the book of Revelation. He does not seek to press beyond these strong, elemental, but reticent biblical symbols. The Wesleys and their age were distrustful of mysticism and speculation. Charles no doubt thought that the biblical pictures of heaven were God-given and that they say all that needs to be said on the matter, or all that, under the conditions of this present life, can be said.

Writing when monarchy was an organising factor both for political life and for the world-picture that one inhabited, Wesley freely used the regal imagery he found in his sources, speaking of 'seeing our heavenly king . . . in yonder dazzling courts above' (93:1.6f., 2.3), of a 'palace of the skies' (97:2.7), a 'dazzling throne' (105:1.4; 106:2.5, 4.1), and of God's 'upper [heavenly] courts' (110:2.1). Through grace the status of royalty is shared by believers, who reign with Christ (97:2.8; 104:1.4) and are 'crowned with glory and gladness' (95:3.4). The saints stand before the Saviour carrying in their hands palms of victory and wearing crowns of royalty (105:1). They are 'more than conquerors at last' (106:3.1).

In Wesley's time only a few people lived in economic security, and many struggled with scarcity and hunger. From this setting, Wesley follows the eschatological parables of Jesus and the depictions of the age to come in the Jewish scriptures, describing heaven as a place of plenty – of eating and drinking, of tasting, and of banqueting:

> The Wine which doth his Passion shew,
> We soon with Him shall drink it New
>   In yonder dazzling Courts above,
> Admitted to the Heavenly Feast
> We shall his choicest Blessing taste,
>   And banquet on his richest Love. (93:2.1–6; also 94)

Describing the sacrament as a heavenly feast, Wesley says:

> Our Cup of Blessing from above
>   Delightfully runs o'er,
> Till from these Bodies they remove
>   Our Souls can hold no more. (99:2)

This rich sensory picture of abundance is, of course, being used symbolically, for as Wesley makes clear, the food of the divine banquet is 'his [Christ's] richest love' and 'the wine of thy eternal love' (93:2.6; 108:2.6; and see 112:2.8).

Both Wesley's theme and the terms in which he expressed it had a model close at hand in Isaac Watts' hymns for the Holy Communion, where he described the Lord's Supper in warmly expressed lines such as, 'where the fresh springs of pleasure rise' (5:2.3), and 'new blessings flow, a sea of joy without a shore' (22:4.3–4). In one stanza Watts had said, 'On earth is no such sweetness found,/ For the Lamb's flesh is heavenly food;/ In vain we search the globe around/ For bread so fine, or wine so good' (18:3).

The image of the marriage feast of the Lamb, which is announced but not described in Revelation 19.6–10, attracted Wesley, and he mentions it often. 'Even now the Marriage-Feast we share' (93:4.2). 'We . . . here begin by faith to eat/ The Supper of the Lamb' (97:2.3–4). But Wesley, like the Apocalypse, lets the picture stand undeveloped (93:2.8–12; 99:4.2; 100:4.4; 107:1.5; 111:2.6; 114:7.4).

Drawing on Revelation 21.2–4, Wesley depicts heaven as the end of suffering and sorrow (93:4.7ff.; 95:3.3; 106:4.5–8). Believers will be led to 'springs of living comfort' (93:4.6), where they will find 'unutterable peace' (94:4.2) and dwell in eternal light, rapture, joy and bliss (94:4.4; 99:4.3; 102:1.7–8; 103:2.1).

Heaven can only be suggested by comparisons. Wesley, in Hymn 101, draws on light and on water, saying that the joys we know in this life are to the joys of the life to come as our feeble lamps are to the sun or as a drop is to the sea. Meanwhile, 'this Divine Communion' gives a foretaste.

1 How glorious is the Life above
       Which in this Ordinance we *taste*;
    That Fulness of Celestial Love,
       That Joy which shall for ever last!

2   That heavenly Life in CHRIST conceal'd
       These earthen Vessels could not bear,
    The Part which now we find reveal'd
       No Tongue of Angels can declare.

3   The Light of Life Eternal darts
       Into our Souls a dazzling Ray,
    A Drop of Heav'n o'reflows our Hearts,
       And deluges the House of Clay.

4   Sure Pledge of Extacies unknown
       Shall this Divine Communion be,
    The Ray shall rise into a Sun,
       The Drop shall swell into a Sea. (101)

Wesley, writing from a busy life, set in a busy age, speaks of heaven as rest. The image has biblical roots in the divine rest on the seventh day of creation, in the law of the Sabbath, and in the land of promise which ended Israel's wandering in the wilderness. It is developed Christologically in Hebrews 3—4. The sacrament looks beyond itself; we who feed now on the 'living bread' at the Supper and are nourished and preserved by it 'feel the earnest in our hearts/ Of our eternal rest' (97:1–2; 98:8.4). 'These mysteries' are a 'pledge of our everlasting rest' (107:1.6).

Heaven as Praise

Heaven, as Wesley the hymn-writer sees it, is a realm of 'rapturous joy and love and praise' (93:1.10). It will be the fulfilment of the most heaven-like activity in which one can engage in this life, singing the glory of God (113:2.4).

Hymn 96 celebrates the unity between the Church in heaven ('they') and the Church now on earth ('we'). Earth and heaven are joined as, through praise, 'we find our heaven on earth begun' (1.4).

The Church triumphant in thy Love
    Their mighty Joys we know,
They sing the Lamb in Hymns above,
    And we in Hymns below.

Thee in thy glorious Realm they praise,
    And bow before thy Throne,
We in the Kingdom of thy Grace,
    The Kingdoms are but One. (96:2–3)

The theme and organisation of the hymn trace to Brevint's remark that the consecrated bread exhibits the Lord's body for our use on earth, but beyond that, 'as to our happiness in heaven, bought with the price of this body, it [the eucharistic bread] is the most solemn instrument to assure our title to it' (V.6).

In a panoramic hymn (105), Wesley describes the heavenly song shared between saints and angels. The saints are seen and heard first, and the morning stars respond:

> 1 Lift up your Eyes of Faith and see
>   Saints and Angels join'd in One,
>   What a countless Company
>   Stands before yon dazzling Throne!
>   Each before his Saviour stands,
>   All in Milk-white Robes array'd,
>   Palms they carry in their Hands,
>   Crowns of Glory on their Head.
>
> 2 Saints begin the endless Song,
>   Cry aloud in heavenly Lays
>   Glory doth to GOD belong,
>   GOD the glorious Saviour praise,
>   All from Him Salvation came,
>   Him who reigns enthron'd on high,
>   Glory to the bleeding Lamb
>   Let the Morning Stars reply.

The angels, who are next in glory to the saints, are first silent as they fall prostrate around the heavenly throne. Then they too begin to sing:

> 3 Angel-powers the Throne surround,
>   Next the Saints in Glory They,
>   Lull'd with the transporting Sound
>   They their silent Homage pay,
>   Prostrate on their Face before
>   GOD and his MESSIAH fall,
>   Then in Hymns of Praise adore,
>   Shout the Lamb that died for All.

The final stanza is the full heavenly doxology as 'all our orders' join in praise. The great 'Amen' ('be it so') of heaven sounds (4.1; see Revelation 5.14):

4   Be it so, They all reply;
        Him let all our Orders praise.
    Him that did for Sinners die,
        Saviour of the favour'd Race,
    Render we our GOD his Right,
        Glory, Wisdom, Thanks and Power,
    Honour, Majesty and Might,
        Praise Him, praise Him evermore! (105)

This hymn, which is based on the sustained vision of the liturgy of heaven
in Revelation 4—7, contains no express reference to the sacrament, but
clearly, Wesley, following ancient tradition, thinks of the Holy Communion as a festal act in which heaven touches earth and communicants
join 'with Angels and Archangels and with all the company of heaven'.

Heaven Now

A recurrent theme of these hymns is that heaven is not only future, it is
present. The sacrament is not only a pledge of heaven to come, it brings
heaven here and now. 'By faith and hope [we are] already there/ Ev'n
now the Marriage-Feast we share' (93:4.1–2). Those who celebrate their
faith are joined with the song of the angels and of the Church triumphant
(96), and they taste now the bread of heaven. 'How glorious is the life
above,/ Which in this ordinance we *Taste*' (101:1.1–2; also 103:2.5–6;
108). In a hymn in Part V Wesley describes the Holy Communion as 'our
heaven begun below' (158:2.4).

Wesley's presentism works in two ways: The Supper brings heaven
near, and it transports the communicants to heaven itself. As the hymns
of Part I could speak of 'yonder cross', in these hymns the speaker points
to 'yon dazzling throne' (105:1.4). At the Holy Communion, the believing communicants, like the seer who was 'in the Spirit on the Lord's Day'
(Revelation 1.10), see the sights and hear the sounds of heaven itself. The
sacrament is a present actualisation of heaven at which communicants
'begin by faith to eat/ The supper of the Lamb' (97:2.3–4). 'Here He gives
our Souls a Taste,/ Heaven into our Hearts He pours' (103:2.5–6).

We have noted that in the exuberant hymns of Part III Wesley describes
the sacrament as a banquet table, a splendid feast. 'Our Cup of Blessing
from above/ Delightfully runs o'er' (99:2.1–2). He speaks of heaven as
'rapturous joy and love and praise' (93:1.10). The word 'joy' appears
in the first hymn and the last hymn of Part III and in 11 others. Heaven

is joy, and the way to heaven is joy. Wesley says all he can to suggest 'a happy, whole eternity' (113:2.6).

Hymn 109

Although Hymn 109 derives from Wesley's consecutive following of Brevint, it seems to have little connection with the theme of Part III. Its tone of entreaty sets it apart from the generally exultant hymns of this section. It is the only first-person hymn in Part III. Wesley's view of heaven is collective; he, like the New Testament, describes heaven in corporate terms, for it is the consummation not so much of one's personal desires, as of the Redeemer's ultimate purposes. The glory of heaven, as Wesley sees it, is a shared glory. Hymn 109 is not only exceptional; it is full of interest:

1 LORD, Thou knowest my Simpleness,*
    All my groans are heard by Thee,
   See me hungring after Grace,
    Gasping at thy Table see,
   One who would in Thee believe
   Would with Joy the Crumbs receive.

2 Look as when thy closing Eye
    Saw the Thief beside thy Cross;
   Thou art Now gone up on high,
    Undertake my desperate Cause,
   In thy Heavenly Kingdom Thou
   Be the Friend of Sinners Now.

3 Saviour, Prince, enthron'd above,
    Send a peaceful answer down,
   Let the Bowels of thy Love**
    Echo to a Sinner's Groan,
   One who feebly thinks of Thee
   Thou for Good remember me.

A communicant comes to the sacrament humble, burdened and hungry – ready to receive with joy even the crumbs from the table (stanza 1).

---

* *my Simpleness:* my unaffectedness, my sincerity.

** *the Bowels of thy Love:* In an old usage, 'bowels' referred to the seat of tender feeling or compassion. The term could be used of God as well as of human beings; see the note on Hymn 82 in Part II, p. 116.

The reigning Christ is asked to look with compassion on the pleading speaker, as he had on the thief at the cross, and to 'be the friend of sinners now'. Wesley draws his tone, ideas, and several of his expressions from Brevint's prayer at the end of Section V: 'O Lord! thou knowest my simpleness, my groaning is not hid from thee; look on a poor sinner at thy table, as thou didst on him who hung by thy cross. O Lord my God! remember me now, when thou art come into thy kingdom' (V.11). (Brevint's words, 'My groaning is not hid from thee' allude to Psalm 38.9.)

The Sacrament and the Final Events

At the Supper, a believer is not only transported to heaven, a realm of fulfilment and joy, but in it one encounters now the end events. This emphasis is not a convention of eucharistic piety, and it owes nothing to Brevint. The communicant is brought before the apocalyptic coming of Christ and the final judgement. The sacrament places one now in the presence of history's finalities.

Just as in Part I Wesley recreated the crucifixion scene and placed communicants at the cross where they beheld (indeed, participated in) Jesus' passion, in Part III he draws on biblical apocalyptic, placing the devout communicant at the return of Christ, the last judgement, and the ushering in of the final age. He speaks in event-images: the archangel's voice, the trumpet of God, heaven and earth fleeing away, and Christ's triumphant coming (93:3).

In Hymn 98, which is particularly full of apocalyptic terms, Wesley refers to disruptions in nature and to the Great White Throne of judgement:

3   He whom we remember here,
     CHRIST shall in the clouds appear,
     Manifest to every Eye,
     We shall soon behold Him nigh.

4   Faith ascends the Mountain's Height,
     Now enjoys the pompous Sight,*
     Antedates the Final Doom,**
     Sees the Judge in Glory come.

---

 * *pompous:* ceremonious, stately.
 ** *Antedates:* anticipates, experiences beforehand.

5   Lo, He comes triumphant down,
     Seated on his great White Throne!
     Cherubs bear it on their Wings,
     Shouting bear the King of Kings.

6   Lo, his glorious Banner spread
     Stains the Skies with deepest Red,
     Dies the Land, and fires the Wood,
     Turns the Ocean into Blood. (98)

The image in stanza 5 of the enthroned Christ descending borne on the wings of cherubim seems to derive from the 'Cherubic Hymn', which in the Byzantine liturgy is sung at the Great Entrance (the bringing in of the Holy Gifts): 'We who mystically represent the Cherubim, sing the Thrice-holy Hymn to the life-giving Trinity. Let us put away all worldly care, so that we may receive the King of All, invisibly escorted by the Angelic Hosts. Alleluia.'[3]

The harsh imagery of nature in turmoil in stanza 6 seems to have been suggested by the apocalyptic description of the consequences of the sounding of the six trumpets of judgement in Revelation 8.7—9.21 (which in turn is based on the plagues of Egypt).

Wesley taps several times in Part III the apocalyptic imagery of 1 Thessalonians 4.13–15 in which Paul pictures Christ appearing in the clouds, manifest to every eye (98:3–4; 100:3.3; 115:2.5). Having come for his followers, Christ conducts them to heaven (100:4.5; 104:1.6; 110:3.6), where the gates are flung open for them (93:3.10–12). The eucharist is, as Richardson puts it, 'the anticipation of the future deliverance of the *parousia* and the inauguration of the new creation'.[4]

In a remarkable emphasis, when Wesley says that faith 'antedates the final doom' (98:4.3) he means that at the sacrament the communicant is present beforehand at the final judgement. The sacrament makes present to faith the redemptive crisis of Jesus' death, but also the vindicating and judging crisis of Jesus' return. By this eschatological symbolism Wesley unites, at least implicitly, redemption and the eucharist with universal history and its consummation – 'the dreadful joyful day' towards which time moves and which waiting believers have already encountered.

In these hymns that are concerned with the end things Wesley seldom mentions judgement and does not speak of hell at all. The character of at least some biblical imagery would suggest severity in depicting history's ultimacies, and in John Wesley's *Journal* he often mentions that he had preached about 'where the worm dieth not and the fire is not quenched'.

But Charles Wesley's terms concerning final things are overwhelmingly positive. The line in which he says that the sacrament 'antedates the final doom' (98:4.3) may be the only place in Part III in which his look ahead expresses an ominous tone. His heaven is the sight of the Saviour and the sound of 'praise and love and joy' (113:2).

The cosmic finalities of which Wesley speaks – the disruption of nature, the radical judgement and overthrow of world order, the vindication of the faithful – are imaginative themes that would test the powers of a Milton. Yet Wesley writes in popular ballad form and in rhymed, neo-classical stanzas and singable meters. A critical reader may judge that as he describes this awesome theme, his forms sometimes seem unequal to the subject matter. Yet he did not search for a rhetoric in which to express the intrinsically inexpressible. Indeed, it would have been awkward if he had strained his resources to do what he could not do. When he wrote for his congregations, he tapped deep emotional associations and a powerful myth-structure that was drawn from Scripture and reinforced by preaching, popular devotion and religious art. The power of what he says is released in readers' minds by forceful words and images that he shared with them.

The Waiting Church

At the Holy Communion the Church is expectant, listening and waiting:

> Then let us still in Hope rejoice,
> And listen for th' Archangel's Voice
>   Loud-echoing to the Trump of GOD. (93:3.1–3)

Wesley understands the Supper as a sign for the Church living between the Lord's departure and his return. It is a showing of the Lord's death until he come:

> 1   Returning to his Throne above
>   The Friend of Sinners cried,
>   Do this in Mem'ry of my LOVE;
>   He spoke the Word, and died.
>
> 2   He tasted Death for every One,
>   The Saviour of Mankind
>   Out of our Sight to Heaven is gone,
>   But left his Pledge behind.

3　　His Sacramental Pledge we take,
　　　　Nor will we let it go;
　　Till in the Clouds our LORD comes back
　　　　We thus his Death will show.

4　　Come quickly, LORD, for whom we mourn,
　　　　And comfort all that grieve,
　　Prepare the Bride, and then return
　　　　And to Thyself receive.

5　　Now to thy gracious Kingdom come,
　　　　(Thou hast a Token given)
　　And when thy Arms receive us home
　　　　Recall thy Pledge in heaven. (100)

Wesley's concluding line, 'recall thy pledge in heaven', draws on Brevint's thesis that pledges 'are recalled and taken back' when the reality they secured is actualised. Sacraments anticipate heaven, but heaven removes the need for sacraments:

Sacraments . . . shall not appear more in heaven than did the cloudy pillar [when the Israelites had arrived] in Canaan . . . Certainly we will have no need either of these sacred images of Christ when we shall see Him face to face, or of these pledges to assure us of that glory which is to be revealed, when we actually possess it. (V.2)

Brevint adds (as Wesley also says in stanza 3), 'But till that day, the holy Communion [remains] . . . as pledge and assurance from the Lord, that in His good time he will crown us with everlasting happiness' (V.2).

Hymn 93

The large, imaginative hymn which opens Part III may well be considered at the close of this chapter, for it gathers much of Wesley's thought on the sacrament and the end things.

The hymn opens (as do five others in the collection: Hymns 8, 9, 13, 60 and 142) with the word 'come'. Christians are called to a sacred meal. But while they *now* are fed at Christ's table (1.1–4), at the same time the table is a place of waiting (1.5).

1   Come let us join with one Accord
   Who share the Supper of the LORD,
      Our LORD and Master's Praise to sing,
   Nourish'd on Earth with living Bread
   We now are at his Table fed,
      But wait to see our Heavenly King;
   To see the great Invisible
   Without a Sacramental Veil,
      With all his Robes of Glory on,
   In rapt'rous Joy and Love and Praise
   Him to behold with open Face,
      High on his Everlasting Throne.

At 1.6, terms of feeding pass to terms of seeing. Although communicants share the living bread, they wait to see their heavenly King 'without a sacramental veil'. The sacraments, while they convey Christ, at the same time obscure the direct sight of him; but sacraments will finally be done away, and unimpeded sight will be granted in a vision of 'rapt'rous Joy and Love and Praise'.

In stanza 2 the imagery returns to eating, drinking and tasting; the sacrament is a pledge of the heavenly feast, where 'We shall his choicest blessings taste,/ And banquet on his richest love' (2.5–6). But in its second half (2.7–12) the stanza depicts an imminent encounter with the coming Christ. The lines use Jesus' parable of the bridegroom and the midnight cry of the bridegroom's arrival – which Wesley mixes with the image of the marriage of the Lamb (Revelation 19.6–9). The sacrament anticipates Christ's coming to gather his Church.

2   The Wine which doth his Passion shew,
   We soon with Him shall drink it New
      In yonder dazzling Courts above,
   Admitted to the Heavenly Feast
   We shall his choicest Blessings taste,
      And banquet on his richest Love.
   We soon the Midnight Cry shall hear,
   Arise, and meet the Bridegroom near,
      The Marriage of the Lamb is come,
   Attended by his Heavenly Friends
   The glorious King of Saints descends
      To take his Bride in Triumph home.

Auditory terms continue in stanza 3, where apocalyptic language (drawn from 1 Thessalonians 4.6) speaks of 'the trump of God' at 'the dreadful joyful day' (3.3f.). Similar terms speak of the final ruin of the world (Revelation 20.10f.), from which believers are delivered (3.1–10). While Christians on earth wait for Christ's coming, in heaven he waits for theirs (3.10–12).

3   Then let us still in Hope rejoice,
     And listen for th' Archangel's Voice
       Loud-echoing to the Trump of GOD,
     Haste to the dreadful joyful Day,
     When Heaven and Earth shall flee away
       By all-devouring Flames destroy'd:
     While we from out the Burnings fly,
     With Eagles Wings mount up on high,
       Where JESUS is on *Sion* seen;*
     'Tis there He for our coming waits,
     And lo, the Everlasting Gates**
       Lift up their Heads to take us in!

In stanza 4 the point of view changes. By anticipation, the final, heavenly joy is experienced now, 'By faith and hope [we are] already there, . . . Suffering and curse and death are o'er,/ and pain afflicts the soul no more' (4.1, 7f.). Line 4.9 describes Christians as 'harbour'd in the Saviour's Breast'. Some biblical expressions speak of resting in 'Abraham's bosom' (Luke 16.22f.) or 'on Jesus' breast' (John 13.25; 21.20). But Wesley, writing in seafaring Britain, suggests by a word an image of a vessel coming from the open sea into a safe harbour.

4   By Faith and Hope already there
     Ev'n now the Marriage-Feast we share,
       Ev'n now we by the Lamb are fed,
     Our LORD's celestial Joy we prove,
     Led by the Spirit of his Love,
       To Springs of living Comfort led

---

  * *Sion:* or *Zion*, the name of a hill in Jerusalem which came to be a name for the city itself, and eventually the city became a symbol for heaven (see Revelation 14.1).

  ** *the Everlasting Gates:* In Psalm 24.7–10 the opened gates welcome the king (the Lord, the ark) to the city. Tradition had used the image Christologically, but Wesley turns the words into a welcome of Christians into heaven.

Suffering and Curse and Death are o're,*
And Pain afflicts the Soul no more
     While harbour'd in the Saviour's Breast,
He quiets all our Plaints and Cries,
And wipes the Sorrow from our Eyes,
    , And lulls us in his Arms to rest!

The last lines allude to the final vision of Revelation 21, 'And God shall wipe away all tears from their eyes' (Revelation 21.4). Wesley's hymn, while it is coherent, is a virtual kaleidoscope of biblical pictures of the end – some of them quite harrowing, and some inexpressibly comforting. Through a succession of biblically derived images (more than twenty of them) this hymn links the present sacramental meal with the future heavenly banquet and with the culmination of universal history.

Wesley's deepest expectation for the future (and the one most connected with eucharistic experience) may well be that a believer looks forward to reunion with Christ, who waits for his people's coming as they wait for his. One sees Jesus face to face, without the mediation of sacraments, and lives with him. In a hymn that is not in this collection, but had been published in *Hymns and Sacred Poems*, 1742, Wesley had said, 'Give me thyself . . . thy presence makes my paradise,/ And where thou art is heaven' (Hymn 403 in the 1780 collection). Believers anticipate eating and drinking with Jesus in his kingdom, regaining Christ's image (102:3.1; 111:2.5) and being united with him, 'One Spirit with Himself to make/ Flesh of his flesh, bone of his bone' (114:6.3–4).

The theme of Part III, 'The Sacrament a Pledge of Heaven', is one that Wesley made his own and in which he developed several emphases which have no parallel in Brevint. Paul Sanders said, 'Brevint in his tract, as other Anglicans, alluded to that consummation in heaven of which earthly communion is a foretaste; but the hymns Wesley patterned after Brevint fairly shout the joy of the early Methodists as they realised that in the Sacrament Christians stand where earth and heaven meet.'[5] Brevint had said clearly enough that the sacrament points to 'the glory to come', but he lacked the visual or auditory imagination to depict that glory as Wesley does. Several of the vivid themes of Wesley's Part III – heaven as praise, the song of the saints and angels, the sacrament as heaven now, the sacramental meeting with the end events – owe nothing to Brevint. Moreover, Wesley sets aside unused Brevint's lengthy and somewhat

---

* *and Curse*: The primal curse which is spoken of in the myth of the fall (Genesis 3.14–19) is lifted in the myth of the end (Revelation 22.3), 'and there shall be no more curse'.

dreary discussion of unworthy reception of the sacrament that fills chapters 9–11a of his Section V. While Brevint tells his readers that the Lord's Supper points to glory to come, through his words, one sees nothing and hears very little. Wesley, by contrast, conveys vision and a sense of ecstasy.

> For all that Joy which now we taste
>   Our happy hallow'd Souls prepare,
> O let us hold the Earnest fast,
>   This pledge that we thy Heaven shall share,
> Shall drink it New with Thee above
> The Wine of thy Eternal Love. (108:2)

Part IV

The Holy Eucharist as it Implies a Sacrifice

Thus far both Brevint's essay and Wesley's hymns have spoken of what God shows and gives in the Holy Communion and of what communicants see and receive. When either writer has referred to sacrifice it has been to the sacrifice of Christ, which is remembered and whose benefits are made accessible in the Lord's Supper. Neither author has spoken of the sacrament as being itself in some sense a Christian sacrifice. They turn now to that theme.

Brevint explains the turn, saying that to recall a sacrifice in faith is, in a sense, to make a sacrifice. Referring to a 'commemorative sacrifice', he says, 'The holy Eucharist . . . becomes by our remembrance, a kind of *Sacrifice* also' (VI.3).

Both Brevint and Wesley believe that the Lord's Supper brings Christ powerfully into the Church's 'now'. At the sacrament believers not only think about, but by faith they are drawn into union with Christ crucified and living. Both writers hold that the sacrament is more than something recalled; it is something done, and the doing has the character of sacrifice.

In the large structure of both Brevint's and Wesley's thought, *sacrifice*, as the church's God-ward action, follows from *sacrament*. Life is offered on the basis of prior grace received. Christian sacrifice is response sacrifice. As Ole Borgen put it:

First come the functions of memorial, means of grace, and pledge of glory to come, and only *then* is the element of sacrifice introduced; it is a God-given plea, which no man can present on his own. It is not because Christ's sacrifice is presented to God that grace is received. Because grace . . . has been received the pleading offer can be made.[1]

Although sacrifice is the particular emphasis of Wesley's Part IV, the theme pervades *Hymns on the Lord's Supper*. The word occurs more than fifty times, in all parts of the collection, and if related terms such as 'oblation', 'offer/offering', 'present', 'receive', 'victim' or 'atone/atonement' are included, its incidence is greatly increased.

Several of the hymns that speak of the eucharist as sacrifice are especially dense and compact. When Wesley has entered one idea, another thought that complements the first seems to come to his mind, and he sets it down, often not supplying the transitions between nor clarifying the relations among the things he introduces. His thought is not disordered, but it is compressed. Particularly in this section, ideas set one another in motion and pass rapidly from one into the next.

The 'Grand Oblation'

Wesley will speak often in Part IV of the eucharist as a sacrifice which Christians make. But to set the priorities of his theme he affirms repeatedly the uniqueness, completeness and adequacy of Christ's self-offering on the cross – his 'grand Oblation' (123:3.7). (Half of the references to sacrifice in Part IV are to Christ's sacrifice.) The redemptive death of the Son of God, Wesley says, is alone equal to the sin of the race. He addresses Christ, saying:

> All hail, Redeemer of Mankind!
> Thy Life on *Calvary* resign'd
>   Did fully once for All atone,
> Thy Blood hath paid our utmost Price,
> This all-sufficient Sacrifice
>   Remains eternally alone: (124:1.1–6)

Neither angels nor human beings could supplement Christ's sacrifice, and Christ himself could not repeat it:

> Angels and Men might strive in vain,
> They could not add the smallest Gain
>   T'augment thy Death's Atoning Power,
> The Sacrifice is all-compleat,
> The Death Thou never canst repeat,
>   Once offer'd up to die no more. (124:1.7–12)

Brevint had earlier said that 'for the expiation of sins, it is most certain

that the Sacrifice of Jesus Christ alone hath been sufficient for it' (VI.2).
Wesley concurs: 'Once offer'd up a spotless Lamb/ In thy great temple
here below,/ Thou didst for all mankind atone' (116:1.3–5). 'Jesus Christ,
the Crucified,/ He who did for all atone' (118:1.2–3; also 120:1.3–4;
122:1.2, 7–8). This conviction was based in the New Testament and had
the consent of the Church. All other sacrifices – those of ancient Israel
or those of Christians – take their reality from the Great Sacrifice of the
Son of God. Wesley will say more than this about sacrifice, but nothing
he says will contradict or qualify his affirmation that Christ's redemptive
work is sufficient and complete.

The Heavenly Priesthood and Sacrifice

Accounts of the atonement must ask how a past act, however momen-
tous, can impinge immediately and decisively on a believer's present. Both
Brevint (in his Section II) and Wesley (in his Part I) have cited the power
of remembering to make the past contemporary. Through the eucharist,
a memorial act, the cross is made present to the communicant and the
communicant is set before the cross.

Now both writers go on to say that in the sacrament the Church does
not simply call to mind (in however active a sense of recalling) Christ's
prior act of sacrifice, but in the eucharist the Church itself makes sacrifice.
But how? In what sense? And how does the Church's act relate to Christ's
act?

The symbolic structures by which both Brevint and Wesley deal with
such questions are drawn largely from the New Testament book of
Hebrews, which proposes that Christ's redemptive work, while it was
a specific, unrepeatable act in history, continues. The work of Christ, in
the Christological contour of Hebrews, passes from Jesus' earthly death
to the right hand of God, '[Jesus] who endured the cross, despising the
shame, and is set down at the right hand of God' (Hebrews 12.2). In his
sacramental hymns, Wesley follows the same pattern, saying: 'From the
Cross where once he died/ Now he up to heaven is gone' (118:1.5–6).

In the heavenly sanctuary, the divine Son is the great high priest, offering at the heavenly altar his sacrifice which belongs to an eternal order.

> He ever lives, and prays
>   For all the Faithful Race;
> In the Holiest Place above
>   Sinners Advocate He stands. (118:2.1–4)

Christ's offering of his blood (that is to say, his life) is the effective redemptive sacrifice, not only as an act in history, but also as a continual advocacy carried out in a priesthood which has no end.

> Thou standest in the Holiest Place,
>   As now for guilty Sinners Slain,
> Thy Blood of Sprinkling speaks, and prays
>   All-prevalent for helpless Man,
> Thy Blood is still our Ransom found,
> And spreads Salvation all around. (116:2)[2]

Brevint had put the matter of Christ's continual sacrifice in his own way:

> The Sacrifice of Jesus Christ being appointed by God the Father for a propitiation that should continue throughout all ages, to the world's end; and withal being everlasting by the privilege of its own order – which *is an unchangeable priesthood* (Heb. 7.24), and by his worth who offered it – that is the blessed Son of God, and by the power of the Spirit by whom it was offered – which is the *Eternal Spirit* (Heb. 9.14) . . . it must in all respects stand everlasting and eternal. (II.8)

Showing to the Father

As to how Christ's work is continued, Wesley is clear that Christ's death was a 'once-for-all' act. He speaks of 'the death thou never canst repeat,/ Once offered up to die no more' (124:1.11–12). He says, however, that Christ's death, once accomplished, is everlastingly 'presented' or 'shown' in heaven, where it always speaks for sinners:

> In the Holiest Place above
>   Sinners Advocate He stands,
> Pleads for us his Dying Love,
>   Shews for us his bleeding Hands.
>
> His Body torn and rent
> He doth to GOD present. (118:2.3–3.2)

The continuing activity of the divine Son is his heavenly 'pleading' or 'presenting' of his own unrepeated act in history. And to the Son's ever-presented sacrifice, the Father continually attends: 'Father, behold thy dying Son!' (124:2.7; also 116:4; 118:3–4).

It is a basic part of Wesley's understanding of the Christian eucharist that at the same time that Christ 'shows' his sacrifice in heaven, the Church on earth, in the sacrament, 'shows' or 'presents' Christ's body and blood to the Father. The Church's repeated act is an earthly counterpart of Christ's continuing heavenly self-presentation. In support of this under-standing, Wesley often refers to 1 Corinthians 11.26, where St Paul, speaking about the Lord's Supper, had said, 'As often as ye eat this bread, and drink this cup, ye do show [*katangello*, proclaim, announce] the Lord's death till he come.' (Sometimes Wesley indicates that he has this text in mind only by the significant way in which he uses the word 'show', as: 'Lo! we to thy justice show/ The passion of thy Son', 122:1.3–4.)

> . . . we beneath
>   Present our Saviour's Death,
> Do as Jesus bids us do,
>   Signify his Flesh and Blood,
> Him in a Memorial shew. (118:4.1–5)

St Paul does not say in 1 Corinthians to whom the Lord's death is shown, but presumably he means that in the Supper the Church exhibits Christ's death to the world or to the spiritual powers of the world. Both Brevint and Wesley, however, interpret Paul to say that while in the Supper the Church shows Christ's death to the world, more importantly the Church in the Supper shows Christ's death to the Father. Brevint explains that the apostle's words 'to set forth the death of the Lord' mean 'to set it forth as well before the eyes of God his Father, as before the eyes of all men' (VI.3). John Wesley concurs; in his *Explanatory Notes upon the New Testament* he paraphrases the words 'Ye do show the Lord's death', to say, 'Ye proclaim, as it were, and openly avow it, to God and to all the world, – till he come, in Glory.'[3]

As Charles Wesley puts it, the Church says to God: 'We again to Thee present/ The blood that speaks our sins forgiven' (121:1.8–9); and to Christ it says, 'Yet may we celebrate below,/ And daily thus [in the sacra-ment] thine offering shew/ Expos'd before thy Father's eyes' (124:2.1–3). The Father is asked to turn his eyes 'to the Tokens of his Death/ Here exhibited beneath' (119:3.3–4).

Neither Brevint nor the Wesleys argued this interpretation of Paul or of the sacrament; it had had some currency among seventeenth-century

Church of England writers, and they both took it for granted. Persons who understood 1 Corinthians 11.26 in this way may well have asked: If Christ's death was offered to God, may not the rite in which the Church shows it forth be an act so identified with the reality it represents that it too is an action offered to God?

In addition to 1 Corinthians 11.26, Wesley's conviction that Christ's sacrifice – and, in it, the Church's sacrifice – is directed to God rested heavily on Hebrews, the work which says more than any other New Testament book about the God-ward thrust of Christ's work. (Ephesians 5.2 also speaks of Christ giving himself as a sacrifice to God, but this text is rather isolated and undeveloped.) Christ, as the obedient Son on earth, addressed his work to God; and now as the eternal priest in heaven he still addresses his work to God. When the eucharistic Church offers its life to God, it does so dependently and in union with the self-offering of the obedient divine Son depicted in the book of Hebrews.

Wesley and his Anglican forebears – basing their sacramental doctrine on their reading of Hebrews – understood that the Church's life is carried before God by its heavenly priest and brother. Rowan Williams, summarising the Anglican tradition in the matter, describes the centrality of Christ's personal action in the eucharist: 'The glorified Christ, crucified and risen, is eternally active towards God the Father on our behalf, drawing us into the eternal movement of self-giving love that the Son or Word directs towards the source of all, the God Jesus calls "Abba."'[4] No doubt it seemed to Wesley that when he held that the Church in its eucharist participates in Christ's on-going, god-ward action, he was simply following the teaching of a basic biblical source and a well-established doctrinal tradition.

Yet some close readers urge caution. Wesley, Brevint and the tradition of sacramental thought in which they both stand, in some respects seem to go beyond the New Testament. While Hebrews does speak of Christ as a priest who has made the once-for-all sacrifice and who continually intercedes for his Church (Hebrews 7.25), it does not expressly describe him as 'showing' or 'pleading' his sacrifice before the Father. And, although Hebrews speaks of Christian sacrifices of praise and alms made in Christ's name (13.15–16), it does not say that the Lord's Supper is itself a sacrifice, nor that in it Christians 'present' or 'show' Christ's body and blood before the Father. (Indeed, Hebrews nowhere mentions the Supper. When it says, 'We have an altar', 13.10, it does not refer to a Christian cultic act.) Critics have argued that ideas which are basic in the sacramental theology of Wesley and his Anglican sources have been read into the thought of Hebrews.

Differences in this matter may be to some extent a matter of temperament. While literal-minded persons may question anything in doctrine or in worship that cannot be supported by close biblical exegesis, others, like Wesley, are more poetic and respond to the suggestion and interpenetration of the images of the scriptures. Wesley's doctrinal readings might be thought to combine the intercessory work of the Great High Priest as described in Hebrews (and in Romans 8.34) with the Lamb at the heavenly throne in Revelation, at the same time taking seriously the union between Christ and his people as portrayed in the later New Testament epistles. Both Wesley and Brevint found in the New Testament, as it was interpreted in their tradition, a powerful imaginative construction. It seemed evident to them that the picture of the living, interceding Christ of Hebrews provided the very basis in reality for the Church's eucharist.

The Mediator

Wesley presents the living Christ as deeply associated with the Father:

> FATHER, behold thy fav'rite Son,
> The Glorious Partner of thy Throne,
>   For ever plac'd at thy Right Hand. (121:1.1–3)

Yet the One who is the Father's 'glorious partner' is also one with his people – with 'us who in thy Jesus stand' (121.1.6). As Christ continually offers himself, he acts in, with and for his people. He is the advocate for sinners, presenting himself for them and them with himself:

> For us He ever interceeds,
> His Heaven-deserving Passion pleads
>   Presenting us before the Throne. (117:2.7–9)

Christ does not, however, plead for sinners by spoken words, but by his sacrificial deed, 'Thy blood of sprinkling speaks, and prays' (116:2.3). (Wesley had made this point in Part I.) Christ's blood – 'the blood that speaks our sins forgiven' (121:1.9) – now echoes through the courts of heaven; God sees (or hears) it and accepts believers 'in the Well-belov'd' (121:1.11).

Wesley depicts Christ's mediatorial role in terms of what Christ shows and the Father sees. The Father is asked to look upon Christ, who is one with his Church, and then to see believers – not as the sinners they are, but to see them through Christ:

1 FATHER, GOD, who seest in me
   Only Sin and Misery,
   See thine own Anointed One,
   Look on thy beloved Son.

2 Turn from me thy glorious Eyes
   To that bloody Sacrifice,
   To the full Atonement made,
   To the utmost Ransom paid.

3 To the Blood that speaks above,
   Calls for thy forgiving Love;
   To the Tokens of his Death
   Here exhibited beneath. (119)

The idea and the wording of the hymn come from Brevint, who had prayed: 'O Lord! who seest nothing in me that is truly mine but dust and ashes, and, what is worse, sinful flesh and blood . . . Turn thine eyes . . . to the satisfaction and intercession of thy Son . . . to the seals of covenant which lie before thee upon this table.' Extending Brevint's repeated word 'to', Wesley asks the Father: 'Turn' your eyes *from* me and *to* Jesus' sacrifice, and *to* the 'tokens of his death' which are 'here exhibited', that is, the bread and wine of the eucharist. The hymn ends,

Then thro Him the Sinner see,
Then in Jesus look on Me. (119:4.3–4)

The Human Need

It is Wesley's purpose in Part IV to point to the divine sacrifice, and he only develops the needy human condition as his principal theme requires. (He lays less emphasis on it than he had in Part I.) He speaks of 'sin' and 'guilt', and in Hymn 119, as above, he says: 'Father, God, who seest in me/ Only sin and misery'. He clearly regards human fault as beyond remedy apart from the grace of the Saviour. Yet he does not linger over human contradiction, and he does not blame or condemn.

Hymn 120, however, reads as an anguished expression of self-judgement. The first five lines speak generally about 'guilty man' and 'the sinner'.

1   Father see the Victim slain,
      JESUS CHRIST the Just, the Good,
   Offer'd up for guilty Man,
      Pouring out his precious Blood,
   Him, and then the Sinner see,
   Look thro' JESU's Wounds on Me.

But line 1.6 ends, and line 2.1 begins, with 'me', and from there to the close, the hymn speaks in the first person singular, ending with 'my heart'.

Stanzas 2–3 develop the speaker's 'me', describing the sinner's desolate state: self-accused, despairing, rejecting life itself – dying, although not made for death. Indeed, the speaker is paradoxically 'Dying at my Saviour's side'. The five lines that begin with the word 'dying' give the passage a sustained tone of loss and despair.

2   Me, the Sinner most distrest,
      Most afflicted, and forlorn,
   Stranger to a Moment's Rest,
      Ruing that I e'er was born,
   Pierc'd with Sin's invenom'd Dart,
   Dying of a broken Heart.

3   Dying, whom thy Hands have made
      All thy Blessings to receive,
   Dying, whom thy Love hath stay'd,
      Whom thy Pity would have live,
   Dying at my Saviour's Side,
   Dying for whom CHRIST hath died.

In 4.1 the struggling sinner puts a question to God: Must those who were made for blessing and life end in death? 'Can it be?' Lines 4.2–6 then give the reply that the sinner finds in Jesus' blood, saying: Without Christ I surely die, but if God is mine through Christ, I hear the voice of pardon.

4   Can it, Father, can it be?
      What doth JESU's Blood reply?
   If it doth not plead for me,
      Let my soul for ever die;
   But if mine thro' Him thou art,
   Speak the Pardon to my Heart. (120)

The Church in Christ

For Wesley, the sacramental action of the Church takes its reality from the definitive divine act at Calvary. The Church's sacrifice does not arise from its own initiative; it is a showing or a pleading of Christ's sacrifice, 'Yet may we celebrate below,/ And daily thus thine offering show' (124:2.1–2). Wesley understands Christ to be deeply united with humanity. He is one of the race, yet at the same time, he is a representative person who encloses the race. When the Church shows Christ's body and blood to the Father, it does not act alone, but it participates in the continual self-presentation that Christ, the Priest-Sacrifice, makes to the Father. In the eucharist, the Church receives Christ's sacrifice which was made in behalf of and is continually available for sinful humanity, and it participates in Christ's offering which was made and is being made to the Father.

As the Church presents itself in Christ and Christ in itself to God, it offers what it has first received. The Church has been gathered into the God-ward movement of the Incarnate Lord, crucified and living.

Wesley takes important suggestions concerning the God-ward thrust of the eucharist from Brevint, who had said:

> Christians . . . represent to God the Father the meritorious passion of their Saviour, as the only sure ground whereon both God may give, and they obtain, the blessings they do pray for. . . [In the sacrament] Christians . . . set out [Christ's everlasting sacrifice] solemnly before the eyes of God Almighty . . . *To men*, it is a sacred *table*, where God's minister is ordered to represent from God his master the passion of his dear Son, as still fresh and still powerful for their eternal salvation; and *to God* it [the sacrament] is an *altar* whereon men mystically present to him the same Sacrifice, as still bleeding and still suing for expiation and mercy. (VI.3)

In his deeply considered Hymn 117, Wesley describes Christ in his heavenly work as closely bonded with his people, as they are one with him. Christ is the principal actor in the Church's eucharist. He who once offered himself to God on the cross still 'in this dreadful Mystery' (in the sacrament) offers himself to God (1.1–3). Moreover, Christians are united with him – wrapped in the smoke of his sacrifice and covered with his blood (1.4–6). They are so bound into him that when he presents himself before God, he presents his people with him (1.9–2.6).

1   Thou Lamb that suffer'dst on the Tree,
And in this dreadful Mystery
   Still offer'st up Thyself to GOD,
We cast us on thy Sacrifice,
Wrapt in the Sacred Smoke arise,
   And cover'd with th' Atoning Blood.

Thy Death presented in our Stead
Enters now among the Dead,
   Parts of thy Mystic Body here,
By thy Divine Oblation rais'd,
And on our *Aaron's* Ephod placed
   We now with Thee in Heaven appear.

2   Thy Death exalts thy ransom'd Ones,
And sets us 'midst the precious Stones,
   Closest thy dear thy loving Breast,
Israel as on thy Shoulders stands;
Our Names are graven on the Hands
   The Heart of our Eternal Priest.

For us He ever interceeds,
His Heaven-deserving Passion pleads
   Presenting us before the Throne;
We want no Sacrifice beside,
By that great Offering Sanctified,
   One with our Head, for ever One. (117)

Wesley uses a series of images to describe the identification of Christ's people with him in his sacrifice. They are: a supplemental offering cast on his sacrifice (1.4, a theme which he will develop in Part IV), wrapped in its sacred smoke and covered with its blood (1.5–6), dead in Christ's death (1.7f.), parts of his body (1.9; 2.12), raised and made holy by his sacrifice (1.10; 2.2, 11), named on the high priest's garment and on his hands and heart (1.11–2.6), and spoken for by the heavenly intercessor (1.10–2.9). The last line sums up: 'One with our Head, for ever One.'

Lines 1.11–2.6 introduce without explanation the image of the high priest's ephod: 'On our Aaron's ephod placed/ We now with thee in heaven appear . . . 'midst the precious stones/ Closest thy dear thy loving breast' (1.11–2.3). The ephod is described in Exodus 28.15–30 as an upper garment of blue linen which was part of the high priest's sacred array. Precious stones which were worked into the ephod were engraved with the names of the twelve tribes – names which spoke of all Israel. The ephod signified that when on the Day of Atonement the high priest went in before the Lord to make sacrifice he carried the people with him (Exodus 28.29f.). Wesley says that the living Christ, in his heavenly priestliness, is 'our Aaron', bearing his people when he enters the holy place of the heavenly tabernacle.

In the next hymn Wesley makes an imaginative extension of the image – an extension that might seem half-whimsical, although it is seriously intended. He says that when believers' names are presented on the high priest's garment, the Father reads them:

All our Names the Father knows,
Reads them on our *Aaron's* Breast.

He reads, while we beneath
Present our Saviour's Death. (118:3.5–4.2)

No use is made of the high priest's ephod in the typology of the New Testament. Wesley's image was anticipated in a suggestion by Brevint, who said that Christ's sacrifice 'sets me among the precious stones of Aaron's ephod (Exodus 27), close to the breast, and on the very shoulders of that eternal Priest, whilst He offers up Himself and intercedes for his spiritual Israel' (IV.14; also VII.2). Wesley seems confident that this image would be clear to hymn-singing congregations.

Continual intercession for his people is a part of Christ's eternal priesthood (Hebrews 7.25). He intercedes by his blood, his saving deed, his wounded humanity. His redemptive action done once on earth and continually presented in heaven is his prayer. According to Wesley, Christ does not simply intercede *for* his people as though he and they were separate. Rather, as he presents himself in their behalf, he presents them in union with himself, 'presenting us before the throne' (117:2.9). The divine intercessor does not ask for his people's earthly well-being, but for their forgiveness.

As Wesley sees it, the deep oneness and exchange between Christ and his people is concretised, actualised in the sacrament. The life that was offered in history and is offered continually in heaven is offered repeatedly in the Church's eucharist. In a hymn in Part II he had said, 'Here [in the sacrament] my dearest Lord I see/ Offering up his Death to God' (64:1.2–3). Christ is active in the sacrament, carrying his people towards God. This divine/human stir is complex. The offering to God of Christ is enclosed in the Church's offering, and the offering of the Church's life is enclosed in Christ. Clearly Wesley does not – could not – consider the

Church's offering to be a propitiatory act arising from the human side to secure divine favour. Christ's sacrifice alone redeems. Yet the sacrament, which is the Church's sacrifice, offered in Christ's sacrifice, is effective. It yields the benefits of Christ's redeeming act. The sacrifice of Christ, represented in the sacrament, 'brings thy grace on sinners down' (125:2.5), and any sacrifice the worshipping Church makes is its response in faith and gratitude to the sacrifice it has first received.

> To us Thou hast Redemption sent;
> And we again to Thee present*
>   The Blood that speaks our Sins forgiven. (121:1.7–9)

To speak of the Church's eucharistic action as *response* may not represent Wesley's mind adequately. Both Brevint and Wesley see Christ and his people as sharers in one life. The Church's act of sacrifice, while it is derivative and responsive, should yet be understood, perhaps more profoundly, as its *participation* in Christ's primal sacrifice. Wesley had said earlier, 'Then let our faith . . . in thy great offering join' (3:4.3). As Christ, the high priest, presents his sacrifice to the Father, the priestly Church, in Christ, presents its sacrifice to the Father. But its sacrifice is wrapped, so to speak, in his. Christ acts in the Church's acts, and the Church acts in his. William Temple spoke in the spirit of Charles Wesley when he said, 'Christ in us presents us with himself to the Father.'[5]

The Eucharistic Sacrifice

The hopeless human condition having been met by the grace of the Saviour, Christians gratefully offer their full humanity to God. In Romans 12.1–2 Paul urged his readers, in response to redemption in Christ, to present themselves – their bodies, their concrete, space-and-time existence – to God as a sacrifice. Similarly, prayer and praise are on the basis of Hebrews 13.15–16 to be regarded as Christian sacrifices made in Christ's name. Christians from very early times had spoken of the Church's weekly eucharist as an act which draws together and gives expression to all of their faithful response to God, and hence as having the character of sacrifice. Wesley would not have thought that when he described the sacrament in sacrificial terms he qualified the New Testament understanding of Christian life as response to grace, but rather such an understanding of the Holy Communion grew directly from it.

---

* *and* [on account of it, in reply to it] *we again to thee present.*

The idea-structure of Hymn 124 illustrates the relation of the sacrificial cross to the sacrificial table. Wesley opens with an exclamation, speaking celebratively to Christ,

1   All hail, Redeemer of Mankind!
       Thy Life on *Calvary* resign'd
         Did fully once for All atone,
       Thy Blood hath paid our utmost Price,
       Thine all-sufficient Sacrifice
         Remains eternally alone:

       Angels and Men might strive in vain,
      They could not add the smallest Grain
         T'augment thy Death's Atoning Power,
      The Sacrifice is all-compleat,
      The Death Thou never canst repeat,
         Once offer'd up to die no more. (124)

Having set out the completeness and finality of Christ's work, Wesley's next word is 'yet' – as though something more may and must be said. He will speak now in the second stanza of what, in the light of Christ's atoning work, we may do:

2   Yet may we celebrate below,
       And daily thus thine Offering shew
         Expos'd before thy Father's Eyes;
      In this tremendous Mystery
      Present Thee bleeding on the Tree
         Our everlasting Sacrifice. (124:2.1–6)

'In this tremendous Mystery' (that is, in the sacrament), we *celebrate*, we *show* your (Christ's) offering, *exposing* it before the Father; we '*present thee bleeding on a tree*'. This turn in thought follows Brevint who, having similarly spoken of the completeness of Christ's sacrifice, continues: 'Nevertheless, this Sacrifice, which by a *real oblation* was not to be offered more than once, is, by an eucharistical and devout commemoration to be offered up every day,' (VI.3.) (On Brevint's and Wesley's emphasis on dailiness, see pp. 221, 223–7.) Alongside Brevint's and Wesley's declaration that Christ's sacrifice alone carries redemptive efficacy, they speak with conviction of the sacrifices that Christians make in life, in suffering and in the eucharist.

Wesley's mind holds things together. If the sacramental grace-giving approach of God to the Church is in Christ's sacrifice, he will say that the Church's response to God is also by sacrifice and in Christ. The Divine Son who is the bearer of the gracious divine address to sinful humanity is also the bearer of the reply that arises to God from redeemed humanity. In the sacrament, Christians offer themselves, with the whole Body, not on their own but as participants in the one availing sacrifice for sin.

The sacrament, as Wesley sees it, looks in two directions, related to the two aspects of Christ's sacrifice – the earthly cross and the heavenly altar. As the hymns of his Part I vividly said, the Holy Communion links the believing Church with the redemptive death at Calvary. It gives now what the cross gave, 'full atoning grace' (123:4.3). Yet at the same time the sacrament (an action of the earth-bound, history-defined Church) is, as Wesley confidently holds, the present earthly correlative of Christ's heavenly sacrifice, the 'image of His sacrifice' (118:5.3).

Brevint had described the connection between the heavenly sacrifice and the earthly sacramental sacrifice when (in John Wesley's economical paraphrase) he said:

> The People of *Israel* in worshipping ever turn'd their Eyes and their Hearts, towards that Sacrifice, the Blood whereof the High priest was to carry into the Sanctuary. So let us ever turn our Eyes and our Hearts, toward Jesus our eternal High Priest, who is gone up into the true Sanctuary, and doth there continually present both his own Body and Blood before God, and (as *Aaron* did) all the True *Israel* of God in a *Memorial*. In the mean Time, we beneath in the Church, present to God his Body and Blood in a *Memorial*, that under the Shadow of his Cross, and Figure of his Sacrifice, we may present ourselves in very deed before him. (VI.3)

Wesley understands the Lord's Supper to be a showing forth of the Lord's death to the Father (his interpretation of 1 Corinthians 11.26). In the eucharist Christians do not simply remember Christ and offer themselves, but they also 'present our Saviour's Death,/. . . Him in a Memorial shew,/ [We] offer up the Lamb to God' (118:4.2, 5f.). In the sacrament the Church presents to God the body and blood of Christ. The one great sacrifice of Christ is not only received; in a profound spiritual exchange, it is also offered to God:

> With solemn Faith we offer up,
>   And spread before thy glorious Eyes
> That only Ground of all our Hope,
>   That precious, bleeding Sacrifice. (125:2.1–4)

In the Lord's Supper the Church does on earth what Christ is always doing in heaven: it sets forth the passion of the Son, presenting to the Father 'the Blood that speaks our sins forgiven' (121:1.9). As we offer up Christ's sacrifice before God's eyes, we ask (perhaps we ask rather abruptly) that the Father see it:

> The Cross on *Calvary* He bore,
> He suffer'd once to die no more,
>   But left a Sacred Pledge behind:
> See here! – It on thy Altar lies. (121:2.1–4)

In lines already quoted, Wesley says of this sacramental showing or presenting of Christ's one sacrifice, 'We . . .'

> . . . daily thus thine Offering shew
>   Expos'd before thy Father's Eyes;
> In this tremendous Mystery
> [We] present Thee bleeding on the Tree
>   Our everlasting Sacrifice. (124:2.2–6)

Wesley has used the terms 'show', 'exhibit' and 'present' to describe the Church's action, but in these lines he adds the term 'expose' – a word that had come to be associated with the Roman cult of the reserved sacrament. Worshippers were to behold and revere Christ as he was held before them in the 'exposition' of the consecrated bread. Wesley uses the language of this highly visual Roman practice, but he inverts its meaning, saying that the Church, in 'this tremendous mystery' (in the Holy Communion), 'exposes' Christ's one offering, not to the awed people, but to the Father. This idea was suggested by Brevint, who had said that 'we present and expose before his [God's] eyes that same holy and precious oblation once offered' (VI.3). Wesley also uses the term 'exhibited', similarly suggesting the monstrance, but in the same inverted sense. 'The tokens of his death/ Here exhibited [to God] beneath' (119:3.3–4).

Wesley proposes that in the Church's eucharistic response, Christ himself is active. As the Church makes eucharist, 'showing' or 'setting forth' or 'exhibiting' Christ's sacrifice before the world and the Father (116:1.2; 124:2; 125:1), in the same act, the living Christ, in the Church, is offering himself to God:

> Thou Lamb that suffer'dst on the Tree,
> And in this dreadful Mystery
>   Still offer'st up Thyself to GOD. (117:1.1–3)

Since in the sacrament the living Christ continues to present his sacrifice to the Father, the interior reality of the Church's eucharist is Christ eternally offering himself. At the Holy Table, in and with the Church's offering, Christ himself presents 'his Body torn and rent' (118:3.1–2; also 41:2.4). The Church offers itself in and with Christ's self-offering, while he offers himself in and with the Church's offering.

Christ is in the Christians' sacrifice, and they are in his. The Church is so united with Christ that, in the Holy Communion, Christians not only die in him (131:2), they appear with him in heaven as sharers in his present offering, 'We now with thee in heaven appear' (117:1.7–12). And perhaps the most daringly stated of all, the Church, in the sacrament, 'presents' Jesus' death and 'offers up the Lamb to God' (118:4). The Father beholds Christ's sacrifice as it is shown in the Church's eucharist (126:5) and sees the communicants in him (121). They are accepted in Christ's acceptance.

When Wesley says that the Church offers Christ in the sacrament, it can seem to some heirs of the Reformation that such doctrine gives Christ into the control of the Church and introduces a quasi-Pelagian factor into the economy of redemption. Such critics hold that all true priestliness belongs to Christ; the Christian eucharist is a thanksgiving act that shows forth what God has done; it is an acknowledgement of (or perhaps a continuance of) God's good gift to humanity. Persons who are of this persuasion are uncomfortable when the eucharist is called a sacrifice, except in the sense that it is an act of thanksgiving. It is properly not an offering up of Christ (which only Christ can do), but a joyful announcement of and a grateful receiving of the sacrifice once offered.

From such a questioning point of view, many of these sacramental hymns can sound very close to the Council of Trent. However, Wesley's complex understanding of sacrifice – on the cross, at the heavenly altar, and in the Supper; Christ in the Church and the Church in Christ – stands in the loose sixteenth- and seventeenth-century Anglican tradition that was his principal intellectual background (a tradition sketched in the Introduction, pp. 15–21). Charles Wesley was referring to the Holy Communion as 'the Christian Sacrifice' in the early 1730s. He no doubt thought that his doctrine rested on good exegetical and theological foundations.

Wesley and his tradition held that the Sacrament of the Table is both a witness to grace once given and also a present enactment of grace. Wesley, however, further thinks that the sacrament expresses the Christian response to grace – a response made in spoken word, in a life of godliness, but also in cultic act. The Holy Communion, which carries the redemptive, grace-imparting movement from God to humanity, also carries the movement of redeemed humanity returning its life to God in thanksgiving and self-offering. Wesley often describes this sacramental 'return' through the image of fire. 'Then let him [Christ] here . . ./ Descend in Blessings from above,/ And [let us] answer by the Fire of Love' (89:2.3, 5–6).

> As Incense to thy Throne above,
>   O Let our Prayers arise
> Wing with the Flames of holy Love
>   Our living Sacrifice. (85:2.1–4)

In Wesley's view, both of these movements are in Christ, and both have the character of sacrifice.

Wesley sees Christ and his people as so united that when the Church offers itself, it offers itself in Christ and Christ in itself. When Wesley understands that in the sacrament Christians offer Christ, he is arguing precisely against the idea that they offer on their own, seeking divine favour. Geoffrey Wainwright proposes that Wesley's doctrine, rather than tending towards Pelagianism, may ward against it: 'Could not the contentious notion "we offer Christ" paradoxically be seen as antipelagian? It could be an acknowledgement that we have nothing else to offer.'[6]

This God-ward movement of the sacrament may be thought of as in some respects like prayer. In prayer the Church addresses its life to God, confident that it is heard. But in true prayer, while God is listener, receiver and responder, God is at the same time giver, prompter and proposer. The Holy Communion, like prayer, is essentially God-given; but it, like prayer, is effective on God, because God in grace wills it so. It is a fresh bestowal of forgiveness; it 'brings thy grace on sinners down' (125:2.5). Brevint had said that in the eucharist we set forth the death of Christ 'before the eyes of the Father', and 'thus the Christians in their prayers do every day insist upon and represent to God the Father, the meritorious passion of their Saviour, as the only sure ground whereon both God may give, and they obtain, the blessing which they do pray for' (VI.3).[7]

'Victim Divine'

The ways of Wesley's mind as he thinks through the eucharist as sacrifice are perhaps best expressed in the large, idea-filled hymn with which he opens Part IV (116), which Rattenbury says 'many people think is his greatest contribution to eucharistic thought'.[8] The hymn throughout is a prayer to Christ. The opening address, 'Victim Divine', puts in two words the paradox of the 'crucified God'.[9]

Wesley begins by saying that we do what we do 'thus' (at the holy table) because of what Christ has done once on earth. At the eucharist we show Christ's death as we claim his grace.

> 1 Victim Divine, thy Grace we claim
>   While thus thy precious Death we shew,
> Once offer'd up a spotless Lamb
>   In thy great Temple here below,
> Thou didst for All Mankind atone,

Then Wesley turns from what Christ once did to speak in stanza 2 of what he is doing now; he is interceding in heaven by his blood:

> Thou didst for All Mankind atone,
> And standest now before the Throne.

> 2 Thou standest in the Holiest Place,
>   As now for guilty Sinners Slain,
> Thy Blood of Sprinkling speaks, and prays
>   All-prevalent for helpless Man,
> Thy Blood is still our Ransom found,
> And spreads Salvation all around.[10]

Wesley returns to speak in stanza 3 of the past redemptive act. Christ's sacrifice opened a way to heaven:

> 3 The Smoke of thy Atonement here
>   Darken'd the Sun and rent the Vail,
> Made the New Way to Heaven appear,
>   And shew'd the great Invisible:
> Well pleas'd in Thee our God look'd down,
> And call'd his Rebels to a Crown.

The words 'Well pleased in Thee our God looked down' refer to the divine approval of Jesus at his baptism (Matthew 3.17; Mark 1.11; Luke 3.22), but the words 'well pleased' are transferred to Jesus on the cross; the Father found Jesus' sacrifice acceptable. Then the acceptance of him passes to others. In the great paradox of redemption, God calls rebels, not to their judgement, but to their coronation.

The thought of stanza 4 returns to the present heavenly sacrifice and its earthly effects:

4   He still respects thy Sacrifice,
    Its Savour Sweet doth always please,
  The Offering smoaks thro' Earth and Skies,
    Diffusing Life and Joy and Peace,
  To these thy lower Courts it comes,
  And fills them with Divine Perfumes.

Depicting Christ's death through the imagery of Jewish burnt offerings, Wesley speaks of the smoke which enwraps the worshippers, carrying them as it ascends to heaven where it pleases God, as it fills earth with blessing. Kathryn Nichols says that stanzas 3–4 bespeak 'the perdurable smoke of Christ's sacrifice which blazes the trail to heaven and disseminates life, joy, and peace'.[11]

This universal *shalom* brought by Christ is especially given in the Holy Communion. (Wesley works the contention-ridden phrase 'real presence' into the last line of his hymn.)

5   We need not now go up to Heaven
    To bring the long-sought Saviour down,
  Thou art to All already given:
    Thou dost ev'n Now thy Banquet crown,
  To every faithful Soul appear,
  And shew thy Real Presence here.

This closely worded hymn brings many aspects of eucharistic reality together: 'We show', at the Church's altar, the death once offered up by Christ on the cross (1.2–4). That death was a sacrifice offered on earth, but it is continued in his heavenly ministry (1.6), where it is eternally presented in 'the holiest place'. Christ's sacrifice is always present and effective for 'helpless man' (2.1–6); it now speaks and prays (2.3), opening a new way for sinners (3.3). God still respects it (4.1–2); Jesus' work pleases God, and brings life, joy and peace to these 'lower courts' (4.3–6). Rattenbury regards Hymn 116 as 'the hymn most expressive of Charles's doctrine of the heavenly sacrifice and its earthly counterpart'.[12]

This hymn, which is unmistakably Charles Wesley's in thought and expression, takes its substance and much of its wording from a passage in Brevint's discussion of the sacrament as a means of grace:

This victim having been offered up both in the fulness of time and in the midst of the habitable world, which properly is Christ's great temple, and thence being carried up to heaven, which is his proper sanctuary, thence He spreads all about us salvation, as the burnt-offering did its smoke, as the golden altar did its perfumes, and as the burning candlestick its lights. And thus Christ's body and blood have every where, but especially at the holy Communion, a most true and *real presence*. When He offered himself upon earth, the vapour of atonement went up and darkened the very sun; and by rending the great veil, it clearly shewed He had made a way into heaven. Now since He is gone up into heaven, thence He sends down on earth the grace that spring continually both from his everlasting Sacrifice, and from the continual intercessions which attend it. So that it is vain to say, *who will go up to heaven?* since, without either ascending or descending, this sacred body of Jesus fills with atonement and blessing the remotest parts of this temple. (IV.11)

Three Centres of Sacrifice

In Charles Wesley's view, three things, (1) Christ's sacrifice once made on earth, (2) his sacrifice eternally presented in heaven, and (3) the sacramental sacrifice that is made repeatedly at the Church's table, are not three discrete acts, but are parts of the one divine act for the reclamation of fallen humanity. These three centres of sacrifice interpenetrate, forming a vital unity.

Wesley never sets his thought out in a complete and linear way. To represent it in a diagram risks oversimplifying its complexity and nuance, but it may also clarify:

(line *a*) As the hymns of Part I had said, the eucharist makes communicants present at the cross, and the cross is, in a sense, present at the Church's table.

(line *b*) At the same time, the heavenly altar is the eternal counterpart of the once-for-all act of the cross, and the cross is the historical act in which the eternal Son was wounded.

(line *c*) The often-repeated eucharistic act presents Christ to the Father, while the living Christ is the reality of the Church's sacrament of the Table.

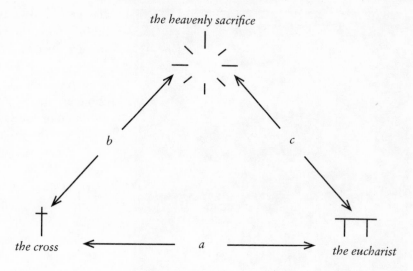

In the hymns of Part IV Wesley does not mount a measured theological argument; he writes poetically and doxologically. In holding together tensively and without resolution emphases that others keep separate, or may even see as opposed to one another, Wesley may be expressing in his own way a sense that, as Kenneth Stevenson has said, eucharistic theology may seem to be 'not a neat, packaged piece of doctrine, but a paradox, a union of opposites, almost a self-contradiction'.[13]

Wesley and his tradition confidently described a correspondence between what the Church does at the holy table and what Christ is always doing in the heavenly sanctuary. The imaginative construction which this parallel yielded may be shown in a visual representation from Wesley's time. The Church of England scholar Richard Wheatly's *A Rational Illustration of the Book of Common Prayer* (originally written in 1710, and significantly revised in 1720) rather quickly established itself as the standard commentary on the Prayer Book.[14] It was clearly written, well informed, and of manageable size. Wheatly's *Rational Illustration* continued to be published and referred to well into the nineteenth century.

Early editions of the book carried as frontispiece a full page engraving which shows a Church of England service of Holy Communion (as illustration below). The scene is in the east end of a rather classically designed church. In the foreground a latecomer who is entering the chancel is being handed the communion order by a verger in black gown and bands. Beyond them is the congregation, which has come up into the chancel following the service of the word, responding to the vicar's invitation, 'draw near with faith'. The people are kneeling, facing away from the

Matth XVIII.19.20 I Cor. XI.23.24.25.26.

viewer and towards the holy table, which stands further to the east, behind a heavy rail. The commandments are mounted on the east wall over the table. The celebrant, in surplice, hood and scarf, is standing at the north (left) end of the table. On it, in front of him are a Prayer Book, two patens, two chalices and two flagons of wine. It is all reverent, orderly and quite plain.

But the engraving shows above the holy table a parallel scene of heavenly splendour. Clouds, borne by three innocent-looking cherubs, shield the congregation from a streaming sunburst. In the centre of the light there is an altar, with the smoke of incense rising from it. Beneath the altar the engraver has printed the reference 'Rev. VIII.3,4'. Standing to the left of the altar is the figure of Christ, garbed in a long, cinctured alb, his arms in the orant position. In a nimbus around his head are written the references 'Heb. IX.11, 23; VII, 26'. The engraving is plain and literal; it requires Scripture texts to make its intention clear. But at the same time it is imaginative and quite splendid. A devout eighteenth-century communicant, looking at the unadorned table and the plainly vested celebrant, sees in and beyond them the heavenly altar at which Christ in glory offers continual sacrifice.

Part IV is the shortest section in *Hymns on the Lord's Supper*, containing only 12 hymns – several of which are, however, especially thoughtful and complex. Brevint's corresponding Section VI, which is also brief and compact, is used by Wesley in every hymn in Part IV.

Six of the 12 hymns in Part IV (119–22 and 125–6) are addressed to the Father. Christians address the one from whom the redemptive divine action originates and to whom the answering human offering is directed.

Significantly, although Wesley's subject in this section is sacrifice and the eucharist, he never speaks of any group within the Church as priestly or doing a priestly work (even though elsewhere in his writings he affirms the priestly character of the Anglican ministry). His pronoun when he speaks of the Church's sacrifice is 'we' – the ecclesial 'we'. It is the believing community which, in Christ, receives and which offers.

Charles Wesley does not himself argue nor defend. He simply affirms his understanding of the sacrament as sacrifice, evidently expecting that others will find his affirmations convincing. He nowhere says more about these themes than he says in these hymns, and John Wesley says nothing that clarifies them further.

*   *   *

ESSAYS

On the Book of Hebrews

Wesley's eucharistic thought, like that of much of the Christian tradition, drew significantly on the New Testament book of Hebrews. This anonymous first-century work, which has few marks of a letter, interprets Christ and his atoning work through the actions of the Levitical high priest on the Day of Atonement – the central place at which, under the Jewish sacrificial system, God covered the people's sin and restored ritual holiness.

The book of Hebrews was written after the Temple in Jerusalem had been destroyed. Its author had probably never seen the Temple, but worked somewhat literarily from the Jewish scriptures, referring not to the Temple in Jerusalem but to the Tabernacle of the exodus accounts. Showing great originality, he proposed that what Jesus did in his life, his death and his present relation to the Church was like what the Jewish high priest did on the Day of Atonement – except that what Jesus did was not a repeated yearly action, carried out in an earthly sanctuary; but being who he was, the eternal Son, his death on the cross outside the gate of Jerusalem was at the same time a sacrifice made in the holy place of the heavenly Temple, and as such it was the true and final sacrifice for human sin. As the writer of Hebrews sees it, Jesus' act was not a supreme instance of the sort of work that the Levitical high priest did; rather, his act gave reality to the shadowy, anticipatory, often-repeated sacrifices of the Levitical system, even as it rendered them obsolete.

The structure of the thought of Hebrews has a two-level, somewhat 'Platonic' character. It speaks of the world of time and historic event, and it speaks also of the eternal world of heaven. Both are real, and Jesus' work belongs to them both. Indeed, in who he is and what he did, he unites these realms. In his redemptive work in history he was a thoroughly human person, a first-century Palestinian Jew. But because he was at the same time the Son of God, his death on earth was also, if one may speak of it so, an event in heaven. The author conceives of heaven on the pattern of the Jewish Tabernacle – or as he would have put it, the Tabernacle was a copy of the order of heaven (see 8.15). Jesus' death in Jerusalem was the world's Day of Atonement. When he died, he was the great, divinely appointed high priest, passing through the veil into the holiest place in heaven itself. Thus his sacrifice was final, made only once, not needing to be repeated each year.

But Christ who died now lives; the one who was united with humanity remains in his heavenly life united with humanity. And because Christ 'ever lives', the effect of his priestly act which was carried out in a single, datable action on earth is continued in his present life in heaven and in relation to God and to the Church. As Francis Frost puts it, 'A blood sacrifice, carried out in time, is taken up into eternity and made eternal in the eternity of the second Person of the Trinity made man.'[15] In Christ's continuing priesthood, the past redemptive event is connected with present sin and need.

Christ's priesthood, as described in the book of Hebrews, has a deeply personal, human side, for Jesus, the heavenly priest, had lived and learned by what he suffered on earth (5.7–9). The sacrifice which he offered was his life of obedience, which contained his death (10.5–7). He can be a compassionate high priest because he knows human experience from the inside. 'Because he himself was tested by what he suffered, he is able to help those who are being tested' (2.18).

The priest is a representative figure who carries a community with him. He acts for it; it acts through him: 'Every high priest chosen from among mortals is put in charge of things pertaining to God on their behalf' (5.1). Jesus continues to act with his people as his care. He remains their intercessor at God's throne (7.25), or to cite another image from Hebrews, he is bound to them as their elder brother (2.11f.).

As Hebrews speaks of him, Jesus, who is heavenly high priest, is also sacrifice. When this great high priest entered the holy place of heaven, the blood that he presented for the people was his own. The sacrificer and the thing sacrificed were one. In Hymn 5 (which is located in Part I, but anticipates many of the themes of Part IV) Wesley combines the image of Christ as sacrifice with that of Christ as priest:

> O Thou eternal Victim slain
> A Sacrifice for guilty Man,
> By the Eternal Spirit made
> An Offering in the Sinner's stead,
> Our everlasting Priest art Thou,
> And plead'st thy Death for Sinners now. (5:1)

Hebrews, followed by both Brevint and Wesley, considered sacrifice a God-ward action – an act of honouring and usually of appeal. When Hebrews speaks of 'offering', it uses the Greek cultic term *prosphero*, to bring or bear forward – a word which comes to figure in early Christian and Eastern liturgical vocabulary. It is the function of priests to offer gifts (5.1), as the Levitical priests did (8.3f.; 9.7, 9; 10.2, 8, 11) and as did Abel (11.4), Abraham (11.17) and Melchizedek (5.5–10; 7.1–10). Supremely, Christ's life and vocation, which are first from God, are offered to God. Jesus is the great priest who offered his prayers and cries (5.7f.), his obedience (5.8; 10.7) – and in sum, himself: 'He has appeared once for all at the end of the age to remove sin by the sacrifice of himself' (9.14, 25ff.; 10.12).

This great high priest in his sacrifice bore sinful human life to God, but did so in a continuing act from which sinners may receive and in which believers, united with Christ, may participate. It is on this model that Brevint can think of the sacrament as a Christian appeal to God or a prayer (6.3–4). Wesley similarly says that the sacrifice is eternal and cannot be repeated, and because it is eternal, it is always accessible. It can be 'shown' or 'presented' before the Father's eyes, as Christians 'plead', not their own worth, but Christ's death (5:1.6).

In the Levitical rite, the high priest on the Day of Atonement entered the holy place alone and then returned to the people (a scene which is set out colourfully in Ecclesiasticus 50.1–21). However, Christ as a representative person, by his priestly sacrifice opened a way into the holiest place for others (Hebrews 5.9; see Hymn 127:2.7–8). Christians through him draw near (Hebrews 10.22), offering continually the sacrifice of praise to God (Hebrews 13.15). As Wesley put it:

> His Flesh is rent, the Living Way
> Is open'd to Eternal Day,
>   And lo, thro' Him we pass to Heaven! (124:2.10–12)

The writer of Hebrews depicts the unity of Christ and his people using some non-priestly images. Jesus, he says, is the elder brother in a family – the 'firstborn', the 'pioneer' (Hebrews 2.10; 12.2), the 'forerunner on our behalf' (Hebrews 6.20). He acted as a representative; what he did makes a crucial difference for the others in the family. When he entered the presence of God, he came in victory, making a way into the holiest place where others may follow. Christ's obedient life and death were offered to God, and since the Church is a people in Christ, its praise and charity (Hebrews 13.16f.) are sacrifices offered to God in the sacrifice of Christ. And if praise and alms are offered to God, Brevint and Wesley would add that in all of life, but particularly in the eucharist, 'We ... with thy Sacrifice ascend' (136:4.2).

Many of the seventeenth-century Anglicans who figured in Wesley's intellectual background had used this New Testament epistle to show the connection between Christ's 'once for all' self-offering at a moment in history and the repeated eucharistic offering of the Church. However, many writers in the Dissenting traditions as well as some Anglican Evangelicals – all of whom have believed wholeheartedly what Hebrews says about Christ and his sacrifice – have seen no connection between the priestly and sacrificial categories of Hebrews and the Church's Sacrament of the Table. Yet Wesley, with a long tradition behind him, held that Christ's sacrifice, made at a moment in history, transcended history. His ongoing priesthood and intercession are the reality in which the faithful, always dependent, eucharistic Church participates. The theological structure of Charles Wesley's *Hymns on the Lord's Supper* rests on his conviction that Christ's priesthood and sacrifice, as he found them set forth in Hebrews, are the eternal reality that underlies the repeated Sacrament of the Table.

* * *

On Jesus' 'Blood'

Jesus' 'blood' is referred to approximately 130 times in *Hymns on the Lord's Supper*, and more than that if one includes adjectives such as 'bloody' and 'bleeding' (or even 'purple' or 'crimson'). It is used 20 times in the 12 hymns of Part IV. Rattenbury remarks, 'The dominant thought of Wesley is the precious blood of Christ, which in some way is implied or described in every hymn of the section.'[16]

The New Testament in narrating Jesus' terrible death does not emphasise its bloodiness. However, the devotional tradition, as it developed in the Middle Ages and after, came to speak in lingering detail of Jesus' hours of suffering – the flagellation, the crown of thorns, the nails, the thrust of the spear, the water and blood. Wesley follows that tradition, speaking often of Jesus' literal crucifixion, emphasising his blood that was shed there. The communicant, in faith, sees 'his body mangled, rent,/ Covered with a gore of blood!' (23:1.3–4). Indeed, the devout believer *feels* Christ's 'gushing blood' (3:4.8). Wesley, however, does not merely describe the first-century scene, but speaks of the blood of the crucifixion as a powerful memory which is recreated in the sacrament and interpreted by a knowledge of the salvation that Christ accomplished. One mourns one's sins and mixes one's sorrows with Christ's blood (6:1.6).

The New Testament says that Jesus himself had established a link between his body and blood and the bread and wine of the cultic meal (Matthew 25.26–9; Mark 14.22–5; Luke 22.14–21; John 6.52–9; 1 Corinthians 10.16). Wesley, following the tradition, often speaks of the sacramental eating of Christ's body and drinking his blood.

> This is the richest Legacy
>   Thou hast on Man bestow'd,
> Here chiefly, Lord, we feed on Thee,
>   And drink thy precious Blood. (42:4.1–4)

(See also 1:4.1, 3, 5; 30:5.2, 8.2; 54:5.2; 58:6.4; 61:3.10; 81:4.4; 153:1.4, among others.) He says to Christ, 'Thy life is to our souls conveyed/ in sacramental blood' (65:3.4).

In antiquity it was understood that sin – which could be a ritual offence or a moral offence; the distinction between the two not being ancient – was something like a pollution or contamination. In breaking a law or taboo, one contracted a defilement which separated one from both God and the covenant community. At its deepest level, this soiled condition could not be dealt with by self-reformation, for the self is itself the problem. Remedy required not regret for the past and a determination to do better, but it required sacrifice – a God-given cleansing, which could deal with the arrears. The sacrifice of the Day of Atonement required the killing of an animal (as not all sacrifices did), and blood represented life (Leviticus 17.11–14). The high priest presented the blood of the sacrificed animal in the Holy Place of the tabernacle to restore the people in the life of the covenant. Through sacrifice, alienations were overcome and communion re-established. From such modes of thought comes the New Testament sense that Christ's blood can cleanse – removing sin and restoring the sinner's relation to God and the holy people.

Several New Testament writers, drawing on this ancient background, saw Jesus' death as a divinely given sacrifice. The blood (the sacrificial living and dying) of Christ removed sin and restored fellowship between sinners and a holy God. Paul, in Romans, speaks of 'atonement through faith in his [Christ's] blood' (3.25) and of being 'justified by his blood' (5.9). Colossians 1.20 says that Christ has 'made peace through the blood of his cross', and Ephesians speaks of 'redemption through his blood' (1.7) and of being brought near to God 'by the blood of Christ' (2.13). The late first-century writing 1 John says that when Christians walk in the light of Christ, 'the blood of Jesus his [God's] Son [continually] cleanses us from all sin' (1.7). Another late New Testament writing, 1 Peter, says that Christians are redeemed 'with the precious blood of Christ' (1.19).

Wesley takes up this biblical and traditional material with conviction: He asks Christ to 'apply to all thy healing blood' (25:2.6). 'Write our protection in thy blood' (41:4.5). 'The virtue [the potency] of thy blood impart' (32:2.3; also 131:3.6). 'Let thy blood my Pardon seal' (79:2.6). Christ's blood, he says repeatedly, is active, effective, performative, 'the blood which once for all atones' (13:2.7). 'His blood for us atones' (132:3.2; also 126:2.3). 'We see the blood that seals our peace' (28:3.1). 'His blood procured our life and peace' (36:3.1; 58:7.2). Wesley speaks of 'his all-cleansing blood' (39:3.4) and 'thy all-atoning blood' (85:3.2). 'Our saviour's blood' is 'with power impressed' (73:1.3). Believers are 'covered with th' atoning blood' (117:1.6; also 68:3.1). We have 'forgiveness in his blood' (125:3.2). Wesley prays 'to Thee whose blood hath purg'd our sin' (133:4.4). He speaks of Christ's sacrificial love as his 'bleeding love' (20:1.1; 90:1.2), and of Christ as 'our bleeding Saviour' (4:1.2; 14:1.7), 'our bleeding Lamb' (105:2.7; 141:8.1), 'our bleeding Prince' (141:4.3), and a 'bleeding Sacrifice' (115:1.5; 125:2.2; 153:2.7).

Wesley often uses the New Testament idea of Christ's death as ransom for lives that had been forfeit through sin. Christ's blood was the price paid for freedom; he 'pays my debt in blood' (2:3.6). 'The purchase-price was blood divine' (45:2.5; and 36:4.2; 37:1.2). 'Thou didst buy our pardon with thy blood' (52:1.2). 'Thy blood hath paid our utmost price' (124:1.4). Believers are 'purchased with the price of his own blood' (156:2.3; and 13:2.6).

Wesley draws heavily on two books, Hebrews and Revelation, which speak often of redemption by the blood of Christ.

The author of Hebrews, thinking in terms of the Levitical system and the Day of Atonement, put the shedding of blood in a focal place, saying that 'under the law almost everything is purified with blood, and without the shedding of blood there is no forgiveness of sins' (9.22). From this general maxim, his thought passes to the work of Christ, who 'entered once for all into the [heavenly] Holy Place, not with the blood of goats and calves, but with his own blood, thus obtaining eternal redemption' (9.12). 'Jesus suffered . . . in order to sanctify the people by his own blood' (13.12).

Hebrews 12.24 introduces the idea that Jesus' blood speaks in behalf of the people. Indeed, as the blood of a new covenant, it speaks more effectively than Abel's blood which cried out to God from the ground (Genesis 4.10). Wesley develops the thought, saying often that Jesus' blood, and not spoken words, is the means by which he intercedes, pleading with the Father for the forgiveness of sinners. 'My blood that speaks your sins forgiven' (1:4.5). 'Father, hear the blood of Jesus . . . Still his blood cries out, "Forgive them"' (14:1.1, 2.3). 'Thy blood of sprinkling speaks and prays,/ All-prevalent for helpless man' (116:2.3–4; also 119:3.1, 4.1; 120:4.2; 121:1.9; 125:4.2). In one hymn, Wesley reverses the image, saying not that the blood speaks to God, but that the witness of God speaks in the mystical blood (92:5.4).

As to the book of Revelation, in the Authorised Version that Wesley used, the book opens praising the heavenly Christ who 'washed us from our sins in his own blood' (1.5). But textual study has shown that the correct reading is not 'washed (Gr. *louo*) us from our sins', but 'loosed (*luo*) us from our sins'. Thus Revelation 1.5 uses not the image of cleansing, but the image of emancipation. Revelation 5.9 says, however, in similar idiom, that Christ has redeemed us to God by his blood. In a related symbol, the seer of Revelation speaks of martyrs washing their garments white in the blood of the sacrificed Lamb (7.14). As the ancient world knew, white clothing that has been stained with blood is almost impossible to restore to whiteness; but paradoxically this blood cleanses. Clothing that had been stained with the martyrs' own blood was made white by being washed in the blood of Christ. The white garments were a sign of the honour due to those who were faithful unto death.

Wesley speaks nine times in *Hymns on the Lord's Supper* of 'the blood applied': 'We long to feel applied the blood for our redemption given' (11:3.4), and 'The sin-atoning blood apply' (31:2.1). As the sacrificial blood in the Jewish system was sprinkled or applied, Christ's blood must be applied or received. 'Apply to all thy healing Blood' (25:3.5; also 16:2.5–8; 20:3.1–2; 31:2.1; 79:1.3; 87:3.2–3; 89:3.5).

Teresa Berger identifies 'the blood applied' as 'a formula for salvation effected'.[17] She traces it to a phrase in Lutheran theology which was taken up by Wesley as 'a short formula for the appropriation and "application" of Christ's work in the life of the individual believer'. Wesley speaks in the same way of 'the death applied' (24:2.3) and 'pardon to our souls applied' (164:4.3). The work of Christ is completed as it is known and elicits inward response.

Wesley stretches language and imagination, exaggerating the quantity of the blood in order to picture or suggest a redemption adequate for sin so extensive and ineradicable. When he does so, he stands in a long tradition that traces to the Middle Ages and continued through the Baroque era and into Wesley's own time – a tradition which found both Catholic and Protestant expressions. In his rhetoric Wesley sometimes indulges in almost garish overstatement, exceeding both biblical restraint and the bounds of what would be accepted (today, and very likely in his day as well) as good taste. He speaks of the saving blood flowing freely (3:3.4; 12:1.3). 'The blood that purges all our stains,/ It starts in rivers from his veins./ A fountain gushes from his side' (24:1.5–2.1). Zechariah had spoken (13.1) of a fountain opened for sin and uncleanness, no doubt having in mind a fountain of water. Wesley makes it a fountain of Jesus' blood in which sinners may wash – indeed, into which they may plunge and from which they may drink: 'Now, e'en now, we all plunge in,/ And drink the purple wave' (27:4.1–2). The believer is 'washed in his all-cleansing blood' (39:3.4; also 106:2.3–4). In an unusual image which to modern readers may suggest something like a transfusion, faith 'pours his [Christ's] blood into our hearts' (71:3.6). In the mind of the ecstatic communicant, the very altar of the church 'streams with blood' (89:4.5). Sinners are totally covered with the blood and by it are protected from judgement – 'hallowed by the streaming blood' (122:3.6–7; 131:3.5). Believers are 'implunged in his atoning blood' (137:4.4). In a hymn outside this collection Wesley urges, 'Fly to those dear wounds of his,/ Sink into the purple flood' (1780 *Collection*, 20.4–5).

This extravagant imagery of blood goes beyond the essentially modest biblical writings. As Rattenbury says, 'This dwelling on the blood of Christ, plunging into it, and so forth, are not expressions which seem to have any justification in the New Testament.'[18] But a further problem may be that the language becomes formulaic – heightening, over-developing and overworking a strong, but limited biblical image. Jesus' blood became a summary term for his saving death, which Wesley used so often and so familiarly in his hymns that it becomes expectable. (It surely became a cliché in the hymns of the later revivalist tradition.) Even a sympathetic reader may tire of the reiterated term. Yet Wesley's insistent reference to Jesus' saving blood shows how single-mindedly he was occupied with human sin and the divine atoning act.

*   *   *

On Jesus' 'Wounds'

Every detail of Jesus' cruel death, as reported in the gospels – the thorns, the nails, the spear – has been taken up into Christian traditions of preaching, devotion and iconography. 1 Peter 2.24 indicates that as early as the first century, Jesus' 'wounds' were becoming a spiritual reference point. (The AV translation used 'stripes' for the Greek *molops*, 'wounds', possibly to correspond with the English word that had been used in Isaiah 53.5.) The motif was embellished by legends and developed in the thousands of crucifixes that were carved and painted in the churches of the medieval and Counter-Reformation West. In one of his most vivid scenes of sacramental realism, Wesley speaks of the wounded Lamb appearing at the Holy Communion (22:2.3). The lines rather suggest a vision of St Gregory that was depicted in several pieces of medieval and Renaissance art, notably in an engraving by Dürer in which the saint is kneeling before an altar celebrating Mass, when the crucified but living Jesus himself steps bodily out from the reredos.

The motif of Jesus' wounds need not be gruesome or morbid; it was a way of speaking paradoxically of a wounded healer or of healing wounds. In a moral, but flawed world, things that are wrong are not set right without pain, and Jesus' wounds were a way for Christians to speak of the hurt that human redemption inflicted on the divine Redeemer. In a hymn in the 1780 collection, Christ says by his wounds, 'I suffered this for you' (34.31–2). In the same collection, Wesley says that dwelling in Christ's wounds makes pain sweet (25.3–4) and that paradoxically,

Jesus' wounds are 'the wounds which all my sorrows heal' (124.19). In *Hymns on the Lord's Supper* Wesley says that the saving wounds are 'still open wide' (122:3.1) – that is, they have not healed over; they are still effective for sinners. In 85:3.1 he speaks of drawing life from the fresh wounds of Jesus.

At times, particularly in Part I of *Hymns on the Lord's Supper*, when Wesley refers descriptively to Jesus' suffering in his passion, 'wounds' become a summary term for the injuries inflicted on him. Wesley identifies the 'five wounds' of Jesus: 'pierc'd his feet, his hands his side' (22:3.3).

Principally, however, Wesley speaks theologically or kerygmatically of Jesus' 'wounds' as received by him on earth, but carried into heaven, where they are enduring demonstrations, in his glorified life, of his identification with sinful humanity. They show the cost to him (that is to say, the cost to God) of human redemption. The Christian imagination, beginning long before Wesley, had conflated the imagery from Hebrews of heavenly priesthood and sacrifice with the regal imagery from Revelation 6 of 'the Lamb as it had been slain' standing before the throne in heaven. The heavenly Christ carries the marks of his earthly suffering and death. His wounds, which he received on earth and still bears, are the glory of heaven.

The marks of Jesus' passion are not simply to be remembered by his followers here; they are, as Wesley sees them, authority for Christ's continued, availing plea for his people. He presents his wounds before the Father, as reminder of his humanity and his sacrifice:

> In the holiest place above,
>   Sinner's Advocate He stands,
> Pleads for us His dying love,
>   Shows for us His bleeding hands. (118:2.3–6)

The Father is asked to 'look through Jesus' wounds on me' (120:1.6).

Charles to some extent took this emphasis from the Moravians who had developed Jesus' wounds as a focus of devotion. John disliked the idiom, and Charles may have thought that he moderated it, for he once made an impatient comment, not about Moravians, but about Roman Catholics, 'What is it that in all their meetings sounds? "Wounds, wounds, & wound holes, nothing else but wounds."'[19]

The emphasis on Jesus' wounds was sustained as a summary term for Christ's saving work in the vocabulary of both evangelicalism and Anglo-Catholicism in the next century, but it has in more recent times largely lost its power and currency. Speech about the saving wounds of

Christ, which is integral to Wesley's thought and vocabulary, must now be moderated if it is to be usable, and it must be explained if it is to be understood. But images that must be explained have lost their immediacy and authority, perhaps beyond recovery. Yet anyone seeking to understand Wesley's hymns must grasp what the wounds of the saviour meant in the context of his imagery and thought.

*   *   *

On Christ as 'Lamb'

In these sacramental hymns Wesley speaks of Christ as 'Lamb' fifty times. The word is short (the sort of word on which Wesley's verse depended), and it reverberates with biblical associations. A reader can at first notice the word, then come to expect it, and then perhaps end by finding its repetition wearying.

The New Testament image of Christ as Lamb traces particularly to the use of lambs in the Levitical system as sin offerings, and especially as the Passover sacrifice, hence Wesley's frequent references to Christ as the true Paschal Lamb. Christians would also have found the biblical basis for the image in Isaiah's reference (53.6, and context) to God's Servant who was 'brought as a lamb to the slaughter' – a passage which in their judgement spoke prophetically of Christ. Wesley makes use of Jewish sacrificial custom, as when communicants by faith identify with Christ as Jewish offerers laid their hands on the sacrificial animal (136:2.5ff.), or when Christians feed by faith on Christ as Jews ate the Paschal sacrifice, 'Still on the Paschal Lamb we feed' (44:1.5; and 3:4.5; 4:1.4; 35:1.1–2; 84:1.8; 106:4.2).

Christian imagination enlarged and universalised the sacrificed lamb of Levitical law to speak of Jesus as the Lamb of God which takes away the sin of the world (John 1.29; also 1 Peter 1.19). The image of the slain but living and triumphant Lamb appears 27 times in Revelation – often as a focus of angelic worship. (Although Hebrews speaks often of Christ's sacrifice, it does not expressly picture him as a sacrificial Lamb.)

In more than thirty instances in *Hymns on the Lord's Supper* Wesley speaks of the Lamb with redemptive sacrifice clearly in mind: 'Thou all-atoning Lamb' (25:3.3), or 'Once offer'd up, a spotless Lamb' (116:1.3), or 'The Lamb for sinners given' (127:2.6). In a dozen instances that are largely celebrational Wesley echoes the praise to the Lamb of Revelation

5, giving glory to the Lamb, as 'Then let our faith adore the Lamb' (3:4.1), 'Our dear triumphant Lamb' (21:9.8), 'Worthy the Lamb of endless praise' (38:1.1), 'O Thou holy Lamb Divine' (136:1.1). As in the vision of Revelation, the one who is worthy of praise is the one who had been slain, 'Thou stand'st the ever slaughter'd Lamb' (5:2.3), 'Glory to the bleeding Lamb' (105:2.7).

In three hymns Wesley encourages loyalty by using the image from Revelation 14.4 of believers following the Lamb faithfully; Christians are 'true followers of the Lamb' (13:3.3; and see 141:8.1; 166:10.3).

Wesley describes 'the Lamb' as present at the sacrament: 'the wounded Lamb appears' (22:3.3; and 53:3.3; 81:2.3; 122:2.6; 126:4.1). In the exchange of the eucharist, Christians 'offer up the Lamb to God' (118:4.6; and see 137:1.4), and the Lamb, as newly slain, is held out to humanity and is seen by God (126:4.1, 5.1; 122:2.6; 133:2.1). Wesley uses the eschatological image of the festal supper at the marriage of the Church and Christ, which Revelation 19.6–19 describes as the marriage supper of the Lamb at which, he says, those who partake of the Holy Communion with faith have begun to eat (93:2.8–9; 97:2.4).

Changes in culture and sensibility since the eighteenth century have made this image of the divinely provided Lamb remote and have reduced its communicative power. Yet for Wesley it was an evocative image by which he could speak of Jewish sacrifices, of Christ, of the cross, of the holy table, and of redemption and eschatology.

Part V

Concerning the Sacrifice of our Persons

HYMNS 128–157

When both Brevint and Wesley say that Christians at the Holy Communion freely give themselves to God in response to grace, they describe this giving in terms of spiritual sacrifice.

Brevint explains that, 'We, beneath, in the Church, present to God his [Christ's] body and blood in a *memorial*; that under the shadow of his cross, and image of his Sacrifice [that is, in the sacrament], we may present ourselves before him in very deed and *reality*' (VI.4).

And Wesley says,

> While Faith th' atoning Blood applies,
> Ourselves a Living Sacrifice
>   We freely offer up to God. (128:3.1–3)

Such spiritualising or moralising of sacrifice is an ancient characteristic of biblical faith. Jewish law, covenant, priesthood and sacrifice were signs of the relation with God into which Israel had been called. Obedience was not burdensome, but was a way of sustaining that relation. The Law held each devout Israelite by interior bonds. Jewish piety emphasised the dedication of the heart that informed the ritual act to the moral conduct that validated it. Thanksgiving is a true sacrifice (Psalm 50.14, 23). A contrite heart is a sacrifice acceptable to God (Psalm 51.17). Indeed, 'To obey is better than to sacrifice' (1 Samuel 15.22). When the Temple was destroyed and cultic sacrifices came to an end, these interior equivalents remained a mark of Jewish spirituality.

Christians from the first saw themselves as priests offering spiritual sacrifices acceptable to God through Christ (1 Peter 2.5). Hebrews is the New Testament book which most urges the finality and completeness of Christ's atoning sacrifice. It gives his sacrifice a moral content, saying that Jesus' fundamental sacrifice lay in his dedication to God's will; his death was the culmination of his life of obedience (Hebrews 10.1–10). Christ's sacrifice finds echo in the lives of believers as praise and alms are Christian sacrifices (Hebrews 13.15f.). Paul, in a central passage, appeals to believers to offer themselves to God as sacrifices that are not slain, but live (Romans 12.1–2). He refers to his own missionary work as sacrificial service (Romans 15.16), and he thinks of his own possible martyrdom in sacrificial terms (Philippians 2.17). Brevint, evidently fearing that such biblically warranted Christian sacrifices often went unrecognised, remarked that it is the error of too many Christians to 'believe, and oftener live, as if under the Gospel there were no other Sacrifice but that of Christ upon the Cross' (VII.1).

The New Testament nowhere speaks of the Lord's Supper in sacrificial terms, yet it was only a small extension of what the New Testament does say for Christians to think that their central church-making, church-and-Christian-sustaining act gathered expressively all of their self-offering; and by the second century, Christians were speaking of the eucharist as a sacrifice. (It was only much later that they began to ask what this sacrifice-talk might mean – who sacrifices? to whom? what is sacrificed? for what purpose?) Both Brevint and Wesley, with a long tradition behind them, are persuaded that in the sacrament Christians present themselves and all they have, in Christ, as a sacrifice to God, 'In this Ordinance Divine/ We still the sacred load may bear' (141:5.1–2). And this eucharistic self-giving is carried out in all of a believer's life.

Christ's Sacrifice and Christian Sacrifices

Both Brevint and Wesley urge that Christians give themselves to God because God has first given in Christ. Brevint opens his chapter on 'the sacrifice of our own persons' saying that while only Christ's sacrifice is expiatory, yet sacrifice is the way in which faithful persons meet and engage with his Great Sacrifice. 'If the Sacrifice of ourselves which we ought to offer up to God cannot *procure* Salvation, it is absolutely necessary [in order] to *receive* it' (VII.1). Believers, he says, respond to sacrifice by sacrifice.

Somewhat similarly Wesley regards the eucharist as a sign of a dual movement. As he has said earlier, God, from the divine side, in the cross and in the sacramental sign of the cross, meets humanity by sacrifice. But when Wesley speaks also of 'the Sacrifice of our Persons', he has in mind a return act of self-giving on the part of Christians.

FATHER, on us the Spirit bestow,
  Thro' which thine everlasting Son
Offer'd Himself for Man below,
  That *we*, ev'n *we* before thy Throne
Our Souls and Bodies may present,
And pay Thee All thy Grace hath lent. (150:1)

Hymn 128

Wesley, as is his practice, sets out the themes of a new section in an unusually full opening hymn. Hymn 128 emphasises that Christ's sacrifice alone is adequate to remove sin. Wesley gives perspective on Christian sacrifices by setting forth the priority, depth, cost and grace of Christ's sacrifice: 'Thy Self our utmost Price hast paid,/ Thou hast for all Atonement made' (128:2.1–2, also 1.1–2).

He establishes first that the self-offering of Christ has alone 'satisfied the inexorably righteous God'. (The lines express Wesley's Anselmian doctrine that Christ's death was a satisfaction offered to the offended righteousness of God.)

1a   All hail, Thou mighty to atone!
     To expiate Sin is thine alone,
         Thou hast alone the Wine-press trod,
     Thou only hast for Sinners died,
     By one Oblation satisfied
         Th' Inexorably righteous GOD:

When Wesley says in the next lines that if the whole Church were to offer itself, it could not remove one sin, he is following Brevint's comment that 'Though the whole church should, in a body, offer up herself as a burnt sacrifice to God,' yet it could not contribute more towards winning redemption or fending off judgement than the bystanders at the cross could to stop the earthquake or the darkness (VII.1).

1b   Should the whole Church in Flames arise,
     Offer'd as one burnt-Sacrifice
         The Sinner's smallest debt to pay,
     They could not, LORD, thine Honour share,
     With Thee the Father's Justice bear,
         Or bear one single sin away.

The God whose righteous demands must be met steps in, and through Christ pays the utmost price.

> 2a   Thy Self our utmost Price hast paid,
>   Thou hast for all Atonement made,
>   For all the Sins of All Mankind;
>   GOD doth in Thee Redemption give:

Having stated thus fully the completeness of Christ's redeeming sacrifice, Wesley asks how this grace can be received:

> But how shall we the Grace receive,
>   But how shall we the Blessing find?

He answers that one receives it by accepting it in faith.

> 2b   We only can *accept* the Grace,
>   And humbly our Redeemer praise
>   Who bought the glorious Liberty:
>   The Life Thou didst for All procure
>   We make by Our Believing sure
>   To us who live and die to Thee.

The line 'To us who live and die to Thee' (2.12) alludes to Romans 14.8f.: 'Whether we live, we live unto the Lord: and whether we die, we die unto the Lord: whether we live therefore or die, we are the Lord's.' Brevint had said that persons attending on Christ's sacrifice do so 'in such a manner as may become faithful disciples, who are resolved to die both for and with their Master' (VII.14).

    Acceptance, however, is not passive; but in receiving divine grace in faith, believers offer themselves to God. (Wesley echoes Brevint VII.1, cited above.)

> 3a   While Faith th' atoning Blood applies,
>   Ourselves a Living Sacrifice
>   We freely offer up to GOD:
>   And none but Those his Glory share
>   Who crucified with JESUS are,
>   And follow where their Saviour trod.

While a communicant makes an act of self-offering, Wesley does not see it as an independent or original sacrifice, but as an act that is joined with the Saviour's sacrifice: 'Our meanest sacrifice receive,/ And to thy own oblation join.' Christ, 'our suffering and triumphant Head', receives the believer's sacrifice and joins it to his own, and Christians, identified with him, are led through suffering to glory.

> 3b Saviour, to Thee our Lives we give,
> Our meanest Sacrifice receive,
>   And to thy own Oblation join,
> Our suffering and triumphant Head,
> Thro' all thy States thy Members lead,
>   And seat us on the Throne Divine.

Sharers with Christ

The final lines of Hymn 128 say that Christ joins the 'mean' sacrifices of believers with his own. Brevint had described the relation of the Christian to Christ saying that 'follow, conform, communion' are 'the most essential clauses in the charter and charge of Christianity' (VII.5).

Wesley enters in Hymn 129 some of the biblical images which express the unity between Christ and the Christian:

> 1 See where our great High-Priest
>   Before the LORD appears,
> And on his loving Breast
>   The Tribes of *Israel* bears,
> Never without his People seen,
> The Head of all believing Men!

Wesley uses again the image of the high priest's ephod (see pp. 158f., above). The high priest's ceremonial garment carried precious stones engraved with the names of the twelve tribes, signifying that when he went before the Lord on the Day of Atonement, he carried his people with him. Christ as priest is so united with his people that he does not act apart from them. When Wesley says that Christ is 'never without his people seen' (129:1.5), he has in mind Brevint's passage:

> As the old Law never introduced Aaron officiating before the Lord without the whole people of Israel, represented ... by the twelve stones on his ephod ... the Gospel most commonly describes Jesus Christ and

his Church, not only as two parties that do nothing without the other, but sometimes as one person alone; as particularly 1 Cor. 12:12 [VII.2] . . . Never did the Son of God intend any more to offer Himself for his people without his people, than did the high priest of the Law to offer himself for Israel without his ephod, the memorial of them. Christ presented Himself to God . . . at the head of all mankind. (VII.6)

In an earlier paragraph Brevint had said pointedly, 'Christ and Christians are and must be continually together' (VII.5).

In stanza 2, Wesley extends the series of biblical images describing the union between Christ and his people:

2   With Him the Corner Stone
        The living Stones conjoin,
    CHRIST and his CHURCH are One,
        One Body and one Vine,
   For us he uses all his Powers,
   And all He has, or is, is Ours.

1 Peter 2.4–8 provides the architectural image of Christ as the corner stone joined to living stones of the Temple (2.1–2). Paul's organic image of the body, its head and members, from 1 Corinthians 12.12–31, lies behind Wesley's line 'Christ and his Church are . . . one body' (2.3–4). In a single line he joins the Pauline image of head and body with the image from John 15.1–8 of Christ and the Church as vine and branches, saying, 'One body and one vine' (2.4). Later, in Hymn 134, Wesley introduces the image of the firstfruits, an early gathering which stood for the entire harvest. He also uses the image of Christ as the elder brother in a family (132:3, based on Hebrews 2.11f., 17; 3.1). The bonding between Christ and his people is a theme that attracts Wesley's imagination.

Christ and Christians are bound together in mind and actions.

3   The Motions of our Head*
        The members all pursue,
    By his good Spirit led
        To act, and suffer too
   Whate'er He did on earth sustain,
   'Till glorious all like Him we reign. (129)

---

* *the Motions:* the inward promptings, active feelings.

By the Spirit, Wesley says, Christians enact and suffer what Christ experienced on earth. They inwardly replicate 'the motions' of their Head (3.1–2). Wesley here follows Brevint, who describes Christians as joined in the spirit and acts of Christ as though they had experienced them in him and with him: 'Christ acts, officiates, and suffers for his body, in that manner that doth become the head; and the church imitates and follows all the motions and sufferings of this heavenly and holy head, in such a manner as is possible to its weak members' (VII.2).

Wesley says to Jesus that we seek to 'die and live with Thee' (130:3.4). 'The Christian lives to *Christ* alone,/ To *Christ* alone he dies' (157:2.3–4). The theme is derived from Paul's motif of dying and rising with Christ (Romans 6.1–11; Galatians 2.20) and of being conformed to Christ's death and resurrection (Philippians 3.10f.). Wesley, however, extends the theme to include more than death and resurrection, developing (or rather sketching in) a thesis that Christ leads his people through the course of his life and sufferings. He prays, 'Thro' all thy States thy Members lead' (128:3.11); and Christians, identifying with him, follow him in the acts of his redeeming life:

1   JESU, we follow Thee,
      In all Thy footsteps tread,
  And pant for full Conformity
      To our exalted Head.

      We would, we would partake
      Thy every State below,
  And suffer all Things for thy Sake,
      And to thy Glory go.

2   We in Thy Birth are born,
      Sustain thy Grief and Loss,
  Share in thy Want and Shame and Scorn,
      And die upon thy Cross.

      Baptiz'd into thy Death
      We sink into thy Grave,
  Till Thou the quick'ning Spirit breathe,
      And to the utmost save. (130:1–2)

Christians, Wesley says, are not merely recipients of Christ's sacrifice; they are united with it. Christians suffer with Christ here (131:1.7–8) as partakers of his grief and shame (133:2.3; 142:7.2–3). They pray that God may take them 'into the fellowship/ Of Jesu's sufferings' (148:2). They bear Christ's cross (131:4, 5); they die with him as 'sharers with the dying God' (131:3.7); they are 'offer'd with the Lamb' (134:4.2) and hang 'with him on the tree' (142:3).

The bond between Christians and Christ is so close that their sacrifice and his constitute one sacrifice: 'We offer up to death with Thee/ A whole burnt sacrifice' (135:2.5–6). Wesley proposes that Christians are carried to heaven in Christ's act: 'We . . . with Thy sacrifice ascend' (136:4.2). Communicants are with Christ not only in his earthly death but in his priestly self-offering in heaven. 'We jointly before God appear/ To offer up ourselves with Thee' (141:7.3–4)

Christ is regarded as a representative, inclusive person. Christians' modest sacrifices are 'conjoin'd to thy [Christ's] great Sacrifice' (133:4.5), in which they share 'by faithful remembrance' (142:1.4; 154 throughout). Christ's sacrifice and theirs are 'mingled in a common flame' (141:8.3). Christians and their sacrifice are caught up in Christ and his sacrifice (134:3.1–2), and the sacrament is an expression of this unitary spiritual action: 'Thou art with all thy Members here,/ In this tremendous Mystery [that is, in the Holy Communion]' (141:7).

In a profound sharing of life, Christ carried out his redemptive work not alone, but in, with and for his people. And his people, for their part, come before God identified with him and his acts. Wesley uses the image of Jewish worshippers laying their hands on the head of an animal that was to be sacrificed.

1   Would the Saviour of Mankind
        Without his People die?
     No, to Him we all are joined
        As more than Standers by.
     Freely as the Victim came
        To the Altar of his Cross,
     We attend the Slaughter'd Lamb,*
        And suffer for his Cause. (131)

Christians freely identify with Christ as he freely gave himself in identification with them. Wesley's lines draw on Brevint's idea, previously cited: 'Never did the Son of God intend . . . to offer Himself for his

---

* *We attend*: we wait upon, serve.

people without his people' (VII.6). Christ's people are not observers, but 'sharers with the dying God/ And crucified below' (131:3.7–8).

2 Him ev'n now by Faith we see:
  Before our Eyes He stands!
 On the suffering Deity
  We lay our trembling Hands,
 Lay our Sins upon his Head,
  Wait on the dread Sacrifice,
 Feel the lovely Victim bleed,
  And die while JESUS dies!

3 Sinners see, He dies for All,
  And feel his mortal Wound,
 Prostrate on your Faces fall,
  And kiss the hallow'd Ground;
 Hallow'd by the streaming Blood,
  Blood whose Virtue All may know,
 Sharers with the Dying GOD,
  And crucified below.

When Wesley says that Christians are much more than beholders of Christ's saving acts, he is reworking a passage from Brevint:

> [Christ] came as a voluntary victim to the altar, being attended by his *Israel*, who, as it were, with their hands, laid all their sins upon his head . . . Because they [the offerers] laid their hands on it [the offered animal] when it was dying, and fell (for prayer and worship) on their faces down to the ground, when it did fall bleeding to death. – they were, as well as the very victim, reputed to *offer* themselves. (VII.6, 7)

Believers are enabled to respond to Christ by the Spirit's inward working. When they cry, it is the Spirit's cry within them.

4 Sprinkled with the Blood we lye,
  And bless its cleansing Power,
 Crying in the Spirit's Cry,
  Our Saviour we adore!

The last four lines stand somewhat apart from the rest of the hymn, for they are addressed to Jesus 'whose cross we bear', asking that his death destroy our sins.

> JESU, Lord, whose Cross we bear,
>   Let thy Death our Sins destroy,
> Make us who thy Sorrow share
>   Partakers of thy Joy. (131:4.5–8)

Supplemental Sacrifices

Wesley seeks to make clear that while Christians' sacrifices are united with Christ's sacrifice, theirs are secondary and dependent. The inadequate offerings of Christians are sanctified as they are joined to Christ's 'great oblation'. Wesley describes this relation of the real but secondary offerings of Christians to the primary offering of Jesus Christ by a biblical image which he found in Brevint (and which may well have had earlier currency). Both authors develop an analogy with the Jewish daily sacrifice in which the worshippers' offerings of meal and drink were joined with the sacrificed lamb. (The offering is described in Exodus 29.38–42, and the regulations are repeated in Numbers 28.3–10.) As Brevint and Wesley spiritualise this image, it speaks of the primary sacrifice of Christ with which the secondary offerings of Christians are associated. His is the basic sacrifice, the lamb; and theirs are the secondary offerings of meal, oil and wine that accompanied it, were supported by it, and were made one with it. (Both Brevint and Wesley find it suggestive that the associated offerings were meal and wine.) Wesley makes frequent use of this comparison (which may seem strained and unpersuasive today), developing it most fully in Hymn 137:

> 1   Ye Royal Priests of JESUS, rise,
>   And join the Daily Sacrifice,
>   Join all Believers in his Name
>   To offer up the Spotless Lamb.

> 2   Your Meat and Drink-Offerings throw
>   On Him who suffer'd once below,[1]
>   But ever lives with GOD above,
>   To plead for us his dying Love.

3   Whate'er we cast on Him alone
Is with His great oblation one,
His Sacrifice doth Ours sustain,
And Favour and Acceptance gain.

4   On Him, who all our Burthens bears,
We cast our Praises and our Prayers,
Ourselves we offer up to GOD,
Implung'd in His atoning Blood.

5   Mean are our Noblest Offerings,
Poor feeble unsubstantial Things;
But when to him our Souls we lift,
The Altar sanctifies the Gift.

6   Our Persons and our Deeds aspire
When cast into that hallow'd Fire,
Our most imperfect Efforts please
When join'd to CHRIST our Righteousness.

7   Mixt with the sacred Smoke we rise,
The Smoke of his Burnt Sacrifice,
By the Eternal Spirit driven
From Earth, in CHRIST we mount to Heaven. (137)

Wesley is following Brevint's thought:

> This Sacrifice did consist of two parts. The first and chiefest was the *Lamb*, that did foreshew the Lamb of God; and the second was the *meat and drink-offering*, made of flour mingled with oil and wine, – all which, being but an additional offering thrown on the Lamb morning and evening, was counted but for one and the same Sacrifice. (VII.10)

Wesley considers the incompatibility of Jesus' 'all-holy' sacrifice and believers' 'human and weak and sinful offerings', and he asks, 'How can the two oblations join?'

1   JESU, to Thee in Faith we look,
    O that our Services might rise
Perfum'd and mingled with the Smoke
    Of thy sweet-smelling Sacrifice.

2   Thy Sacrifice with heavenly Powers
      Replete, All-holy, All-divine,
  Human and weak, and sinful Ours;
      How can the two Oblations join?

By way of answer, stanzas 3 and 4 describe an exchange. Christ's sacrifice imparts its righteousness to the sacrifice of Christians, and 'our mean imperfect sacrifice' is cast on his. (Wesley assumes that his reference in 4.2 to the ritual of the daily sacrifice will be understood.) The two sacrifices are seen by God as one.

3   Thy Offering doth to Ours impart
      Its righteousness and Saving Grace,
  While charg'd with all our Sins Thou art,
      To Death devoted in our Place.

4   Our mean imperfect Sacrifice
      On Thine is as a Burthen thrown,
  Both in a Common Flame arise,
      And both in GOD's Account are One. (147)

Wesley is developing in Part V a complex thesis: Christ's sacrifice alone is redemptive; but Christians are not simply beneficiaries of it. The Holy Communion is an act of Christian sacrifice; it is something done. In receiving the Holy Communion, Christians are crucified with Christ; they are joined with him on his cross. But the sacrificial character of the sacrament does not abridge the solitary authority of the sacrifice of the cross, for in the Lord's Supper, the Church's sacrifice is dependent, united with Christ's prior and plenary sacrifice.

Sacramental thought that moves along these lines (although not necessarily in Wesley's idiom) has, since the mid-twentieth century, become widely heard among theologians, and, since it moderates old doctrinal polarities, it appears in some ecumenical statements on the eucharist. To cite one instance, a generation ago the Scottish Presbyterian Donald Baillie wrote about the sacrament in words which have the sound of Charles Wesley:

When in the sacrament we plead the sacrifice of Christ and in union with him offer ourselves to God, the whole of that process is a giving and receiving in one . . . The very giving of ourselves to God is a receiving of him, and the very receiving of him is already a giving of ourselves. There is no other way of receiving him except by giving ourselves to him: and there is no way of giving ourselves to him except by receiving him. Both of these are happening in every moment when we are worshipping God; and the supreme instrument and medium of that double movement, all in one, is the sacrament which we call the eucharist, or the holy communion, or the Lord's supper.[2]

Despite instances of such agreement, it should be acknowledged that some sharply defined Protestant thought is uncomfortable with this Wesleyan complex of ideas and terms, fearing that to involve Christians so closely in the redemptive act inevitably qualifies the completeness of Christ's work and the total dependence of believers on it. The late Franz Hildebrandt, in his informed but contentious work *I Offered Christ*,[3] examined the sacramental thought of Brevint and Wesley in a broad context and in close detail. His mind was clearly of a different temper from theirs, and he took issue with certain features of their thought. The idea that Christ's people are in some sense with him in his redemptive acts seemed to Hildebrandt to subvert the exclusive saviourhood of Christ and to make Christians in some sense contributors towards their own redemption.

Wesley's response, were he to make it, would no doubt rest in his conviction of the deep bond that persists between Christ and the Church. Wesley's 'high' doctrine of the sacrament is bound up with his 'high' doctrine of the community of Christ. He is clear that the union between Christ and his people is brought about by the initiative of grace. Christ is the Redeemer, and Christians are the redeemed, who, on their own, have nothing to offer but their sin, 'Only sin we call our own' (136:3.1). Christ, in his saving work, gives to his people, and they receive from him. However, as Wesley also emphasises, the incarnate Word takes a redeemed people into his divine life. He unites himself with them, making them forever one with him (133:5.6). Christ acts for the Church, as the Church lives from and in him. He and it constitute a unitary life. As Brevint had said, 'The Gospel most commonly describes Jesus Christ and his Church, not only as two parties that do nothing the one without the other, but sometimes as one person alone' (VII.2). Both Brevint and Wesley cite 1 Corinthians 12.12, 'For as the body is one, and hath many members, and all the members of that one body, being many, are one body: so also is Christ.' The Redeemer, with the Church, constitute the *totus Christus*.

Life that is shared with the Crucified is not easy. Christians suffer with Christ here as partakers of his grief and shame (131:1.7–8; 133:2.3; 142:7.2–3). They pray that God may take them 'into the fellowship/ Of

Jesu's sufferings' (148:2). They bear Christ's cross (131:4.5); they die with him (131:1) as 'sharers with the dying God' (131:3.7), who hang 'with him on the tree' (142:3).

The unworthy sacrifices of Christians are 'conjoin'd to thy [to Christ's] great Sacrifice' (133:4.5). Christians are offered in his sacrifice (135:1.3–5; 136:4), united with it 'by faithful remembrance' (142:1.4; 154 throughout). Christ's sacrifice and theirs are 'mingled in a common flame' (141:8.3). The Redeemer and the redeemed together comprise a single oblation (134:3.1–2):

> The Sav'd and Saviour now agree
>   In closest Fellowship combin'd,
> We grieve, and die, and live with Thee,
>   To thy great Father's Will resign'd;
> And GOD doth all thy Members own
> One with Thyself, for ever One. (133:5)

It is implied in this profound union that those who die with Christ 'shall with Him arise' (4:4.5–8). The union of Christ and his people persists beyond and triumphs over death.

> If his death we receive,
> His life we shall live;
> If his cross we sustain,
> His joy and his crown we in heaven shall gain. (142:8)

Renouncing Sin

It is in the hymns of Part V that Wesley speaks most often and forcefully of death to sin and of living wholly to God. 'The world to me is crucified,/ And I who on his cross have died/ To God for ever live' (135:4.4–6; and see 151:2). Knowing that it was our sins which 'have slain the Prince of Peace, . . . with him we vow to crucify' our sins (133:3.3–6; also 131:4.5–6).

In love – 'amazing love' – 'our God' was crucified. In view of the believer's union with him, Wesley asks whether or not 'our sinful members' (an allusion to Romans 6.13, 19) shall go on living.

> 1 Amazing Love to Mortals shew'd!
>   The Sinless Body of our GOD
>   Was fasten'd to the Tree;
>   And shall our sinful Members live?

He answers 'No, Lord,' and his further comment 'they shall not thee survive' is a way of saying that when Christ died, his people died in him. The unusual expression was suggested by Brevint, who had said that communicants come 'as true and sincere members, that cannot outlive their own Head' (VII.14).

> No, LORD, they shall not Thee survive,
>   They all shall die with Thee.

Sin, Wesley says, shall not continue when the Saviour has died. 'Our sinful members' must be crucified with Christ.

> 2   The Feet which did to Evil run,
>   The Hands which violent Acts have done,
>   The greedy Heart and Eyes,
>   Base Weapons of Iniquity,
>   We offer up to Death with Thee
>   A whole burnt Sacrifice. (135:1–2)

When Wesley itemises those 'base weapons of iniquity', his thought and vocabulary trace to a passage in which Brevint says that Christians who are joined to Christ must

> endeavour to crucify their sinful members, as really as Christ Himself had his sinless body crucified. So that the feet that before did run to evil, the violent hands that did injure, the greedy eyes that did covet, and all those members of the flesh that were weapons of wickedness, may by this cross and Sacrifice be more really bound, and in good measure destroyed.' (VII.9)

In later hymns, Wesley continues in the tone of contrition, a sense of unworthiness, and the determination to put away sin:

> We cast our Sins into that Fire
>   Which did thy Sacrifice consume,
> And every base and vain Desire
>   To daily Crucifixion doom. (141:6)

> JESU, LORD, whose Cross we bear,
>   Let thy death our sins destroy. (131:4.5–6)

Now inflict the Mortal Pain,
   Now exert thy Passion's Power,
Let the Man of Sin be slain,
   Die the Flesh to live no more. (154:4)

In a hymn that is especially full of the language of emotion ('tender fears',
'melt us into gracious tears', 'holy detestation', 'stabbed him [Christ] to
the heart', 'killing anguish'), Wesley prays for a Spirit-given awareness of
sin and sorrow for it:

Come Thou Spirit of Contrition,
   Fill our Souls with tender fears,
Conscious of our lost Condition
   Melt us into gracious Tears,
Just and holy detestation
   Of our Bosom-Sins impart,
Sins that caus'd our Saviour's Passion,
   Sins that stabb'd him in the Heart.

Fill our Flesh with killing Anguish,
   All our Members crucify,
Let th' offending Nature languish
   Till on JESU's Cross it die;
All our Sins to Death deliver,
   Let not One, not One survive;
Then we live to GOD forever,
   Then in Heaven on Earth we live. (151)

Dedication to God

Responding to God's gift, Wesley declares:

Just it is, and Good, and Right*
   That we should be wholly Thine,
In thy only Will delight,
   In thy blessed Service join. (139:3)

---

  * *Just it is, and Good and Right:* Wesley had in mind the opening of the consecration prayer.
The Prayer Book text was 'It is very meet, right, and our bounden duty.' But he may also have
had in mind the Latin Mass which had said, *Vere dignum et justum est.*

Rattenbury remarked, 'The greatest Methodist hymns of consecration are to be found in this section, and it is good to remember that they, in their original setting, were the climax to the Communion service.'[4] Wesley's hymns of consecration use cultic expressions such as 'offer', 'give', 'present' and 'make oblation' for a Christian's self-giving. These terms of priesthood and sacrifice extend beyond the sacramental event to include the presentation to God of one's whole life. Wesley asks Christ:

> Saviour, to Thee our lives we give,
> Our meanest sacrifice receive,
>   And to thine own oblation join. (128:3.7–9)

> By thy pard'ning Love compell'd:
> Up to Thee our Souls we raise,
>   Up to Thee our Bodies yield. (139:1.2–4)

Here, more than in any other part of *Hymns on the Lord's Supper*, Wesley links sacrifice and glory, cross and crown:

> Saviour, to Thee our Lives we give,
> Our meanest Sacrifice receive,
>   And to thy own Oblation join,
> Our suffering and triumphant Head,
> Thro' all thy States thy Members lead,
>   And seat us on the Throne Divine. (128:3.7–12)

> To die with Thee, and live
>   When all my Deaths are past;
> To live where Grief can never rise,
> And reign with Thee above the skies. (149:4.3–6)

Christ now lives, and union with him pledges that those who share his suffering here will share his glory and joy:

> To us who share thy Pain
> Thy Joy shall soon be given,
> And we shall in thy Glory reign,
>   For Thou art now in Heaven. (130:3.7–8; also 131:4.8)

A Christian's Goods

Brevint had ended *The Christian Sacrament and Sacrifice* with his two lengthiest sections: Section VII, 'Concerning the Sacrifice of our own Persons', followed by Section VIII, 'Concerning the Oblation of our Goods and Alms, or the Sacrifice of Justice'. John Wesley, in his abridgement of Brevint retained these two topics, the former of which is also his longest chapter.

However, Charles Wesley in his hymns largely set aside Brevint's Section VIII (a section which is, in fact, somewhat hortatory and repetitious). Perhaps he thought that the sacrifice of one's 'goods' might be taken as implied in the sacrifice of one's 'person'. As Brevint had remarked, 'It is not more fit for worshippers to present their persons without their goods, as it were trees without their sap and fruit' (VIII.12). Or it may have been that Wesley simply thought that by this time he had said the most important things he had to say. In Part V Wesley speaks almost entirely of 'The Sacrifice of Our Persons' and makes only summary comments on 'Our Goods'. But when he does speak of 'goods', he speaks forcefully.

> 1   FATHER, into thy Hands alone
>   I have my All restor'd
>   My All thy Property I own,*
>   The Steward of the LORD.
>
> 2   Hereafter none can take away
>   My Life or Goods or Fame,
>   Ready at thy Demand to lay
>   Them down I always am.
>
> 3   Confiding in thy only Love,
>   Thro' him who died for me,
>   I wait thy Faithfulness to prove,
>   And give back All to Thee. (145)

Wesley expresses his theme of total self-giving (as he had the theme of renouncing sin) with an insistent rhythm of nouns:

---

* *My All thy Property I own:* I acknowledge that everything I have ('my All') is God's property, and I am its steward.

Father, our Sacrifice receive,
  Our Souls and Bodies we present,
Our Goods and Vows, and Praises give,
  Whate'er thy bounteous Love hath lent. (153:2.1–4)

3 If so poor a Worm as I*
    May to thy great Glory live,
  All my Actions sanctify,
    All my Words and Thoughts receive:
  Claim me, for thy Service, claim
  All I have, and all I am.

4 Take my Soul and Body's Powers,
    Take my Mem'ry, Mind, and Will,
  All my Goods, and all my Hours,
    All I know, and all I feel,
  All I think, and speak, and do;
  Take my Heart – but make it new.

5 Now, O GOD, thine own I am,
    Now I give Thee back thy own,
  Freedom, Friends, and Health, and Fame,
    Consecrate to Thee alone;
  Thine I live, thrice happy I,
  Happier still, for Thine I die. (155)

In this hymn Wesley again is following Brevint, who had said, 'Hereafter no man can take any thing from me, no life, no honour, no estate, since I am ready of myself to lay them down as soon as I can perceive that God requires them at my hands' (VII.15).

Christian Resignation

As Wesley sees it, Christian sacrifice means the yielding of oneself and all one has entirely to God and accepting whatever God assigns:

---

* *so poor a Worm as I:* The term 'worm' was used by Wesley (and by other Christian writers well into the nineteenth century) to describe humanity. It appears in the AV Bible (Psalm 22.6, 'I am a worm and no man'; and see Job 25.6). The term in Wesley (as in Watts) refers less to human sinfulness than to human lowliness. One marvels that divine praise can be offered by beings so insignificant.[5]

1 FATHER, behold I come to do
  Thy Will, I come to suffer too
      Thy acceptable Will;
  Do with me, LORD, as seems Thee good,
  Dispose of this weak Flesh and Blood,
      And all thy Mind fulfil.

2 Thy Creature in thy Hands I am,
  Frail Dust and Ashes is my Name;
      Thy Earthen Vessel use,
  Mould as Thou wilt the passive Clay,
  But let me all Thy Will obey,
      And all thy Pleasure chuse.

3 Welcome, whate'er my GOD ordain!
  Afflict with Poverty or Pain
      This feeble flesh of mine,
  (But grant me Strength to bear my Load)
  I will not murmer at thy Rod,
      Or for Relief repine.

4 My Spirit wound (But oh! be near)
  With what far more than Death I fear,
      The Darts of keenest Shame,
  Fulfill'd with more than killing smart,
  And wounded in the tenderest part
      I still adore thy Name.

5 Beneath thy bruising Hand I fall,
  Whate'er Thou send'st I take it all,
      Reproach or Pain, or Loss,
  I will not for Deliverance pray,
  But humbly unto thy Death obey,
      The death of JESU's Cross. (143)

The hymn, written in the 'I' voice, portrays a frail and troubled Christian who is conscious of being in the hands of God and is willing to accept whatever God may choose, 'Do with me, Lord, as seems Thee good' (1.4). Becoming more intense, the hymn speaks of pain and adversity as sent by God, 'I fall beneath thy bruising hand; I take whatever thou sendest, reproach or pain or loss' (5.1–3). The believer does not question or complain or seek for explanation, confident that God has a purpose in everything (2.5–3.1) and pledging to adore God through all (4.5–6).

Wesley seems to have had in mind the struggles of some biblical models: Job in his distress, Jesus in Gethsemane, and Paul's 'thorn in the flesh' (2 Corinthians 12.7–9). His thought, his tone, and his first-person voice all have an immediate model in the opening portion of Brevint's prayer:

> Lo, I come! if this soul and body may be useful to any thing, here they are both, to do thy will, O God. And hereafter, if it please thee to use that power which thou hast, as Creator, over dust and ashes, over weak flesh and blood, over a brittle vessel of clay, over the work of thine own hands; lo, here they are, to suffer also thy good pleasure! I do now protest to my God, that if He please to afflict me either with Pain or dishonour, I will humble myself under it, and be obedient unto death, even unto the death of the cross. (VII.15)

Dying in Jesus' Death

Wesley speaks in the idiom of resignation again in Hymn 154, which urges, 'Let us go and die/ With our dearest dying Lord!' The lines allude to Thomas' pessimistic remark in John 11.16, which Brevint had earlier universalised, saying that at the cross, 'every disciple might . . . be moved to say as Thomas, "let us go and die with him"' (VII.13). The 'uppermost desire' of Christians is to part with their nature's life and meekly to die on Jesus' cross. Having asked for conformity with Jesus' sufferings, the speaker prays, 'Plunge us deep into thy Death' (154:2.3–3.4).

St Paul had said that Christians seek to 'know Christ and the fellowship of his sufferings' (Philippians 3.10). Wesley, however, intensifies the emphasis, saying that believers seek to die with Jesus on his very cross – an idea which appears several times in Part V, but most clearly in two stanzas:

> Beneath thy Bruising Hand I fall,
> . . .
> I will not for Deliverance pray,
> But humbly unto Death obey,
>   The Death of JESU's Cross. (143:5.1, 4–6)

> LORD, Thou seest our willing Heart,
>   Knowest its uppermost Desire,
> With our Nature's Life to part,
>   Meekly on thy Cross t'expire. (154:2)

Hymns 144 and 146 speak of the Christian and the cross of Christ, and
they seem especially enigmatic:

1   Let both *Jews* and *Gentiles* join,
     Friends and Enemies combine,
     Vent their utmost Rage on me,
     Still I look thro' All to Thee.

2   Humbly own it is the LORD!
     Let Him wake on me his Sword:
     Lo, I bow me to thy Will;
     Thou thy whole Design fulfil.

3   Striken by thine Anger's Rod,
     Dumb I fall before my GOD;
     Or my dear Chastiser bless,
     Sing the Pascal Psalm of Praise:

4   While the bitter Herbs I eat,
     Him I for my Foes entreat;
     Let me die, but oh! forgive,
     Let my pardon'd Murderers live. (144)

The hymn, which is also in the first person singular, depicts a righteous
sufferer. Some features of this allusive hymn suggest that the poetic
speaker is Jesus: Jews and Gentiles vented their rage on him (stanza 1); he
sang the Hallel psalms (3.4); he died praying for his murderers' forgiveness (4.2–4). Other features, however, might suit any suffering Christian,
as Christ's passion is made contemporary in Christian experience, and as
a Christian's suffering is interpreted by Jesus' passion. In stanzas 2 and
3 the 'I' of the hymn suffers from others, but also from God, 'my dear
Chastiser' – an idea which Wesley associates with Jesus' passion and, by
derivation, with Christian suffering. Christians in every age have read
their occasions of extremity in the light of Jesus' cross and found that
suffering can be utilised by God's purpose.

    This hymn is modelled on (but not greatly clarified by) a passage from
a prayer of Brevint's:

I do now protest to my God, that if He please to afflict me either with
pain or dishonour, I will humble myself under it, and be obedient unto
death, even unto the death of the cross. Whatsoever happens unto
me, either from the Jews or Gentiles, from my neighbours or from

strangers, since it is my God that employs them . . . I will not hereafter open my mouth before the Lord, who doth strike me, except only to sing this Psalm, after I have eaten some bitter herbs that belong to this Passover, and to entreat Him for the wicked, who perhaps hath maliciously gathered them. (VII.15)

Is the voice of this hymn that of the crucified Jesus, or is it that of a suffering Christian? Or does this unusual hymn demonstrate the two voices mingling, separating, and combining again?

Hymn 146 expresses a similar tone and raises many of the same questions:

1   FATHER, if Thou willing be,
     Then my Griefs a while suspend,
   Then remove the Cup from me,
     Or thy strength'ning Angel send;
   Would'st Thou have me suffer on?
   Father, let Thy Will be done.

2   Let my flesh be troubled still,
     Fill'd with Pain or sore Disease,
   Let my wounded Spirit feel
     Strong, redoubled Agonies,
   Meekly I my Will resign,
   Thine be done, and only Thine.

3   Patient as my great High-Priest
     In his Bitterness of Pain,
   Most abandoned and distrest,
     Father, I the Cross sustain;*
   All into Thy Hands I give,
   Let me die or let me live.

4   Following where my LORD hath led,
     Thee I on the Cross adore,
   Humbly bow like Him my Head,
     All my benefits restore,
   Till my Spirit I resign
   Breath'd into the Hands Divine. (146)

---

* *sustain:* endure, bear up under

The 'I' here seems to be a willingly submissive Christian seeking to live and die in the spirit of Christ. Yet the speaker unmistakably echoes Jesus' agonised prayer in Gethsemane when he asked the Father that the cup might be removed from him, but ultimately prayed 'Thy will be done' (Matthew 26.36–45 and parallels). Some lines even sound as though they were spoken from the cross itself – especially the final giving up of the spirit (Luke 23.46). Christians identify with Christ as he gave himself in identification with them. Christ's people do not come to the cross as observers, but they are 'sharers with the dying God/ And crucified below' (131:3.7–8). The hymn asks the Father that griefs may be removed or that strength be given to endure them to the end. Yet the overriding prayer is that God's will may be done.

The central portion of this hymn takes its theme and many of its wordings from Brevint's prayer:

> What kind soever of suffering hereafter may trouble my flesh, or what kind soever of agonies may, perhaps, worse trouble my spirit, following the example of this high Priest, in the midst of his bitterest pains, O Father, into thy hand I will ever remit my life, and the dearest concernments that attend it. And if thou be pleased that either I live yet a while or not, I will, with my Saviour, bow down my head; I will adore thee under my burden, and humble myself under thy hand; I will give up all, that thou will be pleased to ask, goods, joys, &c. until at last I surrender and give up the ghost. (VII.15)

One cannot but observe the ambiguity of voice in these hymns. The communicant identifies with Jesus in his passion and adopts words that he spoke in Gethsemane and on the cross. Suffering Christians are entitled to identify with the suffering Christ. He has been where they are. Yet such immediacy can sound self-dramatising. Are there essential cautions about Christians placing themselves with Jesus in his passion and death, and do Brevint and Wesley always observe those cautions?

Here again Franz Hildebrandt raises questions. He finds that a Christian's wish to die with Christ on his very cross – a wish that Wesley expresses – goes beyond the boundaries of Scripture and the limits of human prayer: 'We may be enabled to sing: "Whate'er Thou send'st, I take it all," but we are in no position to volunteer "meekly on Thy cross to expire."'[6] That Christians are offerers with Christ, their sacrifice being made one with his, seems to Hildebrandt to be a departure 'from the letter and spirit of Scripture'.[7] Christians, he says, are not to join in Christ's sacrifice, but to receive it and celebrate its completeness.

Hildebrandt admires and commends many of Wesley's hymns, including many from *Hymns on the Lord's Supper*. But in this matter of Christians seeking to be with Christ on his cross, he must dissent. The cross and the sacrament of the cross are, for Hildebrandt, acts of God, which Christians only receive in faith.

However, Charles Wesley's thought in the matter can be given a sympathetic presentation. Wesley does not write as an exegete or a systematician. He is not careless, and his classical training taught him how to construe texts. However, he reads the scriptures as a poet whose synthesising mind works with the imaginatively grasped stuff of images. And it is the way of images to expand and unite. (They unite the things that are imaged with one another and with the image-user.) In these hymns, Wesley seems to combine the sole redeeming sacrifice of Christ (which he affirms repeatedly) with the union (virtually the coinherence) of Christ and the Church which he finds most fully developed in Paul. Christians, as the Apostle sees it, are crucified, buried, risen and ascended with Christ. When Paul says 'I am crucified with Christ' (Galatians 2.20; see also Philippians 3.10), he is, in effect, saying, 'When he died, I died.' Reciprocally, Christ, for his part, lives and suffers and bears witness in the Church. Its prayer is his prayer in it. In its acts of witness, Christ is present, witnessing to himself (2 Corinthians 5.18–20). The Prison Epistles speak in physiological language. Christ is the Church's head, vitally connected to it by joints and sinews (terms which are unexplained) which convey life so that the body is built up in a growth that is from God (Ephesians 4.15–16; Colossians 2.19). One remarkable passage, Colossians 1.24, says that the Church is so much a part of Christ's life that its sufferings supply what is lacking in his sufferings.[8] Christ-and-Church convictions such as these seem to lie behind Brevint's and Wesley's theme.

As a hymn-writer, Wesley composes his work with as much care as his rapid methods allow. He develops in Part V of *Hymns on the Lord's Supper* the themes of: (1) the sole saviourhood of Jesus Christ and the dependence of the Church on him, and (2) the mutuality of Christ and his people, he in them and they in him. Wesley knew the emphasis of Pietist spirituality on the intimate fellowship between Christians and Christ. It was only a step to say that Christians share Christ's very cross and that their self-offering places them with him in his redemptive act. These two emphases need not be in conflict with one another. The themes as they merge and then distinguish themselves are complex, and Wesley's idiom may be uncommon, but his sacramental doctrine is evangelically coherent.

The final truth of the matter for Wesley may well be that the sacrifice of Christians – in cultic act, but also in obedient life – is not so much a demand as it is a gift of the Spirit:

> FATHER, on us the Spirit bestow,
>   Thro' which thine everlasting Son
> Offer'd Himself for Man below,
>   That *we*, ev'n *we* before thy Throne
> Our Souls and Bodies may present,
> And pay Thee All thy Grace hath lent.
>
> O let thy Spirit sanctify
>   Whate'er to Thee we now restore,
> And make us with thy Will comply,
>   With all our Mind and Soul and Power,
> Obey Thee as thy Saints above
> In perfect Innocence and Love. (150)

* * *

ESSAY

Theology and Feeling

In *Hymns on the Lord's Supper* one is made aware of the intensity of the devotion among the followers of the Wesleyan movement. Especially in the early days of the revival, strong emotions were released – sometimes of penitence, and sometimes of ecstatic joy. The emotions occasionally slipped beyond control, and persons cried out or fell to the ground, weeping, shouting, moaning or raging. The destructive emotions could be worked through, and troubled persons be brought to some calmness. But feelings, in their variety and unpredictability, were irrepressible.

Nothing in the social background or the academic careers of the Wesleys had prepared them for this spontaneous, unsought outpouring. They had to ask whether the powerful, potentially disruptive force of emotion, when it was released in the community of faith, was a sign of the stir of God. Or was it more likely to mislead and to carry individuals or the movement itself to extremes? Could it be accepted, subdued and made constructive? Or should it be repressed? If emotion itself was ambiguous, were there criteria to establish, even in extreme experience, the authentic voice of the Spirit?

Many of the Methodist converts had previously known emotion largely as a destructive force in their dissolute lives and disorganised families. But converted persons were encouraged to look to their feelings as a clue to reality. Simple and unlettered but spiritually alert people could, by inward attentiveness, know something of the intimate presence, the tenderness and wonder of God. Yet feelings could deceive. Those who felt themselves close to God could be far off, and those who felt themselves distant could be near. In this matter the Wesleys were not naive.

The issues were not simple. Clearly feeling is not self-validating as a religious criterion. Many people are highly suggestible. Excesses of emotion tend to feed on themselves, and they can pass like a contagion from one person to another. The Wesleys struggled with the ambiguity of 'the religious affections', as did the leaders of the Awakening in the American colonies. Yet despite the complexity of the matter and the possibility of misjudging, in the emotional manifestations that accompanied the Evangelical Revival something important was being expressed about humanity and about Christian faith, against the one-sided account of human reality and of religion that was current in the rationalistic climate of the eighteenth century.

Although the demonstrativeness that their work elicited was new to them, the Wesleys could not dismiss it as they witnessed the unmistakable work of God in the lives of converts, changing their behaviour, establishing order and stability, bringing forth unguessed abilities and courage. While there might be dangers in religious manifestations that uncritically took intense emotions to be the work of God within a believer's heart, there were, as the Wesleys would have seen the matter, even greater dangers in a religion that felt nothing.

The new burst of religious conviction that had been released in eighteenth-century Britain strained against the established order of society and institutional religion. Persons seeking an immediate relation with God tend to be impatient with forms which try to channel it. The God who is known in a fresh and self-authenticating apprehension is not the God of system and predictable order, but the God of the irregular, the paradoxical and the unexpected. If structure and order are eventually affirmed, they will not be affirmed as they had been understood, but as they have been opened by incorporating a reality that lay beyond their earlier confined forms.

Methodists, in their quest for inward assurance, took their feelings to be indices of their relation with God, thus according to feeling some ill-defined theological status. Emotion, however, tends to arise out of immediate impulse and to seem self-validating. To follow it uncritically would yield a disordered and unproductive life. If religious feelings may be affirmed, they must also be socialised, controlled and held accountable in the court of the inner life and of the community of faith.

Wesley does not in *Hymns on the Lord's Supper* use the noun 'feeling', but only forms of the verb 'to feel'. He sometimes uses the noun 'motions' in the now obsolete sense of inward promptings or impulses. (The term survives in the word 'emotion' and when one speaks of being 'moved' by something.) When he says that the members of the body 'all pursue the motions of our Head' (129:3.1–2, and see Brevint VII.2, cited on p. 189), he articulates something like a Christology of feeling. He seems to have in mind some real but undefined correlation between Christ and the inner life of the Christian – as though Christ lives and feels in believers, and believers live and feel in Christ. St Paul suggests something of the sort when in Philippians 1.8 he says that he longs for his fellow Christians 'in the compassion [the *splanxna*, the nobler viscera, the seat of the higher emotions] of Christ Jesus'. Paul's longing for others was Christ's longing in him and his longing was in Christ. If there is the possibility of arrogance in such an identification of one's inner self with the indwelling Christ, both St Paul and Charles Wesley, while recognising the danger, might also have thought that it expressed the daring of faith.

Wesley suggests the theological significance of feeling by his use of the image of fire. Fire exists by burning; if it is at all, it is active, uniting oxygen and fuel. It always moves upward. The term, in Wesley, seems to refer to feeling, but it usually suggests more – an experience that is not self-originated, but is given by or shared by the inner working of the Spirit, leading human life to God.

> Mix'd with the sacred smoke we rise,
> The smoke of his burnt sacrifice;
> By the Eternal Spirit driven
> From earth, in CHRIST we mount to heaven. (137:7)

> 　My feeble Soul would fain aspire,
> In Zeal and Thoughts, and whole Desire
> Lift up to Thee, through JESU's Name,
> As a Burnt-Sacrifice, its Flame. (152:3)

In writing on the Lord's Supper, Wesley describes a varied life of feeling: Communicants ask that they may feel sympathetically with figures at the crucifixion – to feel the pain of Mary (22:2.5–6) and to feel the very death of Jesus (131:2.7–8). The feeling is intensified when one recognises that Christ's suffering was for oneself: 'Sinner, believe; and find him here:/ Believe; and feel he died for you' (71:4.3–4). 'O my God, he dies for me,/

I feel the mortal smart!' (21:7.1–2). At the cross one feels that Jesus' prayer 'Forgive them' is answered: 'Behold him stand as slaughter'd there,/ And feel the answer to his prayer' (140:2.5–6).

As one feels one's sin now, one longs to feel something better. A sinner feels the misery of the stained condition and yearns for newness (32:1.11–12; 149:3.3–4). The soul 'longs to feel [God's] quick'ning breath' (64:2.4).

Feeling is awakened when the realities of redemption are not simply known to be true, but when they are, by the Spirit's inward working, known to be true for oneself: '[We] long to feel applied/ The blood for our redemption given' (11:3.4f.). 'That all may feel the death applied' (24:2.3). 'Sinners see, He dies for all,/ And feel his mortal wound' (131:3.2).

> Come, Remembrancer Divine,
> Let us feel thy Power applying
>   CHRIST to every Soul and mine. (16:2.2–4)

Coming to the sacrament with inner receptiveness, one is open to a deeply felt response. (Self-deception always threatens. One may come seeking an emotional experience, and the search may itself induce the desired feeling.) A believer may be genuinely stirred by what the Supper communicates: 'We feel the double grace is given' (46:4.3). 'With joy we feel its [the eucharist's] sacred power' (62:8.1). In the sacrament 'We now forgiveness have,/ We feel his work begun' (111:2.1–2). 'Receive the sacramental meat,/ And feel the virtue [the power] from above' (71:2.2–3). At the Supper the devout communicant feels the promise of heaven: 'We feel the earnest in our hearts/ Of our eternal rest' (97:1.7–8).

At one moment Wesley speaks as though there were an almost physiological aspect to saving faith:

> The Tokens of thy Dying Love,
>   O let us All receive,
> And feel the Quick'ning Spirit move,
>   And *sensibly* believe. (30:4)

The lines might be thought to anticipate John Macmurray's remark that 'The emotional life is inherently sensuous.'[9]

Charles Wesley not only mentions feeling, he exhibits feeling in the drama and intensity of his thought – his self-abasement and his exultation; his wonder that God should be gracious; his stretching language to speak of that which is beyond speech. His passionate lines express the drama of his gospel and its engagement with the soul. He asks questions of communicants and leads them in frequent exclamations:

> Shall we let Him die in vain,
>   Still to Death pursue our GOD?
> Open tear his Wounds again,
>   Trample on his pretious Blood?
> No; with all our Sins we part:
> Saviour, take my broken Heart! (23:3)

In several places, Wesley sets in a poetic line a long dash that does not interrupt the meter. It is as though he were suggesting a catch of the breath.

> Expiring in the Sinner's Place,
>   Crush'd with the Universal Load
> He hangs! —— adown his mournful Face,
>   See trickling fast the Tears and Blood! (24:1.1–4)

And at times he suggests utter ecstasy:

> The Joy is more unspeakable,
>   And yields me larger Draughts of GOD,
> Till Nature faints beneath the Power,
> And Faith fill'd up can hold no more. (54:5.3–6)

Although the Wesleys in their evangelistic work set forth their message urgently, they did not play to hearers' emotions (a charge which with more cause could be made against George Whitefield). John's published sermons develop in an orderly and measured way. Yet response to the gospel was sought – a new way of seeing things, a radical repudiation of previous ways of life, new commitments, a new informing vision, a new ordering of one's priorities, a new quest for holiness, and a new vision of glory in formerly drab lives. This inward renewal, if it is to endure and to work its way through a convert's life, will (indeed, it must) engage the emotions. It is the response of love to Love.

Yet such renewal, while it draws on wells of emotion, must be set in structures of reality. While emotion may be a part of a believing response to the gospel, it is not to be equated with a believing response to the gospel. If one is eagerly waiting for feelings, the waiting itself can occasion the desired emotions, and the emotions, when they come, can place convictions beyond question or review. At the same time, emotions are not fully under one's control, and when one is counting on feelings, and the desired emotions do not come, one can fall into self-doubt or despair.

Wesley seeks to bring feelings into an objective context. One feels, but not self-indulgently, enjoying one's exquisite sense of feeling. That is the route that led to nineteenth-century sentimentality, Evangelical and Anglo-Catholic. Rather, as Wesley presents the matter, one feels *because of* the reality of God and grace, or the wonder of conversion, or something perceived in the sacrament. Wesley urges communicants to respond to what God has done or is doing, and this response is itself God-given. Wesley prays, 'Open . . . our hearts to know the Lord' (29:2.4). Through the interior witness of the Holy Spirit, God who acts in grace acts also in the inner consent to grace. Yet John Wesley insisted that any supposed inspiration is delusional if it contradicts 'the law and the testimony' (*Journal*, 17 January 1739; he used the expression often).

Charles Wesley argues that one should not abandon the sacrament because the expected interior rewards are not felt. (See pp. 114–19 above.) The communicant stays even when Jesus 'hides his face' (84:2). Valuable though feelings may be, they never take precedence over the clear word of Christ: 'Jesus hath spoke the Word,/ His will my reason is' (84:4.1–2).

Discrimination is always required. Feeling does not make a thing true, although it may be a mode of perceiving the truth of something that is true, but that is not effectively true for one until that truth is recognised in a way that matters inwardly and passionately. Belief lodges in the heart (Romans 10.9), and while in the psychology of the Bible, the heart is not the emotions, the heart is not less than the emotions; it is the interior place where the self determines itself. Wesley would not set feeling against knowing. Rather, for him feeling could be a mode of knowing – an access to reality and certitude. In 92:3.2 he says, 'We know it and feel.'

How much more than this Charles Wesley would say – for instance, how much allowance he would make for differences in temperament – one cannot gather from these hymns. (Clearly he was himself more emotionally direct and volatile than was his more controlled and even-tempered, although more credulous, brother John.) He is open to the voice of feeling, and at times he seems to seek emotional, even sensory validation of faith. Yet he does not insist on emotion nor direct how it must come to expression. Wesley gives no considered discussion of the matter of feeling, important though it is in his thought and religion. What he meant by what he said on the subject in his hymns he says in the hymns themselves or not at all.

After the Sacrament

HYMNS 158–166

Wesley writes for worshippers who would find some act of devotion following the sacrament desirable. He may have had in mind the aids for communicants that were published in the seventeenth and eighteenth centuries which regularly contained post-communion thanksgivings, meditations, resolutions and prayers.

This final section of hymns is informed to some extent by the Holy Communion service of the 1662 Prayer Book, in which, after the communicants have received the body and blood of Christ, a prayer is said, which may be one of thanksgiving or one of self-offering. The people sing or say the *Gloria in Excelsis* – the great early Eastern hymn of praise which in 1552 Cranmer had transferred from the opening position it had held in both the Latin Mass and his 1549 Prayer Book and made it a post-communion doxology. Finally, the people are dismissed with a blessing. This Prayer Book pattern holds its principal actions of thanksgiving, self-offering, praise and blessing until after the sacrament has been received.

Earlier hymns in this collection, especially some towards the end of Part II, had spoken of struggle and frustration, doubtless reflecting the actual experience of at least some communicants. Many hymns had urgently asked Christ to give assurance of his presence or his forgiveness. However, these hymns that follow the sacrament express only gratitude, joy and praise.

The section opens with an uncomplicated hymn in which communicants acknowledge what they have received in the sacrament and in the redemption which the sacrament signifies. They have been given 'the tokens of his dying love' and been richly fed. What they have received is 'heaven begun below'. Tongues have been loosed, and persons made free to praise. Earth and heaven unite to celebrate 'The Lamb for sinners slain,/ Who died to die no more.'

1   All Praise to GOD above
      In whom we have believ'd!
The Tokens of whose dying Love
      We have ev'n now receiv'd.

    Have with his Flesh been fed,*
      And drank his precious Blood:
His precious Blood is Drink indeed,
      His Flesh immortal Food.

2   O what a Taste is This
      Which now in CHRIST we know,
An Earnest of our glorious Bliss,
      Our Heaven begun below!

    When He the Table spreads,
      How Royal is the Chear!
With Rapture we lift up our Heads,
      And own that GOD is here.

3   He bids us taste his Grace,
      The Joys of Angels prove,
The Stammerer's Tongues are loos'd to praise
      Our dear Redeemer's Love.

    Salvation to our GOD
      That sits upon the Throne;
Salvation be alike bestow'd
      On his triumphant Son!

4   The Lamb for Sinners slain,
      Who died to die no more,
Let all the ransom'd Sons of Men
      With all his Hosts adore:

    Let earth and Heaven be join'd
      His Glories to display,
And hymn the Saviour of Mankind
      In one eternal Day. (158)

---

* Lines 1.5–8 are an instance of chiasmus.

It is a frequent doxological theme that praise which is voiced on earth is joined with the praise of heaven. The words at the head of Hymn 161, 'Therefore with Angels and Archangels, &c.', are from the common Preface which leads into the *Sanctus* in the Prayer Book communion rite.

Therefore with Angels and Arch-angels, &c.

1   LORD, and GOD of heavenly Powers,
     Theirs – yet oh! benignly Ours;
     Glorious King, let Earth proclaim,
     Worms attempt to chaunt thy Name.

2   Thee to laud in Songs divine,
     Angels and Arch-Angels join;
     We with them our Voices raise,
     Echoing thy eternal Praise.

3   Holy, holy, holy LORD,
     Live by Heaven and Earth ador'd!
     Full of Thee they ever cry
     Glory be to GOD most high! (161)

In saying that earth and heaven join in praise to the God of both, this hymn draws on classic expressions, largely from the Scriptures. (Expressions of praise tend to be formulaic and to grow from a tradition of prior praise.) Stanza 2 uses the *Sursum Corda*, which unites the Church's eucharistic action with 'Angels and Archangels and all the company of heaven'. Stanza 3 echoes two angelic hymns: it begins with the *Sanctus* from Isaiah's vision in the Temple (Isaiah 6.3), which is repeated in the vision of Revelation 4.8; and it ends echoing the *Gloria in Excelsis*, the angelic song at the nativity (Luke 2.14).

Hymn 163 is a full-throated doxology which begins with the opening line of the *Gloria in Excelsis*, the canticle which in English Prayer Books since 1552 was the congregation's response to the sacrament. Wesley's hymn is a loose paraphrase which draws on the wording and structure of this ancient act of praise, setting its opening words at the head of the hymn.

Glory be to GOD *on high, and on Earth Peace, &c.*

1   Glory be to GOD on high,
     GOD whose Glory fills the Sky;
     Peace on Earth to Man forgiven,
     Man the Well-belov'd of Heaven!

Wesley somewhat expands his source. Stanzas 2–3 are praise to the
Father, and stanzas 4–6 praise to the Son.

2   Sovereign Father, heavenly King,
     Thee we now presume to sing,
     Glad thine Attributes confess,
     Glorious all and numberless.

3   Hail by all thy Works ador'd,
     Hail the everlasting LORD!
     Thee with thankful Hearts we prove,
     LORD of Power, and GOD of Love.

4   CHRIST our LORD and GOD we own,
     CHRIST the Father's only Son:
     Lamb of GOD for Sinners slain,
     Saviour of offending Man.

The text of the *Gloria in Excelsis* incorporates the *Agnus Dei*, which
clearly lies behind Wesley's stanzas 5 and 6 with their themes of hearing
our prayer and granting us mercy. In these Christological stanzas Wesley
makes the ancient Greek canticle speak the soteriological emphases of
the Revival, describing the one who sits at the Father's right hand as our
'Powerful Advocate with God'.

5   Bow thine Ear, in mercy bow,
     Hear, the World's Atonement Thou:
     JESU, in thy Name we pray,
     Take, O take our Sins away.

6   Powerful Advocate with GOD,
     Justify us by thy Blood!
     Bow thine Ear, in Mercy bow,
     Hear, the World's Atonement Thou!

The Spirit is only introduced in the trinitarian seventh stanza, just as the Spirit is mentioned only in the final lines of the *Gloria*.

> 7 Hear, for Thou, O CHRIST, alone,
>   With thy glorious Sire art One,
>   One the HOLY GHOST with Thee,
>   One supreme Eternal Three!

The early Methodists were drawn into close communities of fellowship, praise, prayer, discipline and service – a closeness which must have been especially felt at the Supper. Yet in this collection only Hymn 165 speaks of the eucharistic assembly and the life shared among its members. While many of Wesley's hymns for the Supper speak in the 'we' voice, they convey no sense that communicants form a community whose members interact with one another, helpfully or unhelpfully. Hymn 165 speaks only in positive terms, of happiness, accord, and harmony, of being many and yet one, of joining and meeting, of ties and agreement. This oneness is brought about by Christ in the sacrament – the eucharistic feeding by which Christians are united as they can only be short of heaven itself (4.1–4).

> 1 How happy are thy Servants, LORD,
>   Who thus remember Thee!
>   What Tongue can tell our sweet Accord,
>   Our perfect Harmony!

> 2 Who thy Mysterious Supper share,
>   Here at thy Table fed,
>   Many, and yet but One we are,
>   One undivided Bread.

> 3 One with the Living Bread Divine,
>   Which now by Faith we eat,
>   Our Hearts, and Minds, and Spirits join,
>   And all in JESUS meet.

> 4 So dear the Tie where Souls agree
>   In JESU's Dying Love;
>   Then only can it closer be,
>   When all are join'd above. (165)

Clearly, the hymn speaks idealistically. Persons who join at the sacrament may yet be quite divided, and Methodism, like the New Testament Church, and the churches of the Reformation, experienced tensions, including tensions over the Supper. Yet the Church may hold over against the dividedness of its actual assemblies this fundamental gesture of unity in Christ. Every stanza says that the locus of community is in the sacrament: 'Who thus [in the Church's meal] remember Thee' (1.2); 'Who Thy mysterious supper share' (2.1f.); 'One with the living Bread Divine/ Which now by faith we eat' (3.1f.); 'So dear the tie where souls agree/ In Jesu's dying love [represented in the Supper]' (4.1f.).

Hymns on the Lord's Supper ends with a poem of 22 stanzas, which is clearly not a hymn to be sung, but a final reflection, challenge and prayer to be read and considered by the Church.

It has been a trait of the Christian mind, beginning with the opening chapters of the book of Acts, to idealise the time of the Church's beginnings. In stanzas 1–5 Wesley describes the earliest Christians as 'a simple, lowly, loving race', living in 'holy fellowship' around the communion, which they observed daily and from house to house. (His picture of the harmony of the early Church is based on Acts 2.42–7.) When in stanza 3 Wesley says that the early Christians did not presume to be wiser than their Lord, but obediently kept the memorial of his sacrifice, the lines are his final rebuke to followers of the anti-sacramental 'stillness' teachings.

1   Happy the Saints of former Days
     Who first continued in the Word,
   A simple lowly loving Race,
     True Followers of their Lamb-like LORD.

2   In holy Fellowship they liv'd,
     Nor would from the Commandment move,
   But every joyful Day receiv'd
     The Tokens of expiring Love.

3   Not then above their Master wise,
     They simply in his Paths remain'd,
   And call'd to Mind his Sacrifice
     With stedfast Faith and Love unfeign'd.

4   For House to House they broke the Bread
     Impregnated with Life divine,
   And drank the Spirit of their Head
     Transmitted in the sacred Wine.

5   With JESU's constant Presence blest,
        While duteous to his dying Word,
     They kept the Eucharistick Feast,
        And supp'd in *Eden* with their LORD.

Stanzas 6–9 describe the early Christians taking their flame from 'the altar's fire' and living on earth in a way that would rival the angels. Some of them were faithful even to martyrdom.

6   Throughout their spotless Lives was seen
        The Virtue of this heavenly Food,
     Superior to the Sons of Men
        They soar'd aloft, and walk'd with GOD.

7   O what a Flame of sacred Love
        Was kindled by the Altar's fire!
     They liv'd on Earth like those above,
        Glad rivals of the heavenly Choir.

8   Strong in the Strength herewith receiv'd,
        And mindful of the Crucified;
     His Confessors for Him they liv'd,
        For Him his faithful Martyrs dyed.

9   Their Souls from Chains of Flesh releas'd,
        By Torture from their Bodies driven
     With violent Faith the Kingdom seiz'd,
        And fought and forc'd their Way to Heaven.

In stanzas 10–14 Wesley laments the Church's loss of devotion and power. Lines 10.1–11.2 ask why this decline should have come about. The following lines answer, tracing it to the loss of the daily sacrament (11.3). Coolness has led to disregard of the sacrament, and disregard of the sacrament has led to coldness – 'sad mutual causes of decay'. 'Thine holy Ordinance contemn'd/ Hath let the Flood of Evil in' (14.1–2).

10   Where is the pure primeval Flame,
        Which in their faithful Bosom glow'd?
     Where are the followers of the Lamb,
        The dying Witnesses for GOD?

11   Why is the faithful Seed decreas'd?
        The Life of GOD extinct and dead?
    The daily Sacrifice is ceas'd,
        And Charity to Heaven is fled.

12   Sad mutual Causes of Decay,
        Slackness and Vice together move,
    Grown cold we cast the Means away,
        And quench'd our latest Spark of Love.

13   The sacred Signs thou didst ordain,
        Our pleasant Things are all laid waste;
    To Men of Lips and Hearts profane,
        To Dogs and Swine, and Heathen cast.

14   Thine holy Ordinance contemn'd
        Hath let the Flood of Evil in,
    And those who by thy Name are nam'd,
        The Sinners unbaptiz'd out-sin.

At stanza 15 the hymn begins to address Christ – 'canst Thou not Thy Work revive?' Stanzas 15–17 plead with him to renew his people 'in our degenerate years'. Stanzas 16–17 look beyond the Church and speak of the eucharist 'in its missionary, its worldly dimension'. As Hodges and Allchin observe:

It is not only the faithful remnant who sigh for the coming of Christ; consciously or unconsciously, the nations too mourn his absence. For the return of the Lord amongst his people is of significance for all, and the prayer for the renewal of the Church's Eucharistic life is a prayer that the healing presence may be known among all people.[1]

15   But canst Thou not thy Work revive
        Once more in our degenerate Years?
    O wouldst thou with thy Rebels strive,
        And melt them into gracious Tears?

16   O wouldst Thou to thy Church return?
        For which the faithful Remnant sighs,
    For which the drooping Nations mourn,
        Restore the daily Sacrifice.

17   Return, and with thy Servants sit,
          LORD of the Sacramental Feast,
      And satiate us with heavenly Meat,
          And make the *World* thy happy Guest.

Stanzas 18–22 conclude the poem, carrying the thought to the Church's destiny beyond history. From 19.3 to the end of the hymn, every line contains a verb of appeal, asking God to come, to seal the ransomed saints and complete their number, to erect a Tabernacle here, to send the New Jerusalem down, and to appear among the people, and bring lasting joy.

18   Now let the Spouse, reclin'd on Thee,
          Come up out of the Wilderness,
      From every Spot, and Wrinkle free,
          And wash'd, and perfected in grace.

19   Thou hear'st the pleading Spirit's Groan,
          Thou knowst the Groaning Spirit's Will:
      Come in thy gracious Kingdom down,
          And all thy ransom'd Servants Seal.

20   Come quickly, LORD, the Spirit cries,
          The Number of thy Saints compleat,
      Come quickly, LORD, the Bride replies,
          And make us all for Glory meet.

21   Erect thy Tabernacle here,
          The *New Jerusalem* send down,
      Thyself amidst thy Saints appear,
          And seat us on thy dazzling Throne.

22   Begin the Great Millennial Day,
          Now, Saviour, with a Shout descend,
      Thy Standard in the Heavens display,
          And bring thy Joy which ne'er shall end!

*   *   *

ESSAY

Wesley and Daily Communion

It is in this, Wesley's final hymn, that he commends most expressly the practice of daily communion, although two earlier hymns had suggested it. In 124:2.1–4 he had said, 'Yet may we celebrate below,/ And daily this thine offering shew/ Expos'd before thy Father's eyes;/ In this tremendous Mystery'; and in 137:1.1–2 he had bidden, 'Ye Royal Priests of Jesus, rise,/ And join the daily sacrifice'.

The perennial question of the frequency of communion is, in fact, two closely related questions: (1) As to the *ordo* of Christian worship, how often and when should the Church celebrate the Holy Communion? and (2) as to the practice of the individual believer, how frequently should one, whether lay or cleric, receive the Holy Communion? The Christian cannot communicate frequently if the Church does not celebrate frequently, but any individual might, by personal or community rule, communicate as often as or less often than the Church celebrates.[2]

Brevint had urged more frequent communion, citing the practice of the primitive Christians, who, he said:

did as seldom meet to preach or pray without a Communion, as did the old Israelites to worship without a Sacrifice. On solemn days especially, or upon great exigencies, they ever used this help of sacramental oblation, as the most powerful means the Church had to strengthen their supplications, to open the gates of heaven, and to force, in a manner, God and his Christ to have compassion on them. (VI.4)

John Wesley gave his judgement about the frequency of communion in a discourse which he prepared at Oxford in 1732, setting his recommendations for Christian practice against the background of the custom of the early Church as he understood it:

Let everyone therefore who has either any desire to please God, or any love of his own soul, obey God and consult the good of his own soul by communicating every time he can; like the first Christians, with whom the Christian sacrifice was a constant part of the Lord's day service. And for several centuries they received it almost every day. Four times a week always, and every saint's day beside.[3]

Wesley ratified this opinion by revising and publishing this essay as a sermon in 1787. His early opinion remained his mature opinion.

Stanzas 7–16 of Hymn 166 argue that the Church began by observing the Holy Communion daily, but as that practice was compromised the vitality of the Church diminished. This thesis may have owed something to Jeremy Taylor's widely read life of Jesus, *The Great Exemplar*, 1649. When Taylor reaches the story of the Last Supper, he digresses to speak of 'The Institution and reception of the holy Sacrament of the Lord's Supper' (Discourse XIX). After describing the meaning of the sacrament, Taylor turns to the question, frequently raised, 'whether it were better to communicate often or seldom'. It is clear to him that at first the Christians communicated often. 'At the first commencement of Christianity, while the fervors Apostolical, and the calentures [the warmth] of Infant Christendom did last, the whole assembly of faithful people communicated every day.' This custom continued, Taylor says, for several centuries, but 'it suffered inconvenience by reason of a declining piety, and the intervening of secular interests'. In time, 'it came to once a week', and then to once a fortnight. 'A while after,' Taylor continues, 'it came to once a month, then once a year, then it fell from that too, till all the Christians in the West were commanded to communicate every Easter.' It has proved difficult, he says, for the Church of England to do more than require 'all her children to receive thrice every year at least, intending that they should come oftener'. Taylor summarises the matter:

> It hath fared with this Sacrament as with other actions of religion, which have descended from flames to still fires, from fires to sparks, from sparks to embers, from embers to smoke, from smoke to nothing; and although the publick declension of piety is such, that in this present conjuncture of things it is impossible men should be reduced to a daily communion, yet that they are to communicate frequently is so a duty, that as no excuse but impossibility can make the omission innocent; so the loss and consequent want is infinite and invaluable [beyond valuation].[4]

The opinion that the earliest Christians observed the Lord's Supper daily was widely held in the sixteenth and seventeenth centuries.

Thomas Cranmer, writing in 1550, said, somewhat in passing, that Jesus had ordained the sacrament as 'a daily remembrance in bread and wine'.[5]

The seventeenth-century Prayer Book commentator Anthony Sparrow wrote in his *Rationale upon the Book of Common Prayer*, 1657, that

> In the Primitive Church, while Christians continued their strength of Faith and Devotion, they did communicate every day. This custom

continued . . . But afterward when charity grew cold, and devotion faint, the custom grew faint withal; and within a short time began to be left by little and little; and some upon one pretense, some upon another, would communicate but once a week.[6]

Three reference works, all of them very learned, would have been available to Wesley: the *Apostolici*, 1677, and the *Ecclesiastici*, 1682, by William Cave, and *The Antiquities of the Christian Church*, in ten volumes, 1708–22, by Joseph Bingham. These authorities repeated the pattern, saying that the early Church, in its devotional intensity, observed the sacrament daily; but in time frequency of celebration declined, and devotion slackened.

The seventeenth-century Cambridge theologian and mathematician Isaac Barrow was persuaded that the earliest Christians maintained their faith and courage by observing the Lord's Supper as often as they met. However, he said,

the remitting of that frequency, as it is certainly a sign and an effect, so in part it may be reckoned a cause, of the degeneracy of Christian practice, into that great coldness and slackness which afterward did seize upon it, and now doth apparently keep it in a languishing and half-dying state.[7]

Closer to the time of Wesley, Richard Wheatly, the Prayer Book commentator, seems to have believed that at first the Holy Communion was observed daily. In his *Rational Illustration of the Book of Common Prayer*, 1720, he says, 'We find the Eucharist was always, in the purest Ages of the Church a daily part of the Common-Prayer.' He continues, saying that 'the shameful neglect of Religion with us has made the Imitation of this Example to be rather wished for than expected'.[8]

This sketch (which is very incomplete) of English writers indicates that in his understanding of the frequency of communion in the earliest Church Wesley was following a construction of history that was common among authorities he might have known and trusted.

The English writers who said that the earliest Christians observed the Lord's Supper daily all cited Acts 2.42–7, which says that the first believers in Jerusalem 'continued daily . . . breaking bread from house to house, eating their meat with gladness and singleness of heart, praising God'. But the phrase 'breaking bread' is not specific. It is used in Acts 27.35 of a meal which does not seem to have been the eucharist in the later sense, although the same phrase seems to refer to the communal Lord's

Supper in Acts 20.7 and 1 Corinthians 10.15. Jewish family meals began with the breaking of bread and prayer and ended with the blessing and passing of a cup. All meals were sacred – a thankful communion with God and one another. Evidently in the earliest years of the Church the daily family meal was closer to what developed as the Holy Communion than most household meals came to be in later generations, as the Holy Communion resembled a common meal. The expression 'breaking bread' in Acts seems to describe the earliest Christians as taking meals in common.

From the time when the Church's sacral meal (based, at least in parts of the early Church, on the tradition of the Last Supper) began to be differentiated, the sources point to Sunday as the eucharist day. In the New Testament itself, an emphasis falls on 'the first day of the week' (Acts 20.7; 1 Corinthians 16.2), or 'the Lord's Day' (Revelation 1.10). The late first- or early second-century *Didache* refers, in a redundant but emphatic expression, to 'the Lord's day of the Lord' (14.1). Justin Martyr, writing about AD 150, in his *Apology*, ch. 67, speaks of the day of the Christian assembly as the first day (the day of creation, the day of light) and as 'the eighth day' (the day of the resurrection, the day of the new aeon). The earliest documented rhythm of the Church's eucharistic meal appears to have been weekly, rather than daily.

In the medieval Church the Mass was observed daily (often multiple Masses in the same church each day), but this daily celebration was not an assembly of the Church, but was an essentially private act, required by the clericalisation of the Mass and made possible by the normalisation of non-communicating Low Mass. Ordinarily there was no congregation at the daily Masses, but only a priest-celebrant and a server. People did attend the Sunday Mass in considerable numbers, to be sure, but they received communion only infrequently – sometimes no more than once a year.

When the churches of the sixteenth-century Reformation insisted that at the celebration of the eucharist there be a communicating congregation, the custom of daily celebration was impossible to sustain. However, when the Holy Communion was observed (quarterly or monthly), most of the people who were present and eligible received the bread and wine.

Charles Wesley gives no indication that in his sketch of history he is following sources. Yet these older writers, most of whom he would have known, exhibit a common pattern. At first the vibrant, Spirit-filled Church observed the Lord's Supper daily; but as the sacrament came to be less frequent, the Church's vitality weakened.

It may be that Wesley found that Sparrow, Taylor, Brevint, Wheatly or others who made the same point spoke usefully to an issue that concerned him, and he may have depended on their construction of liturgical history. Or he may have simply made the leap (a leap that is common when Christians appeal to the primitive Church) from 'it must have been so' to 'it was so'.

Hymns on the Lord's Supper Today

Hymns on the Lord's Supper seems to prompt modern-day readers to speak in superlatives. The opening page of this book cited Ole Borgen's estimate of these hymns as 'the greatest treasure of sacramental hymnody that any church ever possessed'.[1] His voice is not alone. The church historian Egil Grislis has ventured that 'no other Protestant denomination has in its possession even a remotely similar treasure of eucharistic poetry'.[2] H. A. Hodges and A. M. Allchin, introducing a selection of Wesley's hymns, say of *Hymns on the Lord's Supper*, 'It would not seem an exaggeration to say that it is one of the finest expressions of Eucharistic devotion to have appeared within the history of the Reformation tradition, equalled perhaps only by the sacramental hymns of N. F. S. Grundtvig in Denmark.'[3] The Canadian liturgical scholar William Crockett has remarked that the Wesleys' sacramental hymns have given to the Methodist people 'a treasury of devotion unique in the history of the Christian Church'.[4] Another Anglican liturgist, Kenneth Stevenson, has said, 'There is a tenderness and strength of biblical allusion in these hymns that mark them off as among the finest to have been written about the eucharist.'[5]

Such comments imply that these hymns have lasting importance. What might be thought to be their contemporary significance?

Hymns on the Lord's Supper ought to remain in the Church's awareness, for it fills a significant place in *the historical record*. The rationalistic eighteenth century was a generally barren period for sacramental doctrine and spirituality. However, Wesley's eucharistic hymns evidence an unexpected and articulate emphasis on the sacrament emerging at a centre of religious conviction, evangelism and social reform. It is almost as though these hymns, along with some other writings of the eighteenth century, represent a subversive Counter-Enlightenment running alongside the prevailing spirit of the age.[6] This minority report should not go unnoticed.

However, to a great extent, the surveys of the eucharistic thought of the period – even those that have concentrated on the Church of England – have slighted the work of Charles Wesley. The story of these hymns – their existence, their initial popularity, and their decline into obscurity – is a part of the story of the Evangelical Revival. And the Evangelical Revival was a shaping force in the religious history and the 'culture wars' of the eighteenth century.

The hymns of this small collection make a notable *theological* statement, bringing the eucharist into vital relation to the Christian message and to the classic Christian encounter with God. Wesley should be recognised as an important continuator of a generally High-Church Anglican tradition of sacramental thought and piety. But his work is not purely derivative. Even when he reaffirms past sacramental teaching and as he reworks Daniel Brevint's *Christian Sacrament and Sacrifice*, Charles Wesley gives a fresh configuration to the tradition in which he stands. The hymns are unusual for the immediacy with which they bring the communicant to the very cross. And Wesley's similar idea that through the sacrament the worshipper is present at history's final things seems to be without precedent. The eucharist, as he sees it, catches one up in the whole panorama of the divine acts. Wesley's understanding of eucharistic sacrifice is imaginative and complex, holding a tensive unity among earthly and heavenly, historical and transcendent aspects of the meeting of God and the believer at the table.

Moreover, Wesley's presentation of the sacrament shows his *passionate involvement* in his theme. Although Wesley is part of the thought world of the eighteenth century, he somewhat restlessly breaks through the general stiffness and reticence of the writings of the period. He does not write confessionally, as though his task as a poet was to anatomise his own experience. Yet he is always engaged. Wesley exclaims; he asks questions; he deals with misunderstandings; he praises God, and he prays; he recognises the reality of spiritual barrenness, yet he encourages others. He dramatically presents the realities that believers may find in 'this mysterious supper'. Despite Wesley's speed and facility in composition, he is never glib nor off-hand. He is a worshipper who seems always to stand in awe of 'the grace on man bestowed' (64:1.1). His doctrine of the Supper is given energy as it is bound up with his spirituality of the Supper.

To find such catholic-sounding terms and ideas as Wesley's appearing at the heart of the Evangelical Revival suggests that these sacramental hymns carry as yet unexplored significance for *ecumenical* discussion. Wesley's preference for biblical vocabulary over speculative terms and his sense that the Church's act in the eucharist is sacrificial, but only as it stands within the great sacrifice of Christ, are emphases that find echoes, after two and a half centuries, in some of the constructive theologians and the unifying inter-confessional conversations and statements of the second half of the twentieth century.

This collection of hymns is, along with all else, a *literary* work. Even unsympathetic readers might agree that while Wesley may not be a great poet, he is a great hymn-writer. Hymns constitute a minor kind of poetry, with its own criteria of excellence. Although many hymns over the generations have been little more than versified piety, the best hymns have been well-crafted and honestly felt expressions of human life engaged with God. Wesley's sacramental hymns show his gift for phrase and versification; they display his intellectual energy; they have theological weight; and the dogma they express is experienced dogma.

The Church does not have an oversupply of believable, unsentimental hymns for the Holy Communion; and persons who have come to appreciate *Hymns on the Lord's Supper* often express their regret that Wesley's work has dropped from use. But it should not be taken for granted that hymns, even good hymns, which for 250 years have not been sustained in the voices and ears of a singing church and been tested by varied and changing experience can be successfully reinstated. (The failure rate in the work of the best hymn-writers, even in their own time, is very high.) There are undeniable barriers. Today's Christians do not talk, write, think and believe just as Charles Wesley did; they inhabit a world, outside and inside themselves, that is in important respects different from his. It is one thing to understand and value these hymns in their own setting, but it is another to suppose that they (or at least that very many of them) could readily find a place in the use and affections of twenty-first-century congregations.

Many of Wesley's words and ideas require today at least some annotation, and lines that must be explained are generally unsuitable for congregational singing. A biblical allusion that must be recognised in order to clarify a line or a hymn may now be quite obscure. But problems arise from a foreign sensibility as much as from an unfamiliar vocabulary of terms and ideas. Even as small a body of written material as Wesley's *Hymns on the Lord's Supper* can make us aware that seismic shifts in world view, in theological convictions, in ways of reading the Bible and expressing Christian devotion separate the early 2000s from the mid-1700s.

A serious obstacle to singing these hymns with conviction lies in Wesley's doctrine of the atonement which figures largely in his thought on the Lord's Supper. He, like many Christians of his era (as well as of eras before and after it), read the death of Christ through categories of penal substitution, according to which Christ, as representative of sinners, suffered on the cross the wrath of the righteous Father. This atonement doctrine is so pervasive in *Hymns on the Lord's Supper* that readers who question it will often find lines of Wesley's they consider attractive and resonant and lines they find problematic standing side-by-side. Persons who are aware of this or other issues raised by modernity cannot simply edit – altering lines or omitting stanzas – without flawing Wesley's usually careful structure and making his thought over into something that might be more congenial, but would not be Wesley. To what extent can the deeply earned, creative eighteenth-century work of Charles Wesley be sung in a culturally strange land?

There is the difficult matter of *music*. Hymns are for the Church and they are written to be sung. If a hymn is to come into widespread use, its words must be carried by a suitable melody. Some hymns have had a long search for a musical setting which, when once it is found, seems inevitable. In his work *The Religious Sublime*, David Morris remarked on the tendency of the medium of print to eviscerate religious passion. 'Despite its simple power, the hymn often looks lifeless and clumsy on the printed page. Its spirit is freed only when the printed words, liberated by the emotional power of music, find their intended expression in song.'[7] The search for good, expressive musical settings makes one look closely at the texts, revealing strengths and felicities in Wesley's lines that might otherwise go unnoticed. But one also finds problem hymns and stanzas. Some of Wesley's accents fall differently in different verses of the same hymn. Some hymns shift their emotional tone sharply, occasionally more than once, and music that would help interpret the opening stanzas might be a mismatch for later stanzas.

These hymns were not meant to be read silently, one following another, running in short lines down the middle of a page. Rather, at a service of Holy Communion a few selected hymns were to be sung, and the thought of each would be internalised as the hymn – its pace and emotional tone set by the music – served as an act of devotion.

Wesley's sacramental hymns largely concentrate on evangelical essentials. Modern-day Christians can recognise in them the God, the perennial word and the central communal act of the Church; and they can recognise themselves. Perhaps some of these hymns (thirty or so of them) could be given a fresh trial with some hope that they might speak to and for present-day communicants. And all 166 of them should be held in the Church's accessible record of eucharistic thought and devotion.

In moving through these hymns – including those that clearly come from their era, not ours – one comes upon new angles of vision, unusual emphases, compressed drama, strong conviction, and striking verbal expressions. Wesley finds an extraordinary range of both doctrinal affirmation and human experience in the Lord's Supper. He does not occupy a tepid middle ground of faith or feeling, but touches extremes of suffering and glory, of hiddenness and epiphany, of estrangement and reunion, of contrition and praise. As one reads his work sympathetically, the generations between the eighteenth century and the present slip away, and one is aware, not of the remoteness and the difficulties, but of the immediacy and the communicative power of this body of hymns. They have the strength of thought and language not only to express the faith of today, but to challenge, inform and enlarge it.

No one else in eighteenth-century Britain saw the Lord's Supper as Charles Wesley saw it, and no one else spoke of it as he did. His imagination was gripped by the eucharistic encounter of Christ with his people, and he cast his thought in vivid, memorable phrases. Readers who do not yet know these hymns have a discovery to make. Readers who already know them can return to them often with surprise and gratitude.

Appendix 1

Names or Descriptive Phrases for the Eucharist in *Hymns on the Lord's Supper*

Although a few of Wesley's *Hymns on the Lord's Supper* do not speak expressly of the Holy Communion, it is the theme of the collection. As Wesley names or describes the sacrament, he exhibits considerable verbal resource. No doubt he simply used expressions as they came to him and was not consciously looking for variety. Yet he shows an extensive vocabulary of phrases.

Wesley's terms are listed here, grouped by their principal noun, set in alphabetical order. The terms 'bread', 'wine', 'flesh', 'body' and 'blood' are very frequent, and they are not listed here completely.

thine own *appointments*, 78:9.1
the *badge* and token this, 13:2.6
the (thy, this) *banquet*, 75:3.3; 110:1.5; 116:5.4
    thy sacramental banquet, 58:4.2
    banquet of immortal food, 61:3.11
    his house of banqueting is this, 81:3.3
    the banquet for all he so freely did make, 92:3.4
    the mystic banquet, 99:3.1
their last *bequest*, 1:1.5
    the dear bequest, 90:1.3
    his dying bequest, 95:1.2
the *blood*, 159:2.3
    This is my Blood which seals the New
        Eternal Covenant of my Grace,
    My Blood so freely shed for You,
        For you and all the Sinfull Race,
    My Blood that speaks your Sins forgiven,
        And justifies your Claim to Heaven. 1:4
    sacramental blood, 65:3.4
    his healing blood, 72:2.5
    the mystical blood, 92:5.4

To thy *Body*, Lord, we flee;/ This the consecrated Shrine,/ Temple of the Deity,/ The Real House Divine. 127:1.5–8

  (Given the flexibility of such New Testament terms as 'body', 'bread' and 'temple', the lines referenced here and perhaps others, which probably in the first instance refer to the Lord's Supper, could refer also to the Church or to Christ.)

this *bread*, 162:3.8

  this expressive bread, 2:1.1

  the bread of life, 2:5.6; 18:1.3; 82:1.3

  living bread divine, 3:1.4; 165:3.1; the living bread sent down from heaven, 30:7.1; 60:2.2; the (our) living bread, 34:1.4; 71:3.4; 84:3.5; 93:1.4; 97:1.2

  this mysterious bread, 29:1.1

  the hallowed bread, 30:2.2; 58:6.1; the hallowed broken bread, 73:2.1

  the bread thy mystic body be, 30:5.3

  everlasting bread, 40:1.4

  the bread of heaven, 56:4.5; the heavenly bread, 90:3.1; 160:3.1

  this (our) sacramental bread, 61:3.7; 88:1.2

  the children's bread, 113:1.1

  the bread impregnated with Life divine, 166:4.1–2

channel(s) of thy (his) grace, 54:4.3; 58:1.4; 86:2.3

  fit channels to convey thy love, 72:2.2

  the blood which in this channel flows, 108:1.4

the royal *cheer*, 91:3.4

  delicious sacred cheer, 160:1.1

his sacramental *clothes*, 39:1.4

this *communion*, 94:1.2

  this divine communion, 101:4.2

  communion of thy flesh and blood, 107:1.3

the *cup*, 95:3.1

  the cup of blessing . . . the bread, thy mystic body, 30:5.1–3

  the cup of blessing, blest by us . . . the hallowed broken bread, 73:1.1, 2.1

our glorious *earnest*, 94:3.3

  the earnest, 94:4.1; 103:2.3; 108:2.3

this *emblem*, 2:1.6; 108:1.2

the *feast*, 60:1.1; 84:3.1; a *feast* 92:2.3

  the sacramental feast, 1:3.1; 44:1.6; 166:17.2

  this eucharistic feast, 4:2.1; 166:5.3

  the monumental feast, 8:5.1

the feast divine, 46:1.4
thy own feast, 76:4.2
the solemn feast, 84:1.7
the feast for thy first followers made, 90:3.3
the spiritual feast, 92:8.2
a soul-transporting feast, 94:1.1; this transporting feast, 99:1.2
figure and means of saving grace, 28:1.4
the altar's *fire*, 166:7.2
thy *flesh and blood*, 3:4.5
  the mystic flesh of Jesus, 71:2.4
  the flesh and blood of Jesus, 73:5.3–4
  Christ's flesh and blood, 158:1.5–8
the sacrificial *food*, 3:4.4
  imperishable food, 81:4.1
  this life-giving food, 92:1.4
  this immortal food, 113:2.1
  this heavenly food, 166:6.2
our *gift*, 153:2.5
our *heaven begun below*, 158:2.4
thy *house*, 77:2.4
  the house of prayer, 77:2.6
  his house of banqueting, 82:3.3
image of his sacrifice, 118:5.3
thine *institution*, 53:3.2
the glorious *instrument* divine, 28:2.3; 56:3.4; 115:1.1
  this choicest instrument, 42:1.3
  if instruments thy wisdom choose, 61:3.4
  an instrument ordained to feed our souls, 73:2.3
  sure instrument of present grace, 94:2.1
  sure instrument thy grace to gain, 107:1.4
  this great instrument, 126:3.3
your precious *legacy*, 1:2.5
  the richest legacy thou hast on man bestowed, 42:4.1f.
the hidden *manna*, 30:6.4
  the manna of thy quick'ning love, 44:3.5; . . . of thy love, 51:4.4
  manna from above, 81:3.6; manna that from heaven comes down,
    84:3.5
  manna that angels never knew, 160:3.3 (also line 2)
the (thy) *means*, 12:4.1; 57:3.6; 58:4.3; 59:1.6; 71:1.6; 76:4.3; 80:1.4;
    80:5.1; 85:5.1; 86:2.4
  figure and means of saving grace, 28:1.4

the means of healing, 53:1.3
the means thy love enjoined, 63:2.5
a sure effectual means of grace, 66:1.4
the sacred means, 73:1.2; 80:5.1
the heavenly everlasting *meat* (food), 3:1.2; 166:17.3
the sacramental meat, 71:2.2
this immortal meat, 112:3.3
this *memorial*, 98:1.1; a memorial, 118:4.5
this divine memorial, 1:5.2
this dear memorial of his love, 54:1.2; that dear memorial, 118:3.1
the memorial of your Lord, 89:1.3
memorial of the (thy) sacrifice, 121:2.5; 123:4.1
the *mystery*, 54:3.1; 56:1.1; these mysteries, 107:1.2
this great mystery, 28:1.3; 98:2.3
the mystery instituted by thee, 56:1.1f.
this dreadful mystery, 117:1.2
this eucharistic mystery, 123:4.2
this tremendous mystery, 124:2.1; 141:7.2
thy great *offering*, 3:4.3
the (this, thine, his) *ordinance(s)*, 15:1.3; 33:1.3; 39:1.3; 62:10.4; 66:2.2;
    77:1.5; 78:10.1; 101:1.2
this (thine) ordinance divine, 53:1.3; 11:4.6; 141:5.1
the heavenly ordinances, 62:1.1
thine holy ordinance, 166:14.1
organs to convey his grace, 59:2.3
thy *sacramental passion*, 141:5.4
the *picture of thy passion*, 87:1.1
this *place of meeting*, 77:2.3
sure *pledges* of his dying love, 71:2.1
the pledge of our hope with Jesus to live, 95:3.2
his pledge, 100:2.4
his sacramental pledge, 100:3.1
recall thy pledge in heaven, 100:5.5
sure pledge of ecstasies unknown, 101:4.1
pledge of our (future possession), 102:1.5; 103:2.3
pledge of our everlasting rest, 107:1.6
this pledge that we thy heaven shall share, 108:2.4
a sacred pledge, 121:2.3
thy *sacramental presence*, 153:1.6
his death-recording *rite*, 1:1.3
the rite thou hast enjoined, 33:2.1

this mysterious rite, 42:3.1; 123:3.6
thy (this) *sacrament*, 64:2.1; 66:1.2; 94:2.2; 123:3.3
our *sacrifice*, 153:2.1
   the daily sacrifice, 166:11.3, 16.4
the sure confirming *seal*, 13:2.2
   the sacramental seal, 30:3.3
our acceptable *service*, 143:4.7
this *shade* which Jesus' cross hath made, 118:5.1–2
the *signs*, 56:3.3; the sign, 71:1.5; 72:1.2
   the sacred sign, 3:1.5; 7:2.3; 11:4.5; 166:13.1
   this authentic sign, 8:2.1; these authentic signs, 44:1.3
   the signs he did ordain, 18:1.2
   the sacred, true, effectual sign, 28:2.1
   these hallowed signs, 47:1.2
   outward signs, 54:3.3; the outward sign of inward grace, 71:1.3
   the real sign, 66:1.3
   a sure communicating sign, 73:2.2
the *Spirit* of their Head, 166:4.3–4
the (thy, his) *supper*, 8:1.1; 92:7.2, 10.4
   the supper of the (your) Lord, 8:1.6; 93:1.2
   his last mysterious supper, 13:1.3; thy mysterious supper, 165:2.1
   the supper of the Lamb, 97:2.1
   they supped in Eden with their Lord, 166:5.4 (restoration of Eden)
the *symbols*, 58:7.1; 73:5.2
a (the) *table*, 84:4.2; 158:2.5
   thy sacred table, 34:1.3; thy table, 97:1.4; 109:1.4; 165:2.2
   a table spread with mystic wine and everlasting bread, 40:1.3
   the table . . . of Jesus our redeeming Lord, 46:1.1–2
O what a *taste* is this!, 158:2.1
title to eternal bliss, 103:2.1
the *tokens*, 72:2.1; the token, 110:3.5
   the token of thy (God's, Jesus') love, 12:2.4; 111:3.1
   the badge and token this, 13:2.1
   the tokens of thy (his) dying (expiring) love, 30:4.1; 158:1.3; 166:2.4
   the tokens of his death, 44:1.2; 119:3.3
   the tokens of thy passion, 79:1.5
   token(s) of thy (his) favour, 82:1.7; 162:1.5
   the tokens of his presence, 89:2.4
   a token of thy glorious kingdom, 100:5.1f.
   a token of fuller union to come, 114:7.2
   the tokens of his death, 119:3.3

the tokens of his flesh and blood, 126:4.3
the awful *types*, 73:3.3 (past)
   type of the heavenly marriage feast, 107:1.5 (future)
the outward *veil*, 73:4.2
the *virtue* of this heavenly food, 166:6.1–2
the *Way* thou hast enjoined, 81:1.5
mystic (mystical) *wine*, 40:1.3; 77:3.4; 95:2.1
   immortal wine, 160:2.6
   the sacred wine, 166:4.4

All of the hymns in this collection are on a single subject and were evidently composed in a fairly short time; inevitably they show some repetition of ideas and words. Yet through these descriptive noun phrases, they display the Lord's Supper in a variety of ways and cast it in a wide range of meanings.

Appendix 2

Wesley's Use of Brevint

Brevint in Wesley's Hymns

The foregoing exposition has identified some of the hymns, stanzas and lines in *Hymns on the Lord's Supper* in which Wesley draws significantly on Daniel Brevint's *The Christian Sacrament and Sacrifice*. However, since this study considers only selected hymns and lines, it has been able to give only an incomplete showing of Wesley's debt to Brevint. Wesley's conception of the sacrament, the general structure of the collection, entire hymns, important ideas, and many words and turns of phrase trace clearly to Brevint.

Although Wesley uses *The Christian Sacrament and Sacrifice* extensively, he uses it quite unevenly. A series of consecutive hymns that are indebted to Brevint may be followed by several that are not. Some passages in Brevint are source for a number of hymns, while other lengthy passages, sometimes of considerable interest and merit, are not used at all. Wesley finds Brevint's closing prayers particularly usable, drawing on them in at least 43 hymns.

In estimating Wesley's use of Brevint, as with identifying his use of the Bible, one cannot be sure that one has located all of the places where Wesley was following Brevint, nor can one be sure that one has not listed places where Wesley was drawing on a widely available vocabulary of sacramental ideas and not specifically on Brevint. Some personal judgement is inevitable. The following lists cite, for the most part, the hymns in which Wesley's borrowing from Brevint is unmistakable, although they also include a few hymns in which his debt to Brevint seems probable, although it may be slight.

Wesley seems to have worked from Brevint's full text, rather than from the abridgement that his brother John made and which was published with *Hymns on the Lord's Supper* (and later separately as well). At least 25 hymns, including some of the more important, draw from passages in Brevint which were not included in John's précis.

In general, Wesley follows Brevint fairly consecutively, only infrequently breaking from the order of ideas he finds in his source.

(In the following summaries, hymns which use Brevint's *The Christian Sacrament and Sacrifice* are shown in standard type, and those that make no use of it are italicised.)

In Part I Wesley uses Brevint in Hymns 2–6, 11–12, 21–3, 27.
He makes no use of Brevint in Hymns *1, 7–10, 13–20, 24–6*.
Wesley uses Brevint in 11 of the 27 hymns.

In Part II Wesley uses Brevint in Hymns 28–9, 31–52, 54–7, 59, 61–70, 72, 74–8, 81.
He makes no use of Brevint in Hymns *30, 53, 58, 60, 71, 73, 79–80, 82–92*.
In the judgement of the present writer, Wesley uses Brevint in 46 of the 65 hymns.

The opening hymn of Part II, Hymn 28, uses Brevint's Section III.1. Then Wesley goes back to the prayer that closed Brevint's Section II for Hymns 29 and 31–3. Evidently some themes of Brevint's prayer in Section II seemed to Wesley to refer more to the present experience of Christ in the sacrament than to its memorial aspect. Then with Hymn 34 Wesley begins his more or less consecutive following of Brevint's Section III on the sacrament as *sign*, which he continues, with a few interruptions, through Hymn 52. In Hymn 53 Wesley sets Brevint aside. Then from Hymn 54 to Hymn 68 (again with a few skips) he draws on Brevint's Section IV, on the sacrament as *means*. Wesley had spoken of the 'means of grace' once in Part I, but he uses the expression 14 times in the hymns of Part II, 13 of them between 56 and 86. (Ten times he simply says 'the Means', capitalising 'Means'.) From Hymns 69 to 78, Wesley (again skipping in a few hymns) uses Brevint's Sections III, IV and I, but somewhat randomly. From Hymn 79 to the end of Part II, Wesley makes no use of Brevint (except for an apparent borrowing in Hymn 81), and his sacramental thought takes independent directions. This is the longest run of hymns in the collection which shows no dependence on Brevint.

In Part III Wesley uses Brevint in Hymns 93–103, 107–9, 112–14.
He makes no use of Brevint in Hymns *104–6, 110–11, 115*.
Wesley uses Brevint in 17 of the 23 hymns.

In 16 hymns of Part III, on the theme of heaven, Wesley follows Brevint's Section V. In Hymn 114 he seems to draw on Brevint's III.7. In some of the hymns of this section, Wesley develops emphases which owe nothing to Brevint, and in a few hymns which do draw on Brevint, the use is slight.

In Wesley's Part IV, on the eucharist as sacrifice, he uses Brevint in important and unmistakable ways in all 12 hymns. In these hymns he largely follows Brevint's quite short Section VI. But he occasionally steps outside it. The important Hymn 116 draws on Brevint's IV.11 (but with a touch of VI.3); Hymn 117 uses IV.14 (with VII.2 and 6); and Hymn 122 uses II.11.

Wesley uses Brevint in all 30 of the hymns of Part V. In a series of four hymns, 143–6, almost every stanza traces directly to a passage in Brevint's VII.15, and a later series, 148–51, traces almost as closely to VII.18.

'After the Sacrament': Wesley makes no use of Brevint in Hymns 158–66.

In the judgement of the present writer there are clear signs of indebtedness to Brevint's words and thought in 116 of Wesley's 166 hymns.

Wesley's Hymns in Brevint's Outline

Brevint's essay *The Christian Sacrament and Sacrifice* is in eight sections, which the author divided into short chapters. Each of these large sections concludes with a prayer, and Section VII contains an additional prayer in ch. 15. Wesley uses these prayer passages of Brevint's in 43 of his hymns. He uses some units of Brevint's work in several of his hymns; some units are used once, although they may be drawn on for an important idea; and substantial units of Brevint are not used at all. (The themes of Brevint's Sections III and IV are combined in Wesley's Part II, and Wesley's Part V corresponds with Brevint's Section VII, but includes a few touches from Section VIII.)

Brevint's Section I, 'The Importance of well understanding the nature of this Sacrament', is brief and methodological, and Wesley wrote no group of hymns that corresponds with it. However, he adopts from Section I Brevint's thesis of a twofold action of sacramental receiving and sacrificial giving, and in Hymns 11, 76, 77, 78, 127 and 153 he uses Brevint's idea that the sacrament is a place of meeting between Christ and the Christian.

Section II: 'Concerning the Sacrament, as it is a Memorial of the Sufferings and Death of Christ':

Brevint's Section II, ch. 1 is used in Hymn 94; ch. 2, in Hymn 6; ch. 3, in Hymns 3, 4, 22; ch. 7, in Hymns 3, 5; ch. 8, in Hymns 3, 5; ch. 9, in Hymns 5, 22; ch. 10, in Hymns 6, 21, 23; ch. 11 (a prayer), in Hymns 2, 3, 4, 6, 27, 29, 31, 32, 33, 39, 122.

Section III: 'Of the Blessed Sacrament, as it stands for a sign of present graces':

Brevint's Section III, ch. 1, is used in Hymn 28; ch. 3, in Hymn 34; ch. 4, in Hymn 34; ch. 6, in Hymns 35, 37; ch. 7, in Hymns 36, 114; ch. 8, in Hymns 31, 37, 38, 74, 75; ch. 9, in Hymn 38; ch. 10, in Hymns 39, 40; ch. 11, in Hymn 45; ch. 12, in Hymns 46, 47; ch. 13 (a prayer), in Hymns 41, 44, 47, 48, 49, 50, 51, 52, 69, 70.

Section IV: 'Concerning the Communion, as it is not a Representation only, but a Means of   Grace':

Brevint's Section IV, ch. 3, is used in Hymn 55; ch. 4, in Hymns 54, 55; ch. 5, in Hymn 56; ch. 6, in Hymns 57, 59, 81; ch. 7, in Hymns 59, 71, 72; ch. 8, in Hymns 39, 57, 59, 61; ch. 10, in Hymn 39; ch. 11, in Hymns 32, 63, 81, 116; ch. 12, in Hymns 42, 62, 76; ch. 13, in Hymns 4, 117; ch. 14, in Hymns 64, 65, 117, 118; ch. 15 (a prayer), in Hymns 43, 62, 66, 67, 68.

Section V: 'Of the Blessed Communion, as being a Pledge of the Happiness and Glory to Come':

Brevint's Section V, ch. 1, is used in Hymn 94; ch. 2, in Hymns 12, 93, 100; ch. 3, in Hymns 93, 96, 97, 99; ch. 4, in Hymn 98; ch. 5, in Hymns 101, 102; ch. 6, in Hymn 103; ch. 11 (a prayer), in Hymns 95, 107, 108, 109, 112, 113.

Section VI: 'Of the holy Eucharist, as it implies a Sacrifice; and first, of the Commemorative Sacrifice':

Brevint's Section VI, ch. 2, is used in Hymns 123, 124; ch. 3, in Hymns 121, 122, 124, 125, 126, 127; ch. 4 (a prayer), in Hymns 118, 119, 120, 121, 126.

Section VII: 'Concerning the Sacrifice of our own Persons':

Brevint's Section VII, ch. 1, is used in Hymn 128; ch. 2, in Hymns 117, 118, 129, 130, 153; ch. 3, in Hymns 128, 129, 130; ch. 4, in Hymns 128, 129, 130; ch. 5, in Hymn 130; ch. 6, in Hymns 117, 129, 130, 131, 132,

134; ch. 7, in Hymns 131, 133, 134, 157; ch. 8, in Hymn 134; ch. 9, in Hymns 133, 134, 135, 137; ch. 10, in Hymns 136, 137; ch. 11, in Hymns 138, 139; ch. 12, in Hymn 140; ch. 13, in Hymns 141, 154; ch. 14, in Hymns 139, 141, 142; ch. 15 (a prayer), in Hymns 143, 144, 145, 146, 155; ch. 16, in Hymn 144; ch. 17, in Hymns 147, 152; ch. 18 (a prayer), in Hymns 144, 148, 149, 150, 151, 152.

Section VIII: 'Concerning the Oblation of our Goods and Alms; or the Sacrifice of Justice':

Brevint's Section VIII, ch. 3, is used in Hymns 155, 156; ch. 5, in Hymns 153, 157; ch. 7, in Hymn 153; ch. 15, in Hymn 155; ch. 17 (a prayer), in Hymn 155; ch. 18, in Hymn 155. The general thought of chs 3, 5, 6, 7, 15, 17–18 is suggested in Hymns 155–7. Wesley makes little use of this lengthy section of Brevint's work.

Wesley does not draw on Brevint in any of the hymns of his final section, 'After the Sacrament'.

Appendix 3

Authorship in Question

Hymns on the Lord's Supper was published under the names of John and Charles, indicating that the volume was a joint project, but saying nothing about which of the brothers was responsible for what features of the work. The abridgement of Brevint's essay was later identified as having been done by John, and the two hymns that were adapted from George Herbert (9 and 160) and the hymn that was translated from Zinzendorf (85) are also taken to be John's work. This was the sort of thing he did well. It is generally assumed that most or all of the other hymns are the work of Charles, the hymn-writing brother.

But the matter of authorship is not so easily settled. John wrote some poetry in addition to his translations of German hymns. Did he contribute hymns to *Hymns on the Lord's Supper* other than those he adapted from Herbert and Zinzendorf? There is no acknowledgement in the collection itself of the known borrowings from Herbert and Zinzendorf; if hymns were included that were by someone other than Charles or John, the text of the hymns would not necessarily have said so. The Wesleys do not even acknowledge how extensively their hymns are indebted to Brevint. Is the work of other authors incorporated in *Hymns on the Lord's Supper* without attribution?

Answers must rely on internal evidence. One must examine the verbal style and the manner of thought in these hymns and ask, 'Knowing what we do of the mind and work of John and of Charles, does it seem likely, or unlikely, possible or impossible, that one or the other of them wrote this piece of verse?' Deciding such things in the absence of documentary evidence is to a large extent a matter of judgement. A reader may become convinced that some idea or some manner of expression is so unlike Charles that one must question whether or not a hymn is really his work. Could it be by John? Or by someone else?

Argument from internal evidence inevitably yields soft results. One critic questions the authorial voice in a hymn and sets forth her or his reasons. But the reasons do not convince another critic. Questions go back and forth. A valuable attempt to give some objectivity to the discussion was made by the early twentieth-century English Methodist scholar Henry Bett, whose slender book, *The Hymns of Methodism* (1913, 1945),[1] based on close study of the Wesleys' poetical works, sought to establish the stylistic marks of the work of John and of Charles. Some later writers have modified Bett's judgements, but most have followed him. Although he clarified many things, Bett himself recognised that his criteria could not set the determination of authorship beyond question.

We give attention to three hymns concerning which questions have been raised.

We begin with *Hymn 62*, which sets forth, with unusual linearity, an extended comparison: 'The heavenly ordinances' (that is, the God-given means of grace) are like the stars of the sky. Although all of the stars witness to their heavenly origin and give their light to the earth, they differ in brightness (stanzas 1–2). Similarly, while the gospel ordinances (which the hymn does not identify) all show the impress of Christ, they differ (stanza 3). All of them give divine light, guiding believers to eternal day (stanzas 4–5), but of them the Holy Communion is first in glory (stanza 6). Surpassing all the heavenly host, it gives 'the light of life Divine' (stanza 7). Nonetheless, while we reverence both the stars and the sacrament, the glory all belongs to God (stanza 8). How foolish for Christians to reject the appointed sacramental means – it is like rejecting the stars and planets! While the present order stands, the sacraments will do their appointed work (stanzas 9–10). This final thought seems to have the 'stillness' controversy in mind.

This hymn is one of the few in the collection which says anything about nature. While the hymn speaks positively about nature, the author does not seem very interested in the theme, but writes in an abstract and formulaic manner, saying only that the heavenly bodies differ from one another in brightness – surely a commonplace idea. The gospel ordinances all display divine power, but among them the Holy Communion is foremost. This lengthy comparison may strike a reader as a rather intellectual device, and it is expressed in lines which seem, by the usual standard of *Hymns on the Lord's Supper*, somewhat flat. The hymn's explanatory manner seems unlike Charles, as though he may not have been deeply engaged by his theme.

Observations like these raised the question of authorship in the mind of Francis Frost.[2] In his essay, 'The Veiled Unveiling of the Glory of God', he proposes that Hymn 62 sounds like a verse development of a simple prose thesis: 'The Lord's Supper is the supreme ordinance of the Christian life.' He suspects (as he does also in Hymns 58 and 93) that John may be the author. Charles' hymns, he says, do not simply versify theological propositions; rather, they grow from an insight perceived intuitively. '[Charles] Wesley', Frost says, 'theologizes poetically.'

Nevertheless, in Brevint's text (in the very section which Wesley is following in Part II of the hymns) there occurs the comment: '[God's] ordinances in the Church, as well as his stars in heaven, differ in glory one from another . . . The blessed Communion must exceed as much in blessings when well used, as it exceeds in danger of a curse when it is not' (IV.12). This idea from Brevint could have suggested Hymn 62 to Charles Wesley.[3] But this observation does not bear on authorship. However, the passage from Brevint may have suggested to Wesley that this hymn about the sacrament (whether it was by John, or by someone else) might suit this location in the collection, and he inserted it. Fr Frost's suspicions are not proved, but they deserve consideration.

The critical eye of Fr Frost also falls on *Hymn 58*. This hymn uses the voice of the lame man at the pool in John 5.1–18 as an imaginative construction through which to express the appeal of a needy person coming to the Holy Communion and pleading for healing. As the hymn spiritualises the gospel incident, the helpless man represents a sinner crying out for salvation or perhaps a communicant seeking assurance. (See p. 65, above.) The 'I' of the hymn has been coming to the sacrament sincerely and often but has found little in the way of inner validation. The despairing 'I' goes through the motions, taking the bread and drinking the wine, but receiving no sense of being met by love and mercy. 'In vain I drink the Hallow'd wine,/ I cannot taste the Love Divine.' The speaker cries for relief.

Much as in Hymn 62, Francis Frost thinks that Hymn 58 is so much an illustration of a thesis that he suspects that John, not Charles, may be the author.[4] Hymns 58 and 62 are in the same stanza form – four four-foot iambic lines, in rhyming couplets, *aabb*. Was someone else writing hymns for the Lord's Supper which the Wesleys judged suitable for inclusion in this book which is otherwise largely Charles' work?

But the other side can also be argued. Hymn 58 is based on the incident of the man at the pool in chapter 5 of John's gospel. Similarly, Hymn 59, the very next hymn, uses the story of the man born blind from John 9, and a later hymn (68, see pp. 105–6) uses the raising of Lazarus, from John 11. These three hymns exhibit the practice of setting oneself inside one of the Johannine healing miracles. They all 'spiritualise' the healing act. They could be thought to form a series within Part V. In sum, along with reasons for setting these hymns outside the collection as possibly by a writer other than Charles Wesley, they could also be thought to represent Charles' mind and work.

Hymn 114 seems also to merit a critical look. It is a sustained comparison between the sleep of Adam from which Eve was brought to be one with Adam, and the death of Christ from which the Church was brought to live in union with him. The sacrament is a sign of this dual story and promise.

The stanzas develop the analogy: *Stanza 1:* A paradox; the First Cause, the one who gives life to all those who live in grace, himself dies; he is made to 'sleep' by the same hand that caused Adam to fall into a deep sleep. *Stanza 2:* From Christ's 'sleep' (his death) comes the blood and water that bring the Church to birth. *Stanza 3:* The Church, a 'second Eve', mother of all the faithful, emerges from this 'sleep'. *Stanza 4:* Christ, a 'heavenly Adam', left his throne above 'that we might all be born of God'. *Stanza 5:* To give birth to the Church, Jesus gave not merely a rib (as Adam did at the creation of Eve), but his heart's blood, his life. *Stanza 6:* Through Christ's death, he and the Church are to one another as Eve was to Adam – 'This at last is bone of my bones and flesh of my flesh' (Genesis 2.23). A question: Will not Christ take his purchase? *Stanza 7:* An answer: Christ's union with the Church, enacted at Calvary (7.3) and betokened 'here' in the eucharist (7.2), will lead to the marriage feast of Christ and the Church in heaven (7.4).

The parallel between Adam and Christ lies deep in the tradition of Christian typology, beginning with the New Testament and sustained in thousands of medieval paintings and windows. The author's immediate source, however, would seem to have been a passage in which Brevint had said:

> Jesus, the second Adam, being seized, as he hung upon the cross, with the deep sleep which God caused to fall upon him, gave this new being to his Church out of that side which at his passion was opened; and the blood and water which then gushed out of his wounds are the true principles of life, by reason of which his spouse, the Church, may be called Eve. (III.7)

Rattenbury, who usually finds something to commend in even Wesley's more pedestrian hymns, expresses a dislike for this hymn, saying that it 'makes a ridiculous and rather repulsive analogy between Adam's rib and Jesus' blood, the one issuing in Eve, the other in the new Eve – the Church of Christ'. He assumes that John acted as editor of *Hymns on the Lord's Supper* and blames the lapse on him, saying, 'Why John permitted it to be printed under his name is a puzzle.'[5]

Charles, to be sure, seldom structures a hymn so plainly around an 'as this, so that' analogy, and this hymn does seem somewhat awkward. Yet the apparent debt of Hymn 114 to Brevint weighs in favour of Charles being the writer. Rattenbury is not so much questioning authorship as he is questioning whether or not the quality of this hymn is up to the general level of the collection. Perhaps the imagery does seem forced, but present-day readers may be more tolerant of strained imagery than were readers of even half a century ago. It may be said in behalf of the hymn that, in its allusive way, it brings into a symbolic and conceptual unity the themes of creation, Christology, atonement, eucharist, and eschatology. Yet the somewhat laboured manner of its thought places it on the list of hymns whose authorship might be questioned.

One might ask about a few other hymns in *Hymns on the Lord's Supper*. Are they by Charles Wesley? If he did not write them, who did? John? Or someone else? There is not much to go on in trying to decide such questions. Yet such matters merit more attention than they have been given in the literature – or than they can be given here.

Notes

Introduction

1 Ole Borgen, *John Wesley on the Sacraments*, Abingdon, Nashville: 1972, p. 17.

2 This is the judgement of F. Hildebrandt and O.A. Beckerlegge, eds, *A Collection of Hymns for the Use of The People Called Methodists*, vol. 7 of *The Works of John Wesley*, Abingdon Press, Nashville, TN: 1983. See Hymn 29 in the same collection and the editors' note, p. 116. A few writers think that Charles' 'conversion hymn' may have been 'And can it be', Hymn 193 in the same work, and see the editors' note.

3 On the number of Wesley's hymns, see Henry Bett, *The Hymns of Methodism*, Epworth Press, London: 1913 (enlarged and reprinted, 1945); E. H. Rattenbury, *The Evangelical Doctrines of Charles Wesley's Hymns*, Epworth Press, London: 1941, pp. 19–20; Frank Baker, *Charles Wesley's Verse: An Introduction*, Epworth Press, London: 1988, pp. 6–10; the quoted words are from Eric Routley, *The Musical Wesleys*, Oxford University Press, New York: 1968, p. 29.

4 The landmark work, *A Collection of Hymns for the Use of The People Called Methodists*, 1780 – 'the Large Hymn Book' – contained 525 hymns, most of them by Charles; but the final editing and the organisation of the volume were the work of John, whose name it carries.

5 Over the years there has been a running discussion of how much of the Wesleys' poetic work is from John and how much from Charles. Henry Bett, *The Hymns of Methodism*, especially ch. 3, 'John Wesley or Charles Wesley?' was a notable effort to draw up criteria to give this enquiry some objectivity. E. H. Rattenbury gave attention to the matter in *Evangelical Doctrines*, pp. 21–5. And in this book, see Appendix 3, 'Authorship in Question', pp. 245–9. It seems responsible to follow the judgement of John C. Bowmer, *The Sacrament of the Lord's Supper in Early Methodism*, Dacre Press, Westminster: 1951, who says concerning *Hymns on the Lord's Supper*, 'On lack of evidence to the contrary, we shall assume that the hymns of this collection are all by Charles' (p. 167).

6 A. C. Outler and R. P. Heitzenrater, eds, *John Wesley's Sermons: An Anthology*, Abingdon Press, Nashville: 1991, p. 502.

7 A letter from John Fletcher Priest, recorded in L. Tyerman, *The Life and Times of John Wesley*, Hodder and Stoughton, London: 1870–71, vol. 2, p. 264. The reference is noted in Kathryn Nichols, 'The Theology of Christ's Sacrifice and Presence in Charles Wesley's Hymns on the Lord's Supper', *The Hymn* 39/4 (1988), p. 29. J. Ernest Rattenbury gathered reports on the large numbers of communicants at some

observances of the sacrament in early Methodism; see *The Eucharistic Hymns of John and Charles Wesley*, Epworth Press, 1948, pp. 2ff. As to how the hymns were used, one possibility is suggested in Bowmer, *The Sacrament of the Lord's Supper in Early Methodism*, p. 87, who cites a diary entry by the Welsh Methodist Howell Harris, speaking of a sacrament service led by Charles Wesley at West Street Chapel in London, 28 August 1743, at which hymns are sung 'between every company of communicants'. The phrase may refer to the custom, continued in some places well through the nineteenth century, of dismissing each table of communicants after all have received the bread and wine, thus creating groups within the congregation, some of which would be retiring from the table while others were coming to it.

8 Rattenbury remarks, 'There can be no doubt that Holy Communion was the central devotion of the Evangelical Revival' (*Eucharistic Hymns*, p. 4). However, Henry Rack enters some realistic cautions, asking what access most Methodists would have had to the sacrament in the early decades of the movement. 'The fact is that eucharistic piety was not, and in fact could not be, the centre of devotion or the norm for every Sunday's worship for Methodists or ordinary Anglicans, and it is unlikely that it ever had been.' *Reasonable Enthusiast: John Wesley and the Rise of Methodism*, Trinity Press International, Philadelphia: 1989, pp. 417–19.

9 Geoffrey Wainwright, 'Introduction' to *Hymns on the Lord's Supper*, Charles Wesley Society, Madison, NJ: 1995, p. xi.

10 An essay that puts this development in a generally positive light is Adrian Burdon, *The Preaching Service: The Glory of the Methodists*, Joint Liturgical Studies 17, Grove Books, Cambridge: 1991.

11 On this story see, among other sources, the rather old, and yet full, insightful, and at times almost despairing article, 'The Sacraments in Early American Methodism', by Paul S. Sanders, *Church History* 26 (1957), pp. 355–71. Ironically, John Wesley undertook his ordinations in order to make the Holy Communion available to the Methodists of North America.

12 Wainwright, 'Introduction' to *Hymns on the Lord's Supper*, p. xii.

13 Published by A. Weekes & Co., London: 1958. The purpose of this slender work, the editor's foreword says, was 'severely practical: to make our present-day parishes know, love, and sing Wesley. This is a treasure entrusted to the Methodist people for the good of the Universal Church', p. ii.

14 Thomas Brett, *A Collection of the Principal Liturgies Used by the Christian Church in the Celebration of the Holy Eucharist . . . With a Dissertation upon Them*, Richard King, London: 1720. Geoffrey Wainwright has surveyed the debt of the Wesleys to the liturgies and theologians of the early Church in '"Our Elder Brethren Join": The Wesleys' *Hymns on the Lord's Supper* and the Patristic Revival in England', *Proceedings of the Charles Wesley Society* 1 (1994), pp. 5–31.

15 Martin Luther, 'Treatise on the New Testament, that is, the Holy Mass', 1520, in *Luther's Works: Word and Sacrament, I,* American edn, vol. 35, Muhlenberg Press, Philadelphia: 1960, p. 99.

16 John Calvin, 'Short Treatise on the Holy Supper of our Lord and only Saviour Jesus Christ', 1540, in *Calvin: Theological Treatises*, Library of Christian Classics, vol. 22, Westminster Press, Philadelphia: 1954, p. 149.

17 John Calvin, *Institutes of the Christian Religion*, ed. John T. McNeill, trans. Ford Lewis Battles, Library of Christian Classics, vol. 21, Westminster Press, Philadelphia: 1960, vol. 2, pp. 1443–5.

18 Richard Baxter, *The Reformation of the Liturgy*, London: 1661. The text of Baxter's 'Savoy Liturgy' can be found in Bard Thompson, ed., *Liturgies of the Western Church*, New American Library, New York: 1961 (and later editions), ch. 12. Baxter's 'epiclesis' is on p. 402.

19 The text is from *The Works of the Late Reverend Mr. Matthew Henry*, London: 1726, a folio volume containing Henry's shorter works, pp. 171 and 175.

20 Bowmer, *The Sacrament of the Lord's Supper in Early Methodism*, p. 61.

21 In 'The Development of the *Collection*', in *The Works of John Wesley*, ed. Hildebrandt and Beckerlegge, vol. 7, p. 23.

22 For an appreciation of Watts' sacramental hymns, see Daniel B. Stevick, '"The Fruits of Life O'erspread the Board," Isaac Watts' *Hymns for the Lord's Supper*', in J. Neil Alexander, ed., *With Ever Joyful Hearts*, Church Publishing, New York: 1999, pp. 227–43.

23 Borgen, *John Wesley on the Sacraments*, p. 281.

24 Two essays which have sought to trace the influence of the Book of Common Prayer in *Hymns on the Lord's Supper* are: J. R. Watson, 'Charles Wesley's Hymns and the *Book of Common Prayer*', in Margot Johnson, ed., *Thomas Cranmer: Essays in Commemoration of the 500th Anniversary of his Birth*, Turnstone Ventures, Durham: 1980, pp. 204–28, and Kathryn Nichols, 'Charles Wesley's Eucharistic Hymns: Their Relationship to the *Book of Common Prayer*', *The Hymn* 39/2 (1988), pp. 13–21.

25 Borgen remarks that Rattenbury in his indispensable work *Eucharistic Hymns*, 1948, makes little use of the seventeenth- and eighteenth-century writings on the sacraments which the Wesleys are known to have read and that he refers to Brevint in John Wesley's abridgement, rather than in the full text. Franz Hildebrandt, in his heavily documented work *I Offered Christ*, 1967, is more interested in locating the Wesley sacramental hymns in relation to Luther and to modern Catholic/Protestant issues than in relation to their own setting in the seventeenth- and eighteenth-century Church of England. He gives little attention either to Calvin and the Reformed tradition or to the Eastern liturgies and theologians.

For many years the principal survey of Anglican sacramental thought was C. W. Dugmore, *Eucharistic Doctrine and Practice in England from Hooker to Waterland*, SPCK, London: 1942, which as an overview has not been fully superseded. Several recent works have reconsidered the tradition. The most comprehensive study is Kenneth Stevenson, *Covenant of Grace Renewed: A Vision of the Eucharist in the Seventeenth Century*, Darton, Longman and Todd, London: 1994. Stevenson collaborated with H. R. McAdoo in *The Mystery of the Eucharist in the Anglican Tradition*, Canterbury Press, Norwich: 1995. A sketch, written with special reference to *Hymns on the Lord's Supper,* is J. Neil Alexander, 'With Eloquence in Speech and Song: Anglican Reflections on the Eucharistic Hymns (1745) of John and Charles Wesley', published in *Proceedings of the Charles Wesley Society* 2 (1995), pp. 35–50; for a revised edition of this essay, see J. Neil Alexander, in *With Ever Joyful Hearts*, pp. 244–60.

26 Joseph Hall, 'A Plain and Familiar Explication of Christ's Presence in the Sacrament of his Body and Blood, Out of the Doctrine of the Church of England. For the satisfying of a scrupulous friend', 1631; bound in *The Remaining Works of the Incomparable Prelate Joseph Hall*, London: 1660, p. 294.

27 Jeremy Taylor, *The Worthy Communicant*, ch. 1, sec. II, in the Heber/Eden edition, London: 1854, vol. 8, p. 23.

28 Taylor, *The Worthy Communicant*, ch. 1, sec. III, p. 31.

29 Taylor's eucharistic liturgy can be found, with a commentary, in W. J. Grisbrooke, *Anglican Liturgies of the Seventeenth and Eighteenth Centuries*, Alcuin Club, SPCK, London: 1958. See also the discussion in H. Boone Porter, *Jeremy Taylor: Liturgist*, Alcuin Club, SPCK, London: 1979.

30 William Law, *A Demonstration of the Gross and Fundamental Errors of a late Book . . .*, 2nd edn, London: 1738. The quoted passages are from pages 109f., 135 and 139f.

31 Waterland's central works on the sacrament, including *A Review of the Doctrine of the Eucharist*, 1738, and four smaller essays, were assembled from his *Works* in a volume, whose editor is not named, published by Oxford University Press in 1880 and usually known by the name on the spine, *The Doctrine of the Eucharist*. The quoted passage is on p. 8.

32 Herbert Thorndike, 'The Laws of the Church', 1659, in *Works*, Library of Anglo-Catholic Theology, vol. 4, pp. 112–13.

33 Jeremy Taylor, *The Great Exemplar*, 3rd edn, London: 1657, pt. III, sec.15, para. 7, p. 522.

34 Simon Patrick, *The Christian Sacrifice*, 2nd edn, London: 1672, p. 23.

35 Robert Nelson, *A Companion for the Festivals and Fasts of the Church of England*, 23rd edn, London: 1773, p. 510.

36 John Johnson, *The Unbloody Sacrifice and Altar*, London: 1718, vol. 2, p. 150. This work was published in the Library of Anglo-Catholic Theology, Parker, Oxford: 1847, pt. II, ch. ii.3.4. vol. 2, pp. 178f.

37 Thomas Deacon, *A Full, True and Comprehensive View of Christianity*, 2nd edn, London: 1748, p. 240.

38 The quotation is from 'The Christian Sacrifice Explained', 1738, in the 1880 collection, p. 419; see note 31.

39 The *Hymns* only identify the introductory essay as 'Extracted from Dr. Brevint'. H. R. McAdoo reports that a 1794 edition of *Hymns on the Lord's Supper* describes the essay as 'Extracted from a late Author, by John Wesley, M.A., Late Fellow of Lincoln College Oxford'. John Wesley later issued his abridgement of Brevint as a separate publication.

40 For many years, there was almost nothing available on Brevint apart from the informative *DNB* article by Canon Venables and the sources it cited. Dugmore (see note 25, above) did not so much as mention him. Similarly G. W. O. Addleshaw's *The High Church Tradition* (1941) skipped over his work entirely. Authors who wrote on Wesley's sacramental hymns necessarily spoke of Brevint, but they made little enquiry into his life or his thought, and they tended to cite him in the abridged text that was printed with *Hymns on the Lord's Supper*. Rattenbury, Borgen and Hildebrandt speak of Brevint, but almost entirely as a source for Wesley.
Recent works have brought Daniel Brevint in his own right into the story of seventeenth-century Anglican writing on the sacrament: Henry R. McAdoo, 'A Theology of the Eucharist: Brevint and the Wesleys', in *Theology*, 97/788 (July/August 1994), pp. 245–56; Kenneth Stevenson, *Covenant of Grace Renewed*, 1994, devotes a chapter to Brevint and Cosin; and Brevint is considered in McAdoo and Stevenson, *The Mystery of the Eucharist in the Anglican Tradition*, 1995. The account of Brevint's life and thought in Stevenson's *Covenant of Grace Renewed*, pp. 98–107, is the best currently at hand.

41 *The Great Exemplar*, pt. III, sec. 15, para. 7, p. 521.

42 E. Venables, in *DNB*, 1900, p. 1200.

43 'The Christian Sacrifice Explained', as in note 38, above, pp. 433f.

44 Geoffrey Wainwright observes Wesley's uneven use of Brevint's work in his paper '"Our Elder Brethren Join": The Wesleys' *Hymns on the Lord's Supper* and the Patristic Revival in England', *Proceedings of the Charles Wesley Society*, 1 (1994), p. 13. The alternation between sequences of hymns which follow Brevint closely and stretches of hymns which do not leads Wainwright to wonder whether in the development of *Hymns on the Lord's Supper* some other and unguessed sources were being 'massively exploited'. Wainwright mentions the subject again in his 'Introduction' to the Charles Wesley Society facsimile edition of the hymns, pp. viiif.

45 Frank Baker, 'Approaching a Variorum Edition of *Hymns on the Lord's Supper*', *Proceedings of the Charles Wesley Society* 2 (1995), p. 8.

46 Information on churches, furnishings and liturgical customs can be found in three books, which represent the insights of three different generations: J. W. Legg, *English Church Life from the Restoration to the Tractarian Movement*, London: 1914; G. W. O. Addleshaw and F. Etchells, *The Architectural Setting of Anglican Worship*, Faber and Faber, London: 1948; and Nigel Yates, *Buildings, Faith and Worship: The Liturgical Arrangements of Anglican Churches 1600–1900*, Clarendon Press, Oxford: 1991.

47 See Donald Davie, *The Eighteenth-Century Hymn in England*, Cambridge University Press, Cambridge: 1993, especially ch. 5, 'The Carnality of Charles Wesley', pp. 57–70.

48 J. R. Watson, *The English Hymn: A Critical and Historical Study*, Oxford University Press, Oxford: 1999, p. 225.

49 Baker, 'Approaching a Variorum Edition', p. 9.

50 Rattenbury, *Eucharistic Hymns*, p. 14.

51 Borgen, *John Wesley on the Sacraments*, pp. 67f.

52 Borgen, *John Wesley on the Sacraments*, p. 69.

53 This book came into circulation in 1658. Its authorship has always been in doubt, but Richard Allestree (1619–81) seems the most likely candidate. It continued in use in Britain through the nineteenth century, and it had some circulation on the Continent. The printing used here is that of 1731. It is no more severe than are other similar works of the period.

54 Sanders, 'The Sacraments in Early American Methodism', p. 359.

55 For an account of this matter, see Bowmer, *The Sacrament of the Lord's Supper in Early Methodism*, ch. 8, 'Admission to the Lord's Supper in Early Methodism', pp. 103–22.

56 The absence of the theme of the resurrection from *Hymns on the Lord's Supper* was observed by Fr Leonid Kishkovsky, see 'The Wesleys' *Hymns on the Lord's Supper* and Orthodoxy', *Proceedings of the Charles Wesley Society* 2 (1995), especially pp. 81–4. See also D. B. Stevick, 'The Altar and the Cross', *Proceedings of the Charles Wesley Society* 5 (1998), pp. 73f.

57 The theme of 'the sacramental universe' was developed by William Temple in *Nature, Man and God*, Macmillan, London: 1951, esp. Lecture XIX, pp. 473–95. It is also introduced elsewhere in his writings.

58 In one of his better-known sacramental hymns, Watts characteristically passes from 'the book of nature' to grace:

Nature with open volume stands
    To spread her Maker's praise abroad,
    And every labour of his hands
    Shows something worthy of a God.

But in the grace that rescued man
    His brightest form of glory shines;
    Here on the cross 'tis fairest drawn
    In precious blood and crimson lines. (10:1–2)

Hymn 216 in the 1780 collection expresses a detailed appreciation of creation, but the hymn is evidently by John, adapting a hymn of Watts which was in turn derived from Psalm 147.

59 Stevenson, *Eucharist and Offering*, p. 168.

60 The best tracing of Wesley's literary sources remains Henry Bett, *The Hymns of Methodism*, as supplemented by Baker, *Charles Wesley's Verse: An Introduction*, Epworth Press, London: 1988, especially ch. 6.

61 Wesley's line is 'Was ever grief or love like thine?' George Herbert's poem 'The Sacrifice' is a narrative of the passion, told from the viewpoint of Jesus. The stanzas consist of three rhyming lines, all of them, until the last, ending with the refrain line, 'Was ever grief like mine?' The final stanza ends 'Never was grief like mine.' Clearly Wesley echoes Herbert. The literary scholar Rosemond Tuve has shown that Herbert's poem in turn echoes the medieval 'reproaches' (the *improperia*), the complaints of Christ against his people, of the Good Friday liturgy. See R. Tuve, *A Reading of George Herbert*, University of Chicago Press, Chicago: 1952.

62 Francis Frost, 'The Veiled Unveiling of the Glory of God in the Eucharistic Hymns of Charles Wesley: The Self-Emptying of God', *Proceedings of the Charles Wesley Society* 2 (1995), p. 94.

63 The best and most accessible study of the literary characteristics of Wesley's work is Frank Baker, *Charles Wesley's Verse: An Introduction*. This study was originally published as the introduction to the author's *Representative Verse of Charles Wesley*, 1964, and revised for separate publication. Baker identifies (by their technical names, which Charles Wesley would have known) the features of Wesley's poetic style, most of which he would have internalised through his study of rhetoric and probably used without thinking about them. Stylistically there is nothing distinctive in *Hymns on the Lord's Supper*, hence the general investigations of Wesley's style illuminate this specific collection. See ch. 2 of Rattenbury's *Evangelical Doctrines* and the material in the introduction (especially pp. 38–55) of vol. 7 of *The Works of John Wesley*, ed. F. Hildebrandt and O. A. Beckerlegge (1983).

64 James Sutherland, *A Preface to Eighteenth Century Poetry*, Oxford University Press, Oxford: 1948, 1963, p. 109. Although it is old, this small book remains a good introduction.

65 Paul Fussell, *Poetic Meter and Poetic Form*, rev. edn, Random House, New York: 1979, p. 10.

66 J. Richard Watson, '*Hymns on the Lord's Supper*, 1745, and Some Literary

and Liturgical Sources', *Proceedings of the Charles Wesley Society* 2 (1995), p. 18. The remark was made in connection with the first stanza of Hymn 116, but it would apply generally to Wesley's six-line stanzas.

67 Rattenbury, *Evangelical Doctrines*, p. 40.

68 'It should indeed be taken as a general rule that the rhymes of the poets of this period represent pronunciations both genuine and linguistically explicable as variants naturally persisting in a time when a received standard was still far from being as fixed as it is today.' A. S. Collins, 'Language 1660–1784', in Boris Ford, ed., *From Dryden to Johnson*, The Pelican Guide to English Literature, Penguin Books, Harmondsworth: 1957, p. 139.

69 Frank Baker has an amused comment in 'Approaching a Variorum Edition of *Hymns on the Lord's Supper*', p. 14.

70 Wordsworth's 'Preface' stands as something of a manifesto, even though it is a surprisingly temperate document. It has been reprinted many times. See *William Wordsworth*, ed. Stephen Gill, Oxford University Press, Oxford: 1984, pp. 595–619.

71 Davie, *The Eighteenth-Century Hymn in England*, p. 69. In another work, Davie says of Wesley's Latinisms: 'They are not threaded on the staple Anglo-Saxon of his diction in order merely to give pleasing variety in sound and pace (though they do that incidentally) but so that Saxon and classical elements can criss-cross and light up each other's meaning.' *Purity of Diction in English Verse*, Oxford University Press, New York: 1953, p. 78.

72 Baker, *Charles Wesley's Verse: An Introduction*, p. 21.

73 Watts' *Works*, ed. Jennings and Doddridge, 1753, London: 1810, vol. 4, p. 122.

Part I

1 Borgen, *John Wesley on the Sacraments*, p. 92.

2 Rattenbury, *Evangelical Doctrines*, p. 199.

3 Rattenbury judged (*Eucharistic Hymns*, p. 16) that Hymns 2, 3, 4 and 8 speak so emphatically of sacrifice that he discussed them not in Wesley's sequence in the hymns about the sacrament as memorial, but with the hymns on sacrifice in Part IV. Such a relocation of these hymns seems mistaken; see Borgen's comment in *John Wesley on the Sacraments*, p. 87.

4 This hymn makes no reference to the Holy Communion, but its passion-centred piety and its sensory appeal are appropriate for the sacrament which 'shows the Lord's death'.

5 Isaac Barrow, 'The Doctrine of the Sacraments', in A. Napier, ed., *The Theological Works of Isaac Barrow*, Cambridge: 1859, vol. VII, p. 517. This small work was not published during Barrow's lifetime.

6 Matthew Henry, *The Communicant's Companion*, 1704, ch. 8, sec. i.

7 Davie, *The Eighteenth-Century Hymn in England*. In ch. 5, 'The Carnality of Charles Wesley', Davie speaks of the 'strong and muscular thought' in Wesley's hymns, commenting that his feeling for language 'was anything but fastidious' and remarking on 'the insistent physicality of his images'.

8 Borgen, *John Wesley on the Sacraments*, p. 88.

9 Milton refers to Christ as 'the mighty Pan/ Who kindly came with them below,' in his poem 'On the Morning of Christ's Nativity', 1629 (published 1645), line 89.

There is a similar reference in Spenser, *The Shepherd's Calendar*, 'May'. Somewhat surprisingly, Dante, referring to God, says 'O Supreme Jove, for mankind crucified' (*Purgatorio* VI. 121, Ciardi translation). Whether or not Wesley knew of such sources and the tradition of thought they represent is not certain. The Christianisation of classical mythology in the early Church is traced in Hugo Rahner's *Greek Myths and Christian Mystery*, Burns and Oates, London: 1963.

10 Watson, 'Literary and Liturgical Sources', p. 19. Watson finds in this hymn an interplay with classical sources, particularly Ovid (pp. 19–26).

11 The reference to the Holy Spirit as 'witness of his dying' traces to the liturgy of *The Apostolic Constitutions*, VIII.12.38, a text which Wesley would have known, either directly or through the work of Thomas Brett's *Principal Liturgies*, 1720, or through Thomas Deacon's *Devotions*, 1734, which used this wording.

12 M. A. C. Warren, *Strange Victory*, SCM Press, London: 1946, pp. 56f.

13 The opening figure of an unknown Traveller suggests Wesley's widely admired, earlier and longer poem 'Wrestling Jacob', 1742, which begins quite hauntingly, 'Come, O thou Traveller unknown/ Whom still I hold, but cannot see.' The poem is widely anthologised. See Donald Davie, ed., *The New Oxford Book of Christian Verse*, Oxford University Press, Oxford: 1981, no. 140.

14 Rattenbury conjectures that this hymn 'must have been a meditation on the *Agnus Dei*' (*Eucharistic Hymns*, p. 25). It is addressed 'Lamb of God'. It contains the pleas 'Let us mercy find' and 'Take all our sins away'. And each stanza ends 'And bid us go in peace.'

15 The incident is told in a long entry for 9 October 1748 in John Wesley's *Journal* (EML edn, vol. 2, pp. 83–90) and in Tyerman's *The Life of John Wesley*, London: 1882, vol. 2, pp. 27f.

16 Donald Davie, *A Gathered Church: The Literature of the English Dissenting Interest, 1700–1930*, Oxford University Press, Oxford: 1978, p. 51.

17 See the survey of these motifs in Ellen M. Ross, *The Grief of God: Images of the Suffering of Jesus in Late Medieval England*, Oxford University Press, Oxford: 1997. Anyone reading this study of medieval iconography with Wesley's sacramental hymns in mind will be struck by the continuity of images of the passion through half a millennium of religious turmoil.

18 The translation is from *Principal Liturgies*, published in London: 1720 by Thomas Brett, an eminent Non-juror. Brett's text, whether or not Wesley knew and used it, gives a period wording.

19 J. K. Mozley's *The Impassibility of God: A Survey of Christian Thought*, Cambridge University Press, Cambridge: 1926, was important as a summing-up of the tradition and of the rethinking that was taking place in the early twentieth century. (Mozley's only reference to Wesley (John) is misleading; he sets him with Pearson and Butler in a list of post-Reformation divines who upheld divine impassibility.) Among those who were questioning divine impassibility, Mozley discusses the Scottish theologian A. M. Fairbairn, the American G. B. Stevens, the independent-minded B. H. Streeter, the impassioned preacher G. A. Studdert-Kennedy, and the philosophical theologian, later Archbishop, William Temple. Since Mozley's landmark survey there has been much literature affirming, in one idiom or another, that God knows, as a redemptive participant, the pain of the world. A survey written today would include Edwin Lewis, *The Creator and the Adversary*, 1950; the Japanese theologian Kazoh Kitamori's work *Theology of the Pain of God*, 1965; Jürgen Moltmann's masterful

The Crucified God, 1973; Rosemary Haughton, *The Passionate God*, 1981; Paul S. Fiddes, *The Creative Suffering of God*, 1988; and much of the work of feminist writers and of the theologians influenced by process thought.

20 'Invitation to Sinners,' 3.6; text quoted in full in John Tyson, ed., *Charles Wesley: A Reader*, Oxford University press, Oxford: 1989, p. 231f.

21 See Daniel B. Stevick, 'The Altar and the Cross: The Atonement in Charles Wesley's *Hymns on the Lord's Supper'*, *Proceedings of the Charles Wesley Society* 5 (1998), pp. 61–80.

Part II

1 Rattenbury, *Eucharistic Hymns*, p. 30.

2 Perhaps this hymn began in Charles Wesley's mind when he realised that some of these words from the catechism – words he had known all his life – with only a little adapting, fell into iambic rhythm.

3 Approximately ten times in hymns outside Part II Wesley asks God or Christ or the Holy Spirit to 'come'. However, the theme belongs principally to the hymns on the sacrament as a present sign and means of grace, being used as a summons 29 times in the hymns of Part II.

4 Borgen, *John Wesley on the Sacraments*, p. 69.

5 Hymn 40 is one of Wesley's passages whose thought form suggests a collect. A brief address to Christ (1.1) is followed by a descriptive clause in the 'who' form (1.2–4), which leads to a compound petition (1.5–2.2), and concludes with a statement of a desired result (2.3–6). This form would have become so familiar from the Prayer Book that it would have seemed to Wesley an inevitable structure into which to cast at least some prayers.

6 Ambrose, *On the Sacraments*, V.1.4. *St. Ambrose on the Sacraments and on the Mysteries*, trans. T. Thompson, ed. J. H. Srawley, SPCK, London: 1950, p. 96.

7 Toplady's first stanza, lines 3–6, reads: 'Let the Water and the Blood,/ From thy riven side which flowed,/ Be of sin the double cure,/ Cleanse me from its guilt and power.' The lines must have puzzled many churchgoers in many traditions.

8 Rattenbury uses (does he coin?) the term in his discussion of the 'Problem of Personation', in *Evangelical Doctrines*, pp. 28–31, saying that the use of 'I' in Wesley 'may be – often is – a piece of dramatic personation; he has put himself in the place of the persons for whom he wrote' (p. 29).

9 Historians of liturgy have supposed that Cranmer took the prayer for the Spirit in his 1549 text from early and Eastern rites. But the English scholar Bryan Spinks has argued persuasively that Cranmer's sources were Western. See Bryan Spinks, '"And with Thy Holy Spirite and Worde": Further thoughts on the Source of Cranmer's Petition for Sanctification in the 1549 Communion Service', in Johnson, *Thomas Cranmer*, pp. 94–102.

10 'A Farther Appeal to Men of Reason and Religion', London: 1745, I.6, p. 5; in the facsimile edition of Wesley's 'Appeals', published in the Library of Methodist Classics by the United Methodist Publishing House, Nashville, TN: 1992. In the standard edition of Wesley's *Works*, the 'Farther Appeal' appears in vol. 8, where the quotation is on p. 49.

Part III

1 Alan Richardson, *An Introduction to the Theology of the New Testament*, Harper, New York: 1958, p. 372.

2 Paul S. Sanders, 'The Sacraments in Early American Methodism', *Church History* 26 (1957), p. 358. Geoffrey Wainwright says, along the same line, 'It was not until the Wesleys' *Hymns on the Lord's Supper* (1745) that the Western church achieved again a rich appreciation of the eucharist as the sign of the future banquet of the heavenly kingdom.' *Eucharist and Eschatology*, Epworth Press, London: 1971, p. 56.

3 Geoffrey Wainwright notes the connection of Wesley's lines with the 'Cherubic Hymn' in '"Our Elder Brethren Join", The Wesleys' *Hymns on the Lord's Supper* and the Patristic Revival in England', *Proceedings of the Charles Wesley Society* 1 (1994), p. 29.

4 Richardson, *An Introduction to the Theology of the New Testament*, p. 375.

5 Paul S. Sanders, 'Wesley's Eucharistic Faith and Practice', *Anglican Theological Review* 48/2 (April 1966), p. 167.

Part IV

1 Borgen, *John Wesley on the Sacraments*, p. 244.

2 The posture in which the risen Christ is depicted is a matter of some interest and some confusion. Wesley (in 116:2.1 and elsewhere, and compare the engraving on p. 170) describes the ascended Christ as a priest standing before the altar in the heavenly Holy Place, the posture of priests when they were making offering (Heb. 10.11). But Hebrews makes the point that when Jesus, the great high priest, had made his final sacrifice, he sat down at the right hand of God (Heb. 1.3; 10.12). The author's confidence that this was so came from his Christological interpretation of Psalm 110.1–2, an interpretation that was probably already a part of Christian tradition by the time Hebrews was written. The regal imagery of the New Testament describes Jesus as seated at the right hand of the divine throne, expressing shared authority (see Matt. 26.64; Acts 5.31; Rom. 8.34; Col. 3.1; Heb. 8.1; 1 Pet. 3.22). (In Stephen's vision, Acts 7.55f., Jesus is standing at the right hand of God.) The priestly imagery of Hebrews has Jesus standing to perform his office and then sitting down to signify its completion. But his priestly work continues. Wesley, in *Hymns on the Lord's Supper*, usually depicts Christ as a priest who is standing.

3 John Wesley, *Explanatory Notes upon the New Testament*, Beacon Hill Press, Kansas City, MO: 1981, reprinted from an undated edition published by the Wesleyan-Methodist Book-Room, London; unpaged.

4 Rowan Williams, Introduction to McAdoo and Stevenson, *The Mystery of the Eucharist in the Anglican Tradition*, p. viii.

5 William Temple, *Christus Veritas*, Macmillan, London: 1924, p. 242. Temple's sentence, which shows his gift for phrase, is quoted with appreciation in C. F. D. Moule, *The Sacrifice of Christ*, Hodder and Stoughton, London: 1956, p. 56, and with distaste by Franz Hildebrandt, in *I Offered Christ*, pp. 58, 68.

6 Geoffrey Wainwright, *Doxology*, Oxford University Press, Oxford: 1980, pp. 272f.

7 Brevint suggested the parallel between prayer and sacrament when he said that we go to the holy communion 'to lay out all our wants, and pour out all our grief and

prayers, and our praises before the Lord'. Communicants have used the sacrament 'as the most powerful means the Church had to strengthen their supplications, to open the gates of heaven, and to force, in a manner, God and his Christ to have compassion on them' (VI.4).

8 Rattenbury, *Eucharistic Hymns*, p. 91.

9 While the words 'Victim Divine' are weighted with significance, the sounds are light. The four syllables contain only one vowel, 'i' – three short 'i's, and one long 'i'. The first and fourth syllables are accented, while the second and third are not.

10 There are 17 's' sounds in stanza 2 of Hymn 116. (More of them occur in the lines immediately before and after.) There are almost as many in stanza 4.

11 Nichols, 'The Theology of Christ's Sacrifice', p. 20.

12 Rattenbury, *Evangelical Doctrines*, p. 226.

13 Kenneth Stevenson, *Accept this Sacrifice: The Eucharist as Sacrifice Today*, Liturgical Press, Collegeville, MN: 1989, p. 11.

14 Wheatly's commentary remained in print through much of the nineteenth century. The frontispiece reproduced and described here is from the 3rd edition, London: 1720. This author's name is variously spelled. The spelling here is that of the 1720 edition.

15 Frost, 'Veiled Unveiling', p. 94.

16 Rattenbury, *Eucharistic Hymns*, p. 98.

17 Teresa Berger, *Theology in Hymns?* Kingswood Books (Abingdon Press), Nashville, TN: 1995, p. 121.

18 Rattenbury, *Eucharistic Hymns*, p. 99.

19 S. T. Kimbrough and O. A. Beckerlegge, eds, *The Unpublished Poetry of Charles Wesley*, Kingswood Books (Abingdon Press), Nashville: 1988–92, vol. 1, p. 192.

Part V

1 When Wesley says that the additional offerings are 'thrown on' the sacrificed Lamb, his expressions 'thrown on' or 'cast on' do not appear in the biblical accounts of the daily offering, but are from Brevint, who spoke of Christian offerings as 'cast on' the offering of Christ.

2 D. M. Baillie, *The Theology of the Sacraments*, Scribners, New York: 1957, p. 122.

3 Franz Hildebrandt, *I offered Christ: A Protestant Study of the Mass*, Muhlenberg Press, Philadephia: 1967. Hildebrandt was a German Lutheran who came to England (later to the USA), where he identified with the Methodist Church.

4 Rattenbury, *Evangelical Doctrines*, p. 225.

5 Isaac Watts, in Hymn 22 of his sacramental collection, says that Christ gave up his life 'to ransom guilty worms from death' (22:2.4). Edward Young (1683–1765), in his long, blank verse didactic poem 'Night Thoughts' which he wrote between 1742 and 1745, and which is known to have influenced the Wesleys, describes the contradictoriness of humanity, 'An heir of glory! a frail child of dust!/ Helpless immortal! insect infinite!/ A worm! A god!' ('Night I', lines 78–80).

6 Hildebrandt, *I Offered Christ*, p. 100.

7 Hildebrandt, *I Offered Christ*, p. 281.

8 Hildebrandt seems to realise that unless he can deal with Colossians 1.24,

his quarrel is not really with Brevint and Wesley, but with the New Testament. He devotes several pages to the text. See *I Offered Christ*, pp. 151–4.

9 John Macmurray, *Reason and Emotion*, Faber and Faber, London: 1950 (first published, 1935), p. 70. William James gave much attention to the physiological aspect of emotion.

After the Sacrament

1 H. A. Hodges and A. M. Allchin, eds, *A Rapture of Praise: Hymns of John and Charles Wesley*, Hodder and Stoughton, London: 1966, p. 38.

2 The two matters – the frequency of the Church's observance of the Supper and the frequency of the people's communion – have been handled differently in the traditions of Western Christendom. By the later part of the early Church the people had come to receive the sacrament infrequently, and until the mid-twentieth century it remained common in Western Catholicism for lay persons to receive the Holy Communion only a very few times a year. However, during those generations the Mass was being celebrated with great frequency, attended in parish churches on Sundays and festal days by large congregations. Usually, however, the people did not receive communion. At the very frequent daily Masses, only the celebrant and the server received; the congregation (when there was a congregation) engaged in pious reflections and made 'spiritual communion'. The major Reformers regarded such non-communicating Low Mass as defective, and they sought to have Word and Sacrament every Sunday. It was their conviction, however, that there could be no true celebration of the eucharist unless there were communicants, for the celebrant's action, which was for the people, was completed in the people's reception. When the long-established habit of non-communicating attendance proved impossible to overcome in Anglican, Lutheran and Reformed bodies, the ideal of weekly communion was generally abandoned, and celebrations were reduced to monthly or quarterly. However, when the eucharist was observed, most of those eligible and attending received the Body and Blood. Thus for four centuries, probably most Protestants were receiving the Holy Communion at least as often as were most Roman Catholics, although their churches observed the Supper less frequently than every Sunday.

3 Wesley, 'The Duty of Constant Communion', in Outler and Heitzenrater, *John Wesley's Sermons*, p. 503.

4 Jeremy Taylor, *The Great Exemplar*, III, 15.19, p. 532. Taylor was right in saying that the early Church observed the sacrament every Lord's Day and that Christians in good standing received. But his description of the frequency with which Christians came to receive the communion in later years is not supportable.

5 Thomas Cranmer, *A Defence of the True and Catholic Doctrine of the Sacrament*, 1550, bk. III, ch. 12. (See G. E. Duffield, ed., *The Work of Thomas Cranmer*, Fortress Press, Philadelphia: 1965, p. 166.) Cranmer is not arguing that daily communion was the practice of the earliest Christians, but that Christ intended that the sacrament not be a yearly 'remembrance', like the Passover, but daily.

6 Anthony Sparrow, *A Rationale upon the Book of Common Prayer of the Church of England*, London: 1657, pp. 274f.

7 Isaac Barrow, 'The Doctrine of the Sacraments', in *Theological Works*, ed. A. Napier, 1859, vol. 7, p. 525.

8 Richard Wheatly, *Rational Illustration*, 3rd edn, 1720, pp. 255f.

Hymns on the Lord's Supper Today

1 Borgen, *John Wesley on the Sacraments*, p. 17.

2 Egil Grislis, 'The Wesleyan Doctrine of the Lord's Supper', *Duke Divinity School Bulletin* 28/2 (1963), p. 110.

3 Hodges and Allchin, *A Rapture of Praise*, p. 36.

4 William R. Crockett, *Eucharist: Symbol of Transformation*, Pueblo, New York: 1989, p. 202.

5 Stevenson, *Eucharist and Offering*, p. 170.

6 As evidence of this counter-current one might note the way in which the rule of reason is questioned in such classic texts as Part IV of Swift's *Gulliver's Travels* (1726) and in Book IV of Pope's *Dunciad* (1742).

7 *The Religious Sublime: Christian Poetry and Critical Tradition in 18th Century England*, University Press of Kentucky, Lexington: 1972, pp.204f. Morris continues: 'It is easy to understand why one eighteenth-century reviewer, judging by criteria of polite literature developed for the medium of print, ridiculed Charles Wesley's hymns as "spiritual Billingsgate". Wesley, of course, addressed his hymns to an audience of unsophisticated literary taste. But, more importantly, he did not intend hymnody to be a form of written composition. For Wesley, print is only the temporary distillate of song. It is as if, for the necessary purposes of storage, a highly volatile gas were bottled as a liquid.'

Appendix 3

1 Henry Bett, *The Hymns of Methodism*, London: 1913; 3rd edn, revised and enlarged, 1945.

2 Francis Frost, 'Veiled Unveiling', p. 91.

3 Jeremy Taylor describes the primacy of the sacrament in similar terms. The substantial discourse 'Upon the Institution and Reception of the Holy Sacrament of the Lord's Supper' which Taylor set in his life of Jesus, *The Great Exemplar*, opens, 'As the Sun among the stars, and Man among the sublunary creatures is the most eminent and noble, the Prince of inferiours, and their measure, or their guide: so is this action, among all the instances of religion, it is the most perfect and consummate.' Part III, sect. 15, 1657 edn, p. 517. Paul makes a similar comparison in 1 Cor. 15.42; he is not, however, speaking of the divine ordinances.

4 Frost, 'Veiled Unveiling', p. 91.

5 Rattenbury, *Eucharistic Hymns*, p. 77.

Bibliography

The Wesleys and Their Period

Period Sources

Baxter, Richard, *The Reformation of the Liturgy*, London: 1661. In a gathered volume, *The Grand Debate . . . for the Review and Alteration of the Book of Common Prayer*, printed in London: 1661. (Baxter's eucharistic text, the 'Savoy Liturgy', is included in Bard Thompson, ed., *Liturgies of the Western Church*, New American Library, New York: 1961, and often reprinted.)

Brett, Thomas, *A Collection of the Principal Liturgies Used by the Christian Church in the Celebration of the Holy Eucharist . . . With a Dissertation upon Them*, Richard King, London: 1720.

Brevint, Daniel, *The Christian Sacrament and Sacrifice: By Way of Discourse, Meditation, and Prayer, upon the Nature, Parts, and Blessings, of the Holy Communion*, Oxford: 1847. (Originally published, 1673.)

Calvin, John, *Institutes of the Christian Religion*, ed. John T. McNeill, trans. Ford Lewis Battles, Library of Christian Classics, vol. 21, Westminster Press, Philadelphia: 1960.

Calvin, John, *Theological Treatises*, trans. J. K. S. Reid, Library of Christian Classics, vol. 22, Westminster Press, Philadelphia: 1954.

Deacon, Thomas, *A Compleat Collection of Devotions . . .*, 1734, vol. 7 of 'Fragmenta Liturgica', ed. Peter Hall, Bath: 1848. The eucharistic text is in Grisbrooke, *Anglican Liturgies*, as below.

Deacon, Thomas, *A Full, True and Comprehensive View of Christianity . . .*, 2nd edn, London: 1748.

Henry, Matthew, *The Communicant's Companion*, 1704. (An edition published by Robert Nelson, Edinburgh: 1839, was compared with the text in a folio volume containing Henry's smaller works, London: 1726.)

Hooker, Richard, *Of the Lawes of Ecclesiastical Politie*, 1635.

Johnson, John, *The Unbloody Sacrifice and Altar. . .*, 2 vols, London: 1714, 1718; reprinted in Library of Anglo-Catholic Theology, in 1847, 2 vols.

Law, William, *A Demonstration of the Gross and Fundamental Errors of a Late Book . . .*, 2nd edn, London: 1738.

Luther, Martin, 'Treatise on the New Testament, that is, the Holy Mass', 1520, in *Luther's Works: Word and Sacrament I*, American edn, vol. 35, Muhlenberg Press, Philadelphia: 1960.

Nelson, Robert, *A Companion for the Festivals and Fasts of the Church of England . . .*, 23rd edn, London: 1773.

Patrick, Simon, *The Christian Sacrifice: A Treatise Shewing the Necessity, End and Manner of Receiving the Holy Communion*, London: 1672.

Patrick, Simon, *Mensa Mystica: or a Discourse Concerning the Sacrament of the Lord's Supper*, 5th edn, London: 1684.

Taylor, Jeremy, *The Great Exemplar*, 3rd edn, London: 1657.

Taylor, Jeremy, 'An Office or Order for the Administration of the Holy Sacrament of the Lord's Supper', in *Whole Works of the Right Rev. Jeremy Taylor*, ed. Reginald Heber, rev. Charles Eden, 10 vols, London: 1854, vol. 10, pp. 616–30. (The eucharistic text is also in Grisbrooke, *Anglican Liturgies*, as below.)

Taylor, Jeremy, *The Worthy Communicant*, London: 1683, in *Whole Works of the Right Rev. Jeremy Taylor*, ed. Reginald Heber, rev. Charles Eden, 10 vols, London: 1854, vol. 8, pp. 1–240.

Thorndike, Herbert, *An Epilogue to the Tragedy of the Church of England*, 1659, in *Works*, 9 vols, Library of Anglo-Catholic Theology, 1844–54. (Pt. III, 'The Laws of the Church', contains Thorndike's discussion of the eucharist.)

Waterland, Daniel, *A Review of the Doctrine of the Eucharist, 1738.* (Contained in *Works*, 10 vols, 1823; later published, with some smaller essays, in 1880; the volume lists no editor and is usually known by the title on the spine, *The Doctrine of the Eucharist.*)

Watts, Isaac, *Hymns and Spiritual Songs*, first published in 1707, in three books; Book III contains the 25 hymns 'Prepared for the Lord's Supper'. Watts' *Works* were edited in six volumes, by Jennings and Doddridge, 1753, printed by John Barfield, London: 1810.

Wesley, Charles, *The Journal of Charles Wesley*, Baker Book House, Grand Rapids, MI: 1980 (reprint of the edition, edited by Thomas Jackson, published by John Mason, London: 1849).

Wesley, John, *The Journal of the Rev. John Wesley AM*, J. M. Dent, London: 1906, 4 vols in Everyman's Library.

Wesley, John, *A Collection of Hymns for the Use of The People Called Methodists*, 1780, vol. 7 in the Bicentennial Edition of *The Works of John Wesley*, edited by Franz Hildebrandt and Oliver Beckerlegge, Abingdon Press, Nashville: 1983.

Wheatly, Richard, *A Rational Illustration of the Book of Common Prayer*, 3rd edn, London: 1720.

Secondary Sources

Addleshaw, G. W. O., *The High Church Tradition: A Study of the Liturgical Thought of the Seventeenth Century*, Faber and Faber, London: 1941.

Alexander, J. Neil, 'With Eloquence in Speech and Song: Anglican Reflections on the Eucharistic Hymns (1745) of John and Charles Wesley', *Proceedings of the Charles Wesley Society* 2 (1995), pp. 35–50; a revised text in J. Neil Alexander, ed., *With Ever Joyful Hearts*, Church Publishing, New York: 1999, pp. 244–60.

Cragg, Gerald R., *The Church and the Age of Reason 1648–1789*, Athenaeum, New York: 1961.

Dugmore, C. W., *Eucharistic Doctrine in England from Hooker to Waterland*, SPCK, London: 1942.

Grisbrooke, W. J., *Anglican Liturgies of the Seventeenth and Eighteenth Centuries*, Alcuin Club, SPCK, London: 1958.

Legg, J. Wickham, *English Church Life: From the Restoration to the Tractarian Movement*, Longmans, London: 1914.

McAdoo, H. R. and Kenneth Stevenson, *The Mystery of the Eucharist in the Anglican Tradition*, Canterbury Press, Norwich: 1995.

Rupp, E. Gordon, *Religion in England 1688–1791*, Oxford Unversity Press, Oxford: 1986.

Stevenson, Kenneth, *Covenant of Grace Renewed: A Vision of the Eucharist in the Seventeenth Century*, Darton, Longman and Todd, London: 1994.

Stevick, Daniel B., '"The Fruits of Life O'erspread the Board", Isaac Watts' Hymns for the Lord's Supper', in J. Neil Alexander, ed., *With Ever Joyful Hearts*, Church Publishing, New York: 1999.

Yates, Nigel, *Buildings, Faith and Worship: Liturgical Arrangements of Anglican Churches 1600–1900*, Clarendon Press, Oxford: 1991.

The Hymns

Baker, Frank, 'Approaching a Variorum Edition of *Hymns on the Lord's Supper*', *Proceedings of the Charles Wesley Society* 2 (1995), pp. 7–15.

Baker, Frank, *Charles Wesley's Verse: An Introduction*, Epworth Press, London: 2nd edn, 1988.

Beck, Brian, 'Rattenbury Revisited: The Theology of Charles Wesley's Hymns', *Epworth Review* 26/2 (1999), pp. 71–81.

Beckerlegge, Oliver A., 'Charles Wesley's Vocabulary', *London Quarterly and Holborn Review* 193 (1968), pp. 152–61.

Beckerlegge, Oliver A., 'An Attempt at a Classification of Charles Wesley's Metres', *London Quarterly and Holborn Review* 169 (1944), pp. 219–27.

Berger, Teresa, '"Finding Echoes": The *Catechism of the Catholic Church* and the *Hymns on the Lord's Supper*', *Proceedings of the Charles Wesley Society* 2 (1995), pp. 63–73.

Berger, Teresa, 'Charles Wesley: A Literary Overview', in S. T. Kimbrough, ed., *Charles Wesley: Poet and Theologian*, pp. 21–9.

Berger, Teresa, *Theology in Hymns? A Study of the Relationship of Doxology and Theology According to 'A Collection of Hymns for the Use of the People Called Methodists (1780)'*, trans. Timothy E. Kimbrough, Kingswood Books (Abingdon Press), Nashville, TN: 1995.

Bett, Henry, *The Hymns of Methodism in Their Literary Relations*, Epworth Press, London: 1913, 1920, rev. edn 1945.

Bett, Henry, 'John Wesley's Translations of German Hymns', *London Quarterly and Holborn Review* 165 (1940), pp. 288–94.

Borgen, Ole E., *John Wesley on the Sacraments: A Theological Study*, Abingdon Press, Nashville: 1972.

Bowmer, John C., *The Sacrament of the Lord's Supper in Early Methodism*, Dacre Press, Westminster: 1951.

Burdon, Adrian, *The Preaching Service: The Glory of the Methodists*, Joint Liturgical Studies 17, Grove Books, Cambridge: 1991.

Charles Wesley Society, *Hymns on the Lord's Supper, 250 Years* (papers from the Sixth Annual Meeting of the Charles Wesley Society, all of them are on *Hymns on the Lord's Supper* and are listed individually in this bibliography), *Proceedings of the Charles Wesley Society* 2 (1995).

Crockett, William R., *Eucharist: Symbol of Transformation*, Pueblo, New York: 1989.

Davie, Donald, *Purity of Diction in English Verse*, Oxford University Press, Oxford: 1953 (esp. ch. 5, 'The Classicism of Charles Wesley').

Davie, Donald, *A Gathered Church: The Literature of the English Dissenting Interest, 1700–1930*, Oxford University Press, Oxford: 1978.

Davie, Donald, *Dissentient Voice*, University of Notre Dame Press: 1982 (especially pertinent is 'The Language of the Eighteenth-Century Hymn', pp. 67–82).

Davie, Donald, *The Eighteenth-Century Hymn in England*, Cambridge University Press, Cambridge: 1993.

Dearing, Trevor, *Wesleyan and Tractarian Worship*, Epworth/SPCK, London: 1966.

Frost, Francis, 'The Veiled Unveiling of the Glory of God in the Eucharistic Hymns of Charles Wesley: The Self-Emptying Glory of God', *Proceedings of the Charles Wesley Society* 2 (1995), pp. 87–99.

Grislis, Egil, 'The Wesleyan Doctrine of the Lord's Supper', *Duke Divinity School Bulletin* 28/2 (1963), pp. 99–110.

Hildebrandt, Franz, *I Offered Christ*, Muhlenburg Press, Philadelphia: 1967.

Hodges, H. A. and A. M. Allchin, eds, *A Rapture of Praise: Hymns of John and Charles Wesley*, Hodder and Stoughton, London: 1966.

Kimbrough, S. T. and Charles A. Green, eds, *Hymns on the Lord's Supper*, with an Introduction by Geoffrey Wainwright, Charles Wesley Society, Madison, NJ: 1995, a facsimile reprint of the 1745 edition with an alphabetical index and a metrical index provided by the editors.

Kimbrough, S. T., ed., *Charles Wesley: Poet and Theologian*, Kingswood Books (Abingdon Press), Nashville, TN: 1992.

Kishkovsky, Leonid, 'The Wesleys' *Hymns on the Lord's Supper* and Orthodoxy', *Proceedings of the Charles Wesley Society* 2 (1995), pp. 75–86.

Manning, Bernard, *The Hymns of Watts and Wesley*, Epworth Press: London, 1942.

McAdoo, Henry R., 'A Theology of the Eucharist: Brevint and the Wesleys', *Theology* 97/788 (July/August 1994), pp. 245–56.

Morris, David, *The Religious Sublime: Christian Poetry and Critical Tradition in Eighteenth Century England*, University Press of Kentucky, Lexington: 1972.

Nichols, Kathryn, 'The Theology of Christ's Sacrifice and Presence in Charles Wesley's Hymns On The Lord's Supper', *The Hymn* 39/4 (1988), pp. 19–29.

Nichols, Kathryn, 'Charles Wesley's Eucharistic Hymns: Their Relationship to *The Book of Common Prayer*', *The Hymn* 39/2 (1988), pp. 13–21.

Noll, Mark A., 'Romanticism and the Hymns of Charles Wesley', *Evangelical Quarterly* 46/2 (1974), pp. 195–223.

Outler, Albert C. and Richard P. Heitzenrater, eds, *John Wesley's Sermons: An Anthology*, Abingdon Press, Nashville: 1991 (texts from vols 1–4 of the Bicentennial Edition).

Rack, Henry D., *Reasonable Enthusiast: John Wesley and the Rise of Methodism*, Trinity Press International, Philadelphia: 1989.

Rattenbury, J. Ernest, *Thoughts on Holy Communion*, Epworth Press: London, 1958.

Rattenbury, J. Ernest, ed., *The Eucharistic Hymns of John and Charles Wesley*, Epworth Press, London: 1948. (Out of print for many years; republished in an

'American Edition' in the USA by the Order of St Luke, Akron, Ohio, 1990; heavily edited and containing some new material on American Methodism.)

Rattenbury, J. Ernest, *The Evangelical Doctrines of Charles Wesley's Hymns*, Epworth Press, London: 1941 (3rd edition, 1954).

Richardson, Alan, *An Introduction to the Theology of the New Testament*, Harper, New York: 1958.

Routley, Eric, 'Charles Wesley and Matthew Henry', *Congregational Quarterly* 33 (1955), pp. 345–51.

Routley, Eric, *The Musical Wesleys*, Oxford University Press, New York: 1968.

Sanders, Paul S., *An Appraisal of John Wesley's Sacramentalism in the Evolution of Early American Methodism*, unpublished Th.D. dissertation, Union Theological Seminary, New York, 1954.

Sanders, Paul S., 'Wesley's Eucharistic Faith and Practice', *Anglican Theological Review* 47/2 (1966), pp. 157–74.

Sanders, Paul S., 'The Sacraments in Early American Methodism', *Church History* 26 (1957), pp. 355–71.

Stevenson, Kenneth, *Accept This Sacrifice: The Eucharist as Sacrifice Today*, Liturgical Press, Collegeville, MN: 1989.

Stevenson, Kenneth, *Eucharist and Offering*, Pueblo, New York: 1986.

Stevick, Daniel B., 'The Altar and the Cross: The Atonement in Charles Wesley's *Hymns on the Lord's Supper*, 1745', *Proceedings of the Charles Wesley Society* 5 (1998), pp. 61–80.

Tyson, John R., ed., *Charles Wesley: A Reader*, Oxford University Press, Oxford: 1989.

Tyson, John R., 'Charles Wesley and the German Hymns', *The Hymn* 35 (1984), pp. 153–7.

Wainwright, Geoffrey, *Eucharist and Eschatology*, Epworth Press, London: 1971.

Wainwright, Geoffrey, 'Introduction' to Kimbrough and Green, eds, facsimile edition of *Hymns on the Lord's Supper*, Charles Wesley Society, Madison, NJ: 1995.

Wainwright, Geoffrey, '"Our Elder Brethren Join": The Wesleys' *Hymns on the Lord's Supper* and the Patristic Revival in England', *Proceedings of the Charles Wesley Society* 1 (1994), pp. 5–31.

Watson, J. R., '*Hymns on the Lord's Supper*, 1745, and Some Literary and Liturgical Sources', *Proceedings of the Charles Wesley Society* 2 (1995), pp. 17–33.

Watson, J. R., 'Charles Wesley's Hymns and *The Book of Common Prayer*', in Margot Johnson, ed., *Thomas Cranmer: Essays in Commemoration of the 500th Anniversary of His Birth*, Turnstone Ventures, Durham: 1990, pp. 204–28.

Watson, J. R., *The English Hymn: A Critical and Historical Study*, Oxford University Press, Oxford: 1999.

White, James, ed., *John Wesley's Sunday Service of the Methodists in North America*, United Methodist Publishing House, Nashville, TN: 1984.

General Index

Index of Hymns

The following entries show hymns that are quoted or discussed in this book. Hymns which are no more than referred to in the text are not indexed.